BATTLING FOR
AMERICAN LABOR

BATTLING FOR AMERICAN LABOR

Wobblies, Craft Workers, and the Making of the Union Movement

HOWARD KIMELDORF

UNIVERSITY OF CALIFORNIA PRESS
BERKELEY   LOS ANGELES   LONDON

University of California Press
Berkeley and Los Angeles, California

University of California Press, Ltd.
London, England

© 1999 by
The Regents of the University of California

Library of Congress Cataloging-in-Publication Data

Kimeldorf, Howard.
    Battling for American labor : wobblies, craft workers, and
the making of the union movement / Howard Kimeldorf.
        p.   cm.
    Includes bibliographical references and index.
    ISBN 0-520-21832-9 (alk. paper)—ISBN 0-520-21833-7
(alk. paper)
        1. Trade-unions—United States—History.   2. Labor
movement—United States—History.   3. Syndicalism—
United States—History.   4. Industrial Workers of the
World—History.   5. American Federation of Labor—
History.   6. Trade-unions—Stevedores—Pennsylvania—
Philadelphia—History.   7. Trade-unions—Restaurant
employees—New York (State)—New York—History.   I.
Title.
    HD6508.K485   1999
    331.88'0973—dc21   99-18366
                                                        CIP

Manufactured in the United States of America

08 07 06 05 04 03 02 01 00 99   10 9 8 7 6 5 4 3 2 1

The paper used in this publication meets the minimum
requirements of ANSI/NISO Z39.48-1992 (R 1997)
(*Permanence of Paper*). ∞

For Robin

Contents

Acknowledgments

Principal funding for this project was generously provided by the Horace H. Rackham School of Graduate Studies and the Office of the Vice President for Research, both at the University of Michigan. Additional funding for field research was provided by the Henry J. Kaiser Family Foundation under the direction of the Walter P. Reuther Library of Labor and Urban Affairs at Wayne State University.

Writing this book has introduced me not only to new ideas but also to new friends and acquaintances whose efforts and contributions appear on every page. I am happy to be able to thank them, however inadequately. The mass of data collected for this study was amplified and enriched by countless archivists and reference librarians. Among those deserving special thanks are Jim Cassedy, Bill Creech, Jerry Hess, Tab Lewis, and David Paynter at the National Archives; Peter Filardo at the Tamiment Institute Library, New York University; Mike Smith at the Archives of Labor and Urban Affairs, Wayne State University; and Richard Strassberg, Director of the Kheel Center for Labor-Management Documentation and Archives, Cornell University. Closer to home, a small army of undergraduates at the University of Michigan spent long hours searching what appeared to be at times an endless loop of microfilm. I would like to single out in particular the contributions of Joana Girardin, Paul Leddy, Renee Lesperance, Mandi Odier, Sean Pratt, Corie Thornton, Tony White, and Beth Wells. The University of Michigan Library staff was, as usual, most helpful. Librarian and sociological fellow traveler Mark Sandler deserves special thanks for his tireless efforts on my behalf.

I benefited from the opportunity to test the ideas in this book before several stimulating audiences, beginning with a presentation to my colleagues at the Center for Research on Social Organization, followed by appearances at the Atlanta seminar in the Comparative History of Labor, Industry, Technology, and Society at Emory University, the American Sociological Association annual meetings, and the Departments of Sociology at Texas A&M University and the University of Oregon. Earlier versions of chapters 2 and 3 appeared in the volume *Waterfront Workers: New Perspectives on Race and Class*, edited by Calvin Winslow and published by the University of Illinois Press; and in the journal *International Labor and Working-Class History*, no. 51, published by Cambridge University Press and reprinted with permission.

I could not have asked for a more supportive and intellectually charged environment in which to write this book, surrounded as I was by colleagues like Duane Alwin, Barbara Anderson, Müge Goçek, Max Heirich, Jim House, Rick Lempert, Jeff Paige, Sonya Rose, Bill Sewell, and Mayer Zald, all of whom provided constructive comments and encouragement along the way. Others who deserve thanks for reacting to this project in its varying incarnations and stages of completion include Peter Cole, Joseph Conlin, Colin Davis, Mel Dubofsky, Larry Griffin, the late Michael Kozura, Darcy Leach, Bruce Nelson, Rob Penney, Charlie Post, Jane Poulsen, Sharon Reitman, Michael Schwartz, Judy Stepan-Norris, Steve Vallas, Cal Winslow, and Bob Zieger. I am especially indebted to Dan Clawson, Bill Friedland, Mike Goldfield, Jeff Haydu, and David Wellman for reading over the entire manuscript and offering their engaged and very thoughtful reactions.

I am grateful to Pat Preston for her highly professional preparation of the manuscript and to Naomi Schneider, my editor at the University of California Press, who expertly guided the manuscript through the review process and into print. It has once again been a pleasure working with Naomi and her talented colleagues, including in particular Sheila Berg and Suzanne Knott.

Over the many years it took to complete this study, my family offered more support and patience than I was entitled to. Fortunately, that is my view and not theirs. Loren, Paul, and Jay each shaped my thinking in ways that I continue to discover. The book, however, is dedicated to Robin, my spouse and best friend, for all that we have shared in life as well as work. In a very real sense, this study would not have been possible without her.

Chapter One

Explaining Union Allegiance

Commenting on the troubled state of industrial relations at the turn of the century, Andrew Carnegie, one of the nation's leading apostles of capitalism, observed a growing "friction between the employer and the employed, between labor and capital, between rich and poor." In workplaces all across America, Carnegie lamented, "rigid castes are formed" based on "ignorance" and "mutual distrust" that only served to widen the already gaping chasm between owners and workers.[1]

Carnegie's vivid depiction of class polarization, while conjuring up nightmarish images for his fellow captains of industry, was like a dream come true for the nation's long-suffering union movement. After sputtering along for years, workplace organization finally and dramatically took off in 1898. By 1904 the U.S. labor movement had upwards of two million members, representing more than a fourfold increase over the previous six years and giving the upstart Americans a larger following than their more established British, German, and French counterparts.[2]

Still, with only about one in twenty nonagricultural wage earners enrolled in unions, American labor had barely scratched the surface. Outside of its core constituency in transportation, mining, and building trades, which together accounted for more than half of all members, union organization was weak or nonexistent. The enlarged labor movement of 1904, despite its recent gains, remained peripheral to the lives of most American workers.[3]

The following summer, as national union membership dipped for the first time in nearly a decade, some two hundred activists, representing forty-three unions, locals, and labor federations from around the country, gathered in Chicago to form a new, more inclusive working-class organization.[4] While most of the delegates were Socialists of one stripe or another, they were—as only the American left can be—deeply divided over just about everything else, from organizing strategies to institutional structure to political participation. About the only point of agreement was that the American Federation of Labor (AFL), then home to roughly 80 percent of the country's union members, was never going to become the true house of labor.[5]

The organization that emerged after eleven days of often heated discussion, the Industrial Workers of the World (IWW), self-consciously defined itself as the antithesis of the AFL. Where the AFL broke up the working class into a multitude of tiny craft unions, the IWW envisioned "One Big Union" consisting of a handful of industrially based affiliates. Where the AFL's membership consisted mostly of native-born, skilled, white craftsmen, the IWW was committed to organizing almost everyone else, targeting in particular the unskilled, recent immigrants, women, and workers of color. Where the AFL monopolized employment opportunities for its current members by restricting union access through closed shops, prohibitive initiation fees, and high dues, the IWW offered a true "communism of opportunity" based on mass recruiting, low initiation fees, and work sharing. And where the AFL advocated an industrial peace based on the sanctity of contracts, the IWW promised unrelenting class war, refusing as a matter of principle to sign labor agreements or any other such "armistice" until the working class secured its final emancipation from capitalism.[6]

These opposing organizational missions reflected the very different ideological forces driving the AFL and the IWW. Under Samuel Gompers's strong stewardship, the federation evolved from tolerating socialism during the early 1890s to vigorously opposing it a decade later as an "industrial crime, against which the trade unions of America will contend to the end."[7] By the time of the IWW's formation in 1905, the AFL had come firmly to embrace American values and institutions, including its system of capitalism, which Gompers, the former Marxist sympathizer turned pragmatist, endorsed as "the best yet devised." The AFL, having long since rejected industrial organization as a means and socialism as an end, stood for trade unionism, pure and simple. Organizing had become a business, much like any other, seeking "more, more, more" under the existing economic arrangements.[8]

If the rebellious IWW sought more of anything, it was revolutionary fervor. Staking out a position to the left of the Socialist party, the
Wobblies, as members of the IWW were known, rejected the grad-
ualism of electoral politics. "The ballot box is simply a capitalist concession," insisted one delegate at the IWW founding convention.
"Dropping pieces of paper into a hole in a box never did achieve
emancipation for the working class." Shunning the political arena as
the incubator of "slowshulism," the Wobblies concentrated their efforts at the point of production, where they believed capitalism was
most vulnerable to attack.[9] Theirs was the socialism, not of "dentists,"
as Trotsky once referred to the middle-class constituency of the
American Socialist party, but of the downtrodden and dispossessed
proletarian masses—a kind of "socialism," as Wobbly leader "Big Bill"
Haywood put it, "with its working clothes on."[10]

The ensuing clash between the AFL and the IWW thus provided
the clearest possible choice for American workers, now in a position
to choose between two organizations anchoring opposite ends of the
ideological spectrum. "The choice," as Socialist leader Eugene Debs
saw it, was "between the A.F. of L. and capitalism on one side and
the Industrial Workers and Socialism on the other." Framed in this
way, the increasingly bitter rivalry between the AFL and the IWW
came to be seen as a crucial test of working-class consciousness, serving as a sort of proletarian referendum for the rank and file. Voting
with their feet, some two million to three million workers passed
through the IWW over the next several years. Most, however, remained only briefly, such that the number of card-carrying Wobblies
in any single month seldom averaged more than sixty thousand. When
the final count was taken shortly after World War I, the AFL, at more
than four million strong, emerged as the clear winner, easily defeating
the Wobblies.[11]

Important lessons have been drawn from the AFL's landslide victory. Writing in 1928, Selig Perlman claimed to find "added strength"
for his influential new theory of job consciousness in "the events of
the day," pointing specifically to the inability of Socialists and Wobblies "to hold their own" in the contest for union loyalty. Following
Perlman's lead, succeeding generations of scholars have regarded the
AFL's triumph as evidence of an underlying conservatism among the
rank and file.[12] In choosing to milk capitalism rather than overthrow
it, so the argument goes, American workers were simply following

their bellies, not their heads, instinctively craving the AFL's pork chops while rejecting the Wobblies' more cerebral offerings of final emancipation. Although there has been a lively scholarly debate over the years concerning the sources of this proletarian conservatism, few observers question its role in driving organized labor to the right during the opening decades of the twentieth century, away from groups like the Wobblies and into the waiting arms of the AFL.[13]

This study offers an alternative account for American labor's disengagement with the left at this critical historical juncture. Challenging a wide range of theories that attribute the failure of the IWW as well as the success of the AFL to an ideologically deficient rank and file said to be suffering from some form of "collective brain damage," it begins by uncoupling observable organizational outcomes from interior psychological states, seeking in that way to disentangle the institutional results of collective action from the consciousness of the participants themselves.[14] Whether American workers were "ideologically incorporated," "falsely conscious," or "brain damaged" in some other way cannot possibly be known from anything they may have done or failed to do—at least not without subjecting the rank and file to some kind of retrospective group psychoanalysis. Knowing only that a majority ultimately sided with the AFL is hardly evidence that they did so out of agreement with the ideological conservatism of its top leaders.[15]

Whatever the rank and file may have thought of men like Sam Gompers, they behaved on the job in ways that can hardly be described as conservative. Their greater institutional distance from the political radicalism of European labor did not prevent the feisty Americans from waging an all-out battle against their employers, marked by levels of mobilization, intensity, and violence second to none.[16] This unusual combination of political quiescence and industrial revolt has baffled observers for years, leading most students of the problem, particularly graduates of the long-established exceptionalist school, to "solve" the puzzle of American labor by hoping to find the missing piece of European-style radical labor politics.[17] While the search for an indigenous political radicalism has generated many valuable insights into the character of working-class movements on both sides of the Atlantic, it has diverted attention away from gaining a deeper understanding of that piece of the puzzle that is overwhelmingly present: the distinctive *industrial* radicalism of American labor.[18]

Taking a closer look at this industrial radicalism—dismissed by most academic observers as a harmless "mere economism"—is the principal objective of this study.[19] In place of sweeping generalizations about the essentially "liberal" or "bourgeois" character of American workers and their unions, it offers a concrete historical analysis of union loyalty, asking why a segment of American workers was drawn earlier this century to the IWW, why most of them eventually left the Wobblies for the archrival AFL, and how, at a more interpretive level, their behavior can be understood in terms other than those handed down by the dominant paradigm of proletarian conservatism.

These questions are taken up through an investigation of two particularly revealing histories of union succession occurring over roughly the same period on the Philadelphia docks and in the hotel and restaurant industry of New York City. In both settings, unorganized workers were approached in 1913 by rival Wobbly and AFL delegates; and in each case, after considering their options, they allied with the IWW. Some twenty years later, the longshoremen and culinary workers found themselves inside the AFL, thus completing the same journey from the far left of the trade union ideological spectrum to the far right.

Although both groups covered the same ground, they did so by following very different paths. In Philadelphia the organizational transition was more abrupt, coming on the heels of a long and generally successful IWW reign that began in 1913 when the port's three thousand longshoremen, then evenly divided between white ethnic immigrants and African Americans, formed Local 8 of the IWW's Marine Transport Workers' Industrial Union (MTW). For more than a decade, Local 8 had its way on the waterfront, virtually running the port by relying on militant direct action and labor solidarity. As its power crested during World War I, the Wobbly union was strong enough to force recognition from the same federal government whose ongoing investigations of radical and subversive activities singled out the Quaker City longshoremen as a serious threat to national security. It was not to last, however. By 1926 Local 8 had been driven out of business, with most of its former members, including several prominent IWW leaders, defecting to the rival AFL union.[20]

Local 8's association with the IWW from 1913 to 1926 made it the single most durable example of Wobbly unionism at the time. During that same span of years, literally hundreds of IWW locals passed into and out of existence: hardly any lasted beyond a particular strike or job action; those that did, typically survived as paper organizations with wildly fluctuating memberships and few regular dues payers. In contrast, Local 8 remained viable throughout most of its thirteen-year existence, maintaining a stable and growing membership. If Local 8, as one of its leaders claimed, "was an outstanding example of what the I.W.W. could do" in building a durable working-class base, its eventual failure demonstrated just as clearly the limits of Wobbly unionism.[21]

New York's culinary workers forged a more typical relationship with the IWW, turning to the Wobblies for leadership in the midst of a faltering citywide walkout of six thousand hotel workers in 1913. The IWW's dramatic intervention, accompanied by the usual incendiary rhetoric and threats of sabotage, captured the attention of the national media and the local police far more than the loyalties of the immigrant, mostly male strikers. With the collapse of the walkout, the Wobblies withdrew from the field, leaving behind an empty organizational shell as a hollow reminder of their earlier presence.

Rebuilding on the Wobblies' foundation, a new industrial union, also independent of the AFL, was formed in 1916, the International Federation of Workers in the Hotel and Restaurant Industry. After drawing twenty thousand hotel and restaurant workers into a dramatic citywide strike, the syndicalist International Federation was dislodged in 1920 by the still more inclusive and equally aggressive Amalgamated Food Workers. For the next several years, the independently left-wing Amalgamated waged a tireless campaign to organize the city's waiters, waitresses, cooks, dishwashers, chambermaids, and hotel workers, often with stunning success. By 1934 the aging Amalgamated was pushed aside by the newly formed Food Workers Industrial Union, whose Communist officers led the city's culinary workers into the mainstream AFL union, thus bringing to a close more than two decades of self-sustaining industrial unionism.[22]

In following their divergent trajectories from the IWW to the AFL, Philadelphia's racially diverse longshoremen and New York's overwhelmingly white and increasingly female culinary workers offer an intriguing contrast, ideal for observing the same organizational dynamics at work among two radically different labor forces located in distinct industrial settings. It is precisely the contrasting character of these trajectories, coupled with the small number of cases under comparison, that calls for a method of "parallel demonstration" in which the objective is to build a generalizable argument by demonstrating its "common applicability" to a wide range of contexts; in this instance, seeking a unified explanation for the convergent outcomes in Philadelphia and New York—cases that represent contrasting demographics, industries, and patterns of union succession—as the basis for advancing a more general interpretation of American labor.[23]

Why, then, did the longshoremen remain with the IWW for more than a decade before abruptly bolting to the AFL while the hotel and restaurant workers followed a more circuitous route, passing through no fewer than three independent industrial unions before finally being absorbed by the AFL? What accounts for these distinct yet ultimately convergent trajectories? Specifically, why were both groups of workers initially attracted to the IWW?[24] Once inside the IWW, why did the longshoremen remain for so long while the culinary workers left almost immediately to form a new organization? Why did both groups of workers, many of them former card-carrying Wobblies or radicals of one stripe or another, eventually turn to their old nemesis, the AFL, for relief? And, more generally, what does this history of organizational succession suggest about the alleged conservatism of American workers?

Proletarian Conservatism

In the highly competitive academic marketplace of ideas, the thesis of proletarian conservatism has at times operated as a virtual monopoly. Its influence has been such that, prior to the renewal of labor history in the 1960s, few scholars were willing to take issue with the dominant view, expressed years ago by Henry Pelling, that a "lack of class consciousness" constituted a "permanent characteristic of American labor." The only real debate has been over its permanency: most students have characterized the American proletariat as a "class without consciousness" from the moment of its inception, whereas others have sought to locate the failure of class consciousness in the harsh realities of late-nineteenth-century industrial capitalism. But whatever its source—whether a congenital defect in thinking or a product of history—"the lack of class consciousness," as Paul Edwards argues, "has been a well-known feature of American workers." So well known, in fact, that a new generation of radical historians has recently joined the consensus, exemplified by Michael Kazin's insistence "that American workers have seldom been motivated by a class consciousness worthy of the name."[25]

Scholars who dug still deeper into the inner psychic worlds of American workers found not only a limited awareness of class but also what appeared to some as a fondness for capitalism itself. Confirming the conventional wisdom, Gerald Grob, in his influential study of nineteenth-century labor ideologies, described the rank and file as "expectant capitalists." "Above all," he concluded, "the fact remains that the American worker has been by tradition and by history inclined toward a capitalistic outlook, a phenomenon well recognized" by observers across the political spectrum. Indeed, even committed Socialists saw the American worker as someone who, in the words of former Socialist party leader Michael Harrington, "thinks and speaks well of capitalism." Having thus become "the principal upholders of the capitalist system," as American unionists have been described, their love of capitalism flowed naturally from an inability to think of themselves as members of a class—another of those "well-known" and "well-recognized" historical "facts" that have led a long procession of scholars to ask, as John Diggens recently has, "Why is the American working class so conservative?"[26]

But is this really the right question? How do we know that American workers were ever "so conservative" or, for that matter, enamored of capitalism and utterly lacking in class consciousness?[27] Most such claims rest on little more than inference. With only the most limited access to the private mental worlds of the rank and file, conclusions about what they were thinking at an earlier point in time have often been inferred from what they actually did—in this case, deriving proletarian conservatism from the act of joining the AFL. Such reasoning, argue Reeve Vanneman and Lynn Cannon, rests on a crude "psychological reductionism" that ends up reducing institutional outcomes to some presumed mental state, as if the failure of radical groups like the IWW was primarily attributable to a deep-seated psychic disorder—what might be termed the anticlass, procapitalist complex—plaguing the rank and file.[28]

Locating the left's failure in worker psychology is one of the few common threads tying together a diverse range of theories aimed at explaining the relative weakness of socialism within the American labor movement. It is perhaps most apparent in many of the culturally based explanations that posit a tension of some kind between the collectivist, egalitarian, and revolutionary traditions of socialism, on the one hand, and the ostensibly individualistic, meritocratic, and pragmatic beliefs of American workers, on the other. Whether the particular ideological shortcoming is conceptualized as Leon Sampson's peculiar brand of Americanism that substituted for socialism, Louis Hartz's ever-vigilant liberalism that guarded against conservative aristocratic traditions, or Seymour Martin Lipset's vigorous antistatism that fostered distrust of political remedies based on centralized authority, the principal obstacle to working-class radicalism is seen as residing inside the heads of the rank and file.[29]

A similar psychologizing strategy operates just beneath the surface of the most widely accepted materialist explanations for the failure of socialism: the opportunism of the two-party system, the openness of the class structure, and the ethnic and racial heterogeneity of the labor force. Each rests on a psychological profile of the rank and file as suffering from the same anticlass, pro-capitalist complex. It is routinely argued, for example, that the two-party system was unassailable because, in the end, most workers never broke with the prevailing liberal consensus undergirding American capitalism;[30] that social mobility was an effective antidote to class protest only to the degree that working people embraced the nation's cultural values of individualism, personal achievement, and material gain;[31] and that ethnic and racial identities proved so durable precisely because the laboring poor failed to think of themselves as belonging to the same class.[32] And so it goes, with every failed outcome ultimately traced to a corresponding failure of working-class consciousness.

This master narrative of failed consciousness has not gone unchallenged, particularly in recent years. With the "new" labor historians leading the way, the received view of American workers as "conservative by birth" has become a favored target of attack. Focusing on nineteenth-century processes of class formation, scholars have uncovered a broad insurgent current, awash in Republican ideology and dedicated to preserving preindustrial values of artisanal independence and community autonomy in the face of encroaching industrial capitalism. No longer a simple story of ideological incorporation leading to working-class quiescence, the new revisionist history highlights a youthful and contentious proletariat, radicalized by a class-based "producerist" consciousness, launching forms of collective action in Gilded Age America that rival those of their Western European contemporaries.[33]

This is essentially where social scientists have picked up the story, seeking to understand why, as Kim Voss poses the question, these earlier "radical attitudes and actions on the part of American workers were eventually transformed into a weak and conservative labor movement" dominated by the AFL.[34] In redirecting scholarly attention away from explaining the absence of ideological radicalism toward identifying the sources of its conservative metamorphosis, recent research by sociologists, political scientists, critical legal scholars, and others has largely abandoned the psychological reductionism of old: if working-class political insurgency was short-lived, it is no longer primarily attributable to some presumed psychological shortcoming in the form of either a failed "false" or an impotent "job" consciousness but rather to the structure of American society, which robbed the rank and file, even the most radical, of the capacity to mobilize and effect more sweeping changes.[35]

This line of argument, informed by resource mobilization perspectives and the "new institutionalism," shifts the analytical focus from the ideational to the material, downplaying the role of worker mentalities as the source of earlier left-wing failures.[36] Thus Amy Bridges argues that the Workingmen's parties of the 1830s ultimately failed, not because their message was rejected, but because their working-class supporters were concentrated in cities, where they constituted a minority of the electorate.[37] The revolutionary anarchist movements that flourished in Chicago and elsewhere a generation later met a similar fate, not because they were too radical, but because, in Eric Hirsch's words, "elites ... brutally and violently invaded" and destroyed the ethnically based urban "havens" that sustained an oppositional political culture among recent working-class immigrants.[38] Similarly, the solidaristic Knights of Labor collapsed during the 1880s, not because they violated the spirit of individualism, but because, as Voss and others have argued, they were unable to withstand the combined weight of repression by employers and the state.[39]

This growing body of work is fine as far as it goes. The problem is that it does not go far enough. Neither the revised portrait of nineteenth-century worker radicals nor the structuralist explanations for their defeat have altered the received view of early-twentieth-century trade unionists as fundamentally conservative. All that has changed is the assignment of cause and effect: the rank and file's anticlass, pro-capital complex—its "well-known" lack of class consciousness and love of capitalism—is now seen as more of a *consequence* rather than a *cause* of the AFL's ascendancy during the 1890s. For most students of twentieth-century American labor, however, the federation still represents the coffin of proletarian radicalism, with its cautious business unionism entombing a conservative rank and file.[40]

Having long since buried the indigenous radicalism of the Workingmen's parties, the revolutionary anarchists, and the Knights of Labor, the craft unionists thus remain cast in their stereotypical role as the gravediggers, not of capitalism, but of worker insurgency. As this familiar plot unfolds, their main protagonists at the time, the Wobblies, appear briefly on the historical stage as compassionate but slightly delusional Don Quixotes, sadly out of touch with the political realities of twentieth-century American capitalism and its hold over the minds of most workers. Preaching their revolutionary message to the unconverted, "the I.W.W.," observed Robert Hoxie in 1920, "faces a perpetual dilemma." "The bulk of the American workmen," he wrote, "want more here and now for themselves and their immediate associates and care little for the remote future or the revolutionary ideal. These will have none of the I.W.W. . . . . [W]e find it difficult to escape the conclusion that the Industrial Workers of the World as a positive social factor is more an object of pathetic interest than of fear." Hoxie was only partly right: the real pathos of the Wobblies was that they failed despite having their finger on the syndicalist pulse of the American working class.[41]

Syndicalism and American Workers

What most contemporary observers saw as the "weak" and "spasmodic" character of the direct-actionist IWW proved to Hoxie's satisfaction that there was "no syndicalist problem of consequence in this country." Characterizing syndicalism as "a doctrine of despair" fundamentally at odds with the "optimism" of American workers, Hoxie concluded that "the conditions are not here for its growth." Much the same argument was advanced a few years later by Perlman

in his landmark comparative study, *A Theory of the Labor Movement.*
Like Hoxie, he wrote syndicalism out of the American class experience altogether. While conceding that syndicalism had become in
several Western European countries "an easy plaything for the gusts
of wind blowing from Soviet Russia," it failed to reach the shores of
the United States where, in Perlman's classic formulation, a "job-
conscious" trade union movement, represented by the AFL, reigned
supreme.[42]

The AFL thus came to be seen as the organized expression of a
"homegrown" job consciousness in contrast to an alien and potentially
subversive syndicalism associated with groups like the IWW. Although most Wobbly leaders explicitly rejected the syndicalist label—
in part because of its sinister "foreign" connotations—the term stuck.
And for good reason: like the self-described syndicalist movements
sweeping parts of Europe, Latin America, and Africa at the time, the
IWW saw capitalism as exploitive and the political state as oppressive;
both could be overthrown, the Wobblies believed, only by the direct
economic action of a unified proletariat whose "new unions" represented the nucleus of a future society in which workers would collectively own, manage, and administer industry for the benefit of all.[43]

The IWW's expansive syndicalist vision appeared sharply at odds
with the AFL's myopic trade union focus. Federation leaders, having
long since made their peace with capitalism, targeted individual employers, not the system. They directed their organizational efforts at
giving workers a fatter paycheck and more say on the job, not unifying
them as a class or instilling a revolutionary consciousness. Their unions were vehicles of piecemeal reform in the present, not staging
platforms for an unrealized working-class utopia. In short, the AFL
was a business, not a social movement.

These are essentially the terms in which the IWW and the AFL
have been traditionally viewed by students of American labor. From
this familiar perspective, the Wobblies appear "as the only major labor
organization in the U.S. which seriously and consistently challenged
the capitalist organization of production." Holding down the center
of "radical labor leadership" in early-twentieth-century America, the
IWW exemplified a truly "class-conscious movement."[44] Whereas the
revolutionary Wobblies "made thousands of laborers and farmers the
enemies of capitalism," the role of AFL leaders, in Debs's memorable
phrase, was "to chloroform the working class while the capitalist

class goes through its pockets." Led by the "virulently antiradical" Gompers, the trade unions were bastions of "procapitalist and antisocialist" ideology, standing as the country's strongest "bulwark against revolution."[45]

The ideological contrast was certainly undeniable. But so, too, was the commitment to a kind of *practical* syndicalism that led both organizations—in waging the day-to-day struggle against the rule of capital—to eschew the political arena in favor of the workplace, to generally prefer the immediacy of direct action at the point of production to the uncertainty of legislative action in the halls of Congress. However much AFL leaders warmed up to capitalism, they remained cool toward the state as either an object or an instrument of working-class reform. If their belief in voluntarism grew mostly out of past political failures rather than from a principled rejection of politics as such, the effect was the same in forcing most AFL affiliates, like their IWW counterparts, to rely primarily on building up economic power on the job. So, despite their divergent views on the desirability of capitalism and revolution, the IWW and the AFL shared, as Will Herberg observed years ago, a "definite affinity to syndicalism . . . with its stress on proletarian direct action and its marked distrust of government and the state."[46]

Yet this "affinity to syndicalism" has seldom been recognized by students of twentieth-century American labor. Instead, most scholars have followed Lipset in seeing the "essential traits of American trade unions"—most notably the reliance on militant direct action—as the product of a national "value system" that simultaneously "depreciated a concern with class" while valorizing "individual achievement" as measured chiefly by "pecuniary success." It follows that the peculiarly American recourse to "violent and militant tactics" reflects the dominant cultural "emphasis on ends as contrasted to means" that leads most wage earners in the United States "to compare themselves individually with other workers who are relatively close to them in income and status." Driven by the resulting high levels of "individual discontent," American workers have thus lashed out at their immediate employers with an uncommon aggressiveness, seeking "to win economic and social objectives by whatever means are at hand."[47]

The nation's "value system" is likewise the implicit starting point for Kazin's recent interpretation of early-twentieth-century labor militancy as an evolved species, not of syndicalism, but rather an "elastic

and promiscuous" populism. Rejecting Lipset's assertion of a seam-
less national culture spun from individualism, Kazin spins a more
patchworked cultural yarn in which savvy union leaders, having failed
to reach ordinary workers through the Marxist vocabulary of class,
discursively constructed their followers as "average men" battling an
"unscrupulous" and "unworthy elite." This "oppositional discourse,"
rooted in a culturally accepted mode of "populist persuasion" that
elevated "the people" above "class," compelled wage earners to vigorously exercise their "rights" of industrial citizenship on the job,
often through violent and confrontational means.[48]

If most observers have missed the syndicalist affinities of American
labor it is because they usually have been looking in the wrong places.
Focusing on a national "value system" that is conceived from the
outset as classless is unlikely to turn up evidence for a class-based
syndicalism. As a result, most cultural explanations for the peculiari-
ties of American unionism have not only overlooked its obvious affinities to syndicalism, they have, in addition, failed to really examine
the nature of what it is they claim to be explaining: invariably seeing
American labor's distinctive reliance on direct action at the point of
production as a simple reflection of individualism, populism, antistatism—almost anything, that is, except syndicalism.[49]

The view from the ground, however, offers a much better vantage
point from which to observe the syndicalist practices that undergirded
labor organizations as diverse as the IWW and the AFL. In immediate
aims, according to IWW authority Melvyn Dubofsky, "one could not
easily distinguish the behaviour of the Wobblies from those of more
conventional trade unions. Like members of the craft unions affiliated
with the AFL, IWW activists struggled to raise wages, reduce hours,
and improve working conditions." Moreover, in pursuing their common objectives, the IWW and the AFL relied mainly on the activity
of workers themselves, not the neutrality of the state or the majesty
of the law. Finally, whatever lasting gains both organizations made
came largely from extending their control over the job, often using
the same methods of direct action aimed at disrupting production.[50]

Autonomous self-activity, direct action at the point of production,
and an emphasis on workers' control were all part of a diffuse "syndicalist impulse" that, as David Montgomery has convincingly argued,
defined the struggles of American workers for nearly two decades
following the birth of the IWW. Between roughly 1909 and 1922 this

"new unionism" pushed strike activity to record levels in the United States. At its peak in 1919 more than four million workers officially went out on strike—nearly one out of every four wage earners in the country. That this industrial insurgency extended so far beyond the organizational boundaries of the IWW led Montgomery to question "the customary image of the IWW as representing conduct and aspirations far removed from the 'mainstream' of American labor development."[51]

In construing syndicalism as a *practice* of resistance rather than a theory of revolution, Montgomery grasped what was most relevant about the IWW experience, unlike Hoxie and others who, focusing on the Wobblies' limited ideological appeal, came up empty-handed.[52] Put simply, it was neither the Wobblies' increasingly resonant critique of capitalism nor the unremarkable character of their immediate union objectives that made them a part of labor's mainstream but the fact that they were anchored in the same syndicalist waters as the AFL. Washing across the industrial landscape of early-twentieth-century America, syndicalism represented a fluid mix of organizational practices that combined the institutional brawn of pure and simple trade unionism with the mobilizing muscle of contemporary working-class insurgency to produce a kind of "syndicalism, pure and simple"—defined by its point-of-production focus, aggressive job control, and militant direct action.

In competing for the allegiance of American workers, the IWW and the AFL tapped into different dimensions of this diffuse syndicalism. The AFL's approach might best be characterized as "business syndicalism."[53] Grounded in the restrictionist practices that Perlman saw as the essence of "job consciousness," the AFL's syndicalism carved out its jurisdictions along craft or narrowly drawn occupational lines, carefully regulated enrollment in relation to local labor market conditions, and elaborated rigid work rules to protect its existing job territory and monopolize employment opportunities for current union members. In contrast, the IWW practiced a form of "industrial syndicalism." Rejecting the exclusionary logic of craft unionism, the Wobblies' syndicalism was organized along more inclusive occupational or industrial lines, relied on an expanded membership as the basis of mass mobilization and disruption, and used its control over the job to challenge traditional managerial prerogatives over hiring, firing, and the organization of work.[54]

Driven by these competing organizational logics, business syndicalism and industrial syndicalism generated corresponding ideal-typical patterns of collective action. Business syndicalism depended on establishing, strengthening, and enforcing the labor contract. It thus privileged the solidarity of small numbers over mass disruption, generally limiting organizing campaigns and strike activities to specific groups of workers directly implicated in each dispute. In contrast, industrial syndicalism avoided contractual relations that in any way restricted its freedom of movement. Operating for the most part from outside the emerging system of "industrial legality," as Antonio Gramsci termed the growing formalization of collective bargaining, it drew strength from the rank and file's spontaneity, creativity, and emergent solidarities.[55]

These rival syndicalisms were rooted in differential disruptive capacities. Business syndicalism grew mostly out of the experiences of strategically located skilled workers, whose centrality in production and irreplaceability maximized their disruptive potential while their minimal numbers facilitated self-organization and collective action. It was a wickedly effective combination that gave early-twentieth-century craftsmen what Luca Perrone has termed "reserve power": the capacity to secure their objectives merely by threatening to actualize their widely recognized disruptive potential. Such was the basis of early contract unionism, as powerful craft workers and relatively vulnerable employers came together to coordinate their "mutual" interests in sustaining high levels of economic growth through industrial peace and stability.[56]

Industrial syndicalism grew out of the differently structured disruptive capacities of the less skilled. Theirs was the power of large numbers, as magnified by strategic timing. Lacking the positional advantages of craft workers, their ability to disrupt production depended on the exercise of "situational power": the capacity, unconstrained by time contracts and labor agreements generally, to take direct action whenever the balance of class forces was most favorable. To be effective, this power had to be repeatedly actualized and demonstrated, not held in reserve. Capitalizing on the element of surprise and seizing on moments of employer vulnerability, less skilled workers were drawn to industrial syndicalism as their weapon of choice.

What distinguished these two variants of syndicalism, then, was not only that one was led by revolutionaries while the other was not. It was not just that one opened its membership doors more widely than the other. Nor simply that one refused to sign contracts while the other saw that as its principal objective. More fundamental than any of these programmatic differences were the contrasting logics of collective action on which they rested: the AFL's reliance on small numbers, reserve power, and contractualism versus the IWW's dependence on mass mobilization, situational power, and unrestricted direct action. As ideal types, business syndicalism and industrial syndicalism thus represented alternative routes of class formation that led craftsmen and less skilled workers toward opposite ends of the same syndicalist continuum.

Although tradesmen and common laborers generally followed divergent organizational trajectories, their paths sometimes crossed. Many of the most highly skilled trades regularly went into battle armed with nothing more than the logic of business syndicalism. And in many cases that was enough to secure their objectives. But whenever their conventional arsenal lacked sufficient fire power, highly skilled machinists, engineers, carpenters, railroad workers, and others did not hesitate to grasp, if only momentarily, the more potent "organizational weapon" of industrial syndicalism, wielding it with sometimes deadly force against combative employers or resistive government officials.[57]

Much like those craftsmen who found it advantageous at times to support more inclusive forms of organization and even defy the tenets of contractualism, less skilled workers were drawn periodically into the orbit of business syndicalism. Textile operatives, miners, and other laborers employed in the emerging mass production industries sometimes pulled back from the logic of industrial syndicalism by restricting their membership or signing time contracts, particularly when, as was often the case, doing so appeared to offer them the best chance of staying organized in the face of overwhelming odds.

In short, economic location and patterns of collective action were highly correlated, though not perfectly so. Clearly, there were times when craftsmen selectively borrowed from the repertoire of industrial syndicalism, just as there were times when less skilled workers opportunistically appropriated elements of business syndicalism. But such "times" were just that: exceptional moments whose very infrequency proved the general rule that skill and organizational logics were—for most workers, most often—linked in ways that systematically drew craftsmen toward business syndicalism and less skilled workers toward industrial syndicalism.

Understanding syndicalism as the driving force behind early-twentieth-century worker mobilization has far-reaching implications, suggesting that the IWW and the AFL—despite trading in very different ideological currencies—often functioned as flip sides of the same syndicalist coin, having been forged out of the same base elements of productionism, job control, and direct action. This common amalgam, although bearing distinct organizational imprints, served as a uniform medium of exchange for Wobblies and craft unionists alike, providing a shared syndicalist standard as the basis for working-class organization.

Recognizing the substantial overlap in syndicalist practices, however, is not in any way to deny the vast organizational distance separating the IWW from the AFL—a gulf that was all too real for countless workers who, by virtue of their occupation, skill level, citizenship status, race, ethnicity, or gender, found themselves on one side or the other of what was usually a wide and unbridgeable chasm.[58] But what separated most rank-and-file Wobblies from their trade union counterparts had little to do with any of the presumed differences in worldviews, ideological attachments, degrees of class awareness, or stages of consciousness that have become the stock-in-trade for students of American labor. Contrary to conventional wisdom, the ground-level war between the IWW and the AFL was seldom fought over questions of reform versus revolution, job versus class consciousness, even political conservatism versus radicalism. Rather, as the following case studies seek to demonstrate, for many American workers the contest between the IWW and the AFL was fundamentally about which practice of syndicalism—industrial or business—would define the main current of labor development in the United States.

This way of thinking about the rivalry between the IWW and the AFL offers a particularly useful framework for analyzing the dynamics of union succession on the Philadelphia waterfront and in New York's culinary industry. In both settings the great majority of unorganized and less skilled workers turned initially to the IWW's industrial syndicalism. Rival AFL organizers, advocating a business syndicalism of craftism and contractualism, found themselves isolated from the rank-and-file movement developing on the docks and inside the hotels and restaurants. While the newly organized longshoremen and culinary workers ended up following very different institutional paths over the next two decades, they remained fiercely loyal to the industrial syndicalism of their birth, so much so that the rival AFL union operating in each industry was unable to make any inroads until it embraced many of the same organizational practices. Even after the Wobblies were gone, important elements of their industrial syndicalism lived on for a time, within the shell of the triumphant AFL.

In choosing between both organizations, then, the longshoremen and the culinary workers were not guided by a narrow and defensive job consciousness that uniquely "fit" the AFL but rather by an expansive and combative industrial syndicalism that was more closely identified with the IWW—and to which the AFL in large part later adapted itself. What was striking in both cases was the continuity of syndicalist organizational practices, even as the rank and file was moving from one end of the ideological spectrum to the other, from the left-wing IWW to the right-wing AFL. Few among the thousands of longshoremen and culinary workers who made that journey bore any resemblance to the "job-conscious" conservatives in whose image scholars have routinely portrayed—and arguably distorted—the way that class was experienced at the point of production by ordinary American workers.[59]

Conceiving of the rank and file as practicing syndicalists of one kind or another, rather than as political Neanderthals or primitive militants, invites a fundamental rethinking of the peculiar dualism that has defined the American working class. The seeming contradiction between its political conservatism, on the one hand, and its industrial radicalism, on the other, turns out, on close inspection, to be a problem only for those who assume that workers are by nature either politicized socialists or economistic conservatives. Once unionists are examined under the lens of syndicalism, however, this superficial distinction can be shown to hide more than it reveals, obscuring as it does the rich history of syndicalist practices that—while avoiding the political area—were hardly conservative and that—while focusing on the job—threatened at times the stability of the capitalist economic order. Therein lies the significance of syndicalism in the formation of the American working class.

These issues are explored more fully through separate analytical narratives that trace the history of organizational succession in Philadelphia and New York. Chapters 2 and 3 narrate the struggle for union supremacy on the docks. Chapters 4 and 5 do the same for the culinary industry. All four chapters focus on the world of work, not out of some misguided commitment to a kind of "theoretical economism," but because that was the principal site of contestation between the IWW and the AFL: the workplace, the union hall, and the picket line provided the main public arenas in which their competing visions and practices of class organization were fought out, debated, and ultimately decided.[60]

The approach taken here is also deeply historical in recognizing that the formation of union loyalty, like that of class, is indeterminant to the extent that organizational allegiance is the product of multiple, path-dependent struggles whose outcomes are historically contingent. This irreducibly historical dimension calls for a degree of narrative integrity that can only come from moving "contextual" variables like timing, sequence, and events from the margins of sociological analysis to the explanatory center.[61] The result is a grounded work of historical sociology that takes the patient reader down the same path blazed years ago by the pioneering longshoremen and culinary workers whose struggles are chronicled in the following pages.

Chapter Two

Industrial Syndicalism on the Philadelphia Waterfront

In May 1913, when Philadelphia's three thousand longshoremen joined the IWW as members of Marine Transport Workers' Local 8, no one expected much of anything from their new affiliation. There was no reason to think that this IWW local would be any different from countless others that had come and gone in recent years. After all, the port's long-suffering dockworkers seemed a most improbable match for the impatient, ideologically driven Wobblies. Confident shipowners gave the relationship "at most three months," while the Wobblies, sensing the rank and file's lack of passion, welcomed the affair as a harmless fling. But as their spring romance deepened, the longshoremen found themselves drawn into a marriage of convenience in which they needed the IWW's industrial syndicalism as much as the IWW needed their strength in numbers. It proved to be a most durable relationship, enabling Local 8 to virtually rule the city's waterfront for the next several years.

As part of a national organization that is less known for its deeds than its good intentions, Local 8 accomplished things that other IWW affiliates could only dream of. It forged an ethnically mixed, racially divided, mostly unskilled labor force with little history of collective action into a unified and powerful body that, at its height, brought resistant employers, hostile government officials, and rival unionists to their knees. For more than a decade, the port's longshoremen ran the docks, driving up wages, improving conditions, and controlling hiring. It was a most impressive record of accomplishment—never equaled, before or since, by any other IWW local.[1]

Local 8's stunning success, however, unleashed a firestorm of controversy within the IWW. In 1920 the national leadership turned on the port's longshoremen, accusing them of functioning like a "reactionary craft union" at the expense of their revolutionary convictions. Walter Nef, a leader of Local 8, later wrote of his growing frustration with the Chicago headquarters of the IWW, whose officers "always looked upon the longshoremen's union as an ordinary craft union only being part of the I.W.W. instead of the A.F. of L." "They considered the Longshoreman as too conservative," Nef recalled, "only jobites."[2]

Much the same explanation dominates the few scholarly studies that have looked into the sources of Local 8's success. In the 1931 classic, *The Black Worker,* Sterling Sperro and Abram Harris characterized the Philadelphia local as an "exception" to the IWW's emphasis "on revolutionary propaganda." Local 8 succeeded where others failed because, in their words, "it was a good business union, capable of winning recognition from employers and of improving working conditions. . . . In its day-to-day relations with employers in the port it differed not one whit from a conservative union of the A.F. of L." A nearly identical conclusion was reached by Herbert Northrup nearly fifteen years later. In *Organized Labor and the Negro,* Northrup drew the same facile distinction between Local 8 as "an avowed revolutionary organization" and its actual functioning as "a practical business union" not unlike the AFL. The latest version of this argument appears in a recent article by the historian Lisa McGirr, author of the most comprehensive published study yet of the Philadelphia longshoremen. While praising Local 8 as "a progressive and innovative union," McGirr attributes its success to job control and interracial solidarity; except for the latter, she concludes, comparisons with the AFL are "indeed accurate."[3]

This chapter throws a very different light on the character of Wobbly unionism on the Philadelphia docks. Focusing on the origins and consolidation of Local 8 before World War I, it argues against compressing this history into the conventional AFL mold of "job-conscious" unionism. While Local 8 managed to control the job as effectively as any craft union, its ability to do so rested on a logic of collective action that was fundamentally at odds with the membership exclusiveness and rigid contractualism that defined the AFL's business syndicalism. What drew the port's unskilled maritime workers to the IWW was not job control itself but rather the underlying logic of collective action that made it possible: the Wobblies' industrial syndicalism of labor solidarity and unrestricted direct action. Local 8's immediate objectives may have been little different from its AFL rival, but the longshoremen's means of achieving them—through the practice of industrial syndicalism—certainly were.

Open-Shop Port

The spirit of independence that made revolutionary Philadelphia the cradle of American unionism came much later to the local waterfront. Lagging more than a century behind the city's union printers, who are generally credited with conducting the new republic's first strike in 1786, the port's longshoremen finally struck out on their own in the summer of 1898 when they spontaneously quit work. The union of record at the time, the three-year-old American Longshoremen's Union, was itching for a fight. Its president, Edward McHugh, a former international organizer with the British Dockers' Union, offered to place his entire treasury at the disposal of the strikers. Emboldened by the promise of financial support, the wildcatters dug in and scored a rare victory over the shipowners.[4]

But the celebration was short-lived. When it came time to pay up, McHugh told his stunned followers in Philadelphia that the union's general secretary had, before his recent disappearance, siphoned off the treasury, leaving the organization bankrupt. Facing angry creditors and a disillusioned membership, the American Longshoremen's Union was forced to close its doors a few months later, leaving its unfinished organizational business to the upstart International Longshoremen's Association (ILA), whose leaders, having condemned the recent walkout, met with uniform distrust from the rank and file. Recognizing the futility of their efforts, the ILA's field organizers immediately withdrew from the port. After a decade-long absence, they returned in 1909 with a charter for a new longshore local. Following a brief, ultimately ineffectual, flurry of activity, the union's representatives were pulled, the recently chartered local was abandoned, and the longshoremen were once again on their own.[5]

The ILA's collapse was merely the latest in a long string of organizational failures stretching back to 1885, when the Knights of Labor first attempted to crack the Philadelphia waterfront. Preaching the gospel of solidarity, the Knights' Local Assembly of dockworkers attracted fewer than two hundred members at its peak, before quietly passing out of existence. Its successor, McHugh's American Longshoremen's Union, managed to survive a bit longer in the field but was no more successful in building a durable base of support on the docks. The ILA's demise was simply more of the same, notable only insofar as it left Philadelphia as the only large North Atlantic port without a meaningful union presence.[6]

The open shop was partial payback for the economic and moral debts incurred by earlier unions. Financial malfeasance by the American Longshoremen's Union, followed by the ILA's sectarian refusal to bail out the strikers, broke not only the back of dockside unionism but the men's spirit as well. This early history of union corruption and opportunism hung like a dark cloud over the waterfront, casting a long shadow of cynicism and doubt that paralyzed the longshoremen for years to come. If there was a silver lining in any of this, it was visible only to local waterfront employers whose open-shop convictions drew strength from labor's apparent weakness.

Employer intransigence was also fueled by the privatized character of port ownership. Long after New York and many other large ports had "gone public" under the auspices of municipal port authorities, most of Philadelphia's thirty-seven miles of commercial waterfront remained in private hands. A 1914 report prepared by the city's newly formed Board of Commissioners of Navigation enumerated a total of 159 piers, of which 77 were described as "principal piers." Of this latter group, only 8 were public facilities owned by the city. The majority, 44, were owned and operated by the railroads, chiefly the Philadelphia and Reading Railroad and the Pennsylvania Railroad. With 38 piers between them, both rail lines effectively controlled the port's voluminous export traffic in coal and petroleum-based products extracted from the state's interior. The city's expansive sugar piers, which handled fully one-sixth of the nation's refined sugar, were also under private control. Led by the powerful Spreckles Company, the sugar industry owned 7 piers—almost as many as the entire city of Philadelphia. Four of the remaining piers were owned by steamship companies, with the rest widely scattered among private investors and wealthy families involved in the import/export business.[7]

Control over key dockside facilities gave the traditionally antiunion railroad and sugar interests a prominent voice within the city's diverse shipping community. As industry outsiders, they were clearly not in a position to dictate employer policy, which was largely set by steam-ship companies and their waterfront subsidiaries. But their significant investment role in the port's infrastructure, coupled with their virtual monopoly over the coal and sugar trade—two of Philadelphia's lead-ing cargoes—strengthened the stance of the railroads and sugar re-finers, enabling them to lean on local waterfront employers to keep shipping costs down by keeping unions off the docks.

The resulting combination of early labor miscues and employer intransigence slowed the advance of unionization in Philadelphia and, in doing so, fostered a more inclusive workforce characterized by a high degree of ethnic and racial diversity. Since Philadelphia was the last major North Atlantic port to organize, in 1913, its waterfront workers were spared the exclusionary union practices that produced a more homogeneous labor force elsewhere. On the Boston water-front, where strong unions were established under Irish control as early as 1847, long-standing membership prohibitions against "blacks"—aimed at keeping out Italians and African Americans—had the intended effect of maintaining a virtually all-white labor force that was 85 percent Irish, with the balance consisting of older immigrants from Northern and Western Europe.[8]

Even New York's weaker and more fragmented dockside unions had sufficient strength and unity of purpose to create a labor force in their own image. Neatly segregated as if by decree, Manhattan's "white" locals, clustered around the Chelsea waterfront, were re-served for the Irish much as Brooklyn came to be dominated by Ital-ians. African Americans, like the "black" Italians before them, entered the industry as strikebreakers. But because they lacked an organiza-tional base within the union, African Americans failed to make the same inroads before World War I and thus remained a small fraction, about 6 percent, of the port's seventeen thousand longshoremen.[9]

The racial homogeneity and ethnic balkanization found on the un-ionized waterfronts of Boston and New York were strikingly absent in open-shop Philadelphia. Untouched by restrictive craft unions, and therefore lacking any history of membership exclusion based on race or ethnicity, workers of different colors and nationalities competed for jobs on a more or less equal footing, often managing to secure regular, if intermittent, employment. Although precise data on the port's ethnic breakdown are not available, it appears that Poles were the most numerous, perhaps representing close to one-fourth of

Philadelphia's three thousand dockworkers in 1910. They were followed in descending order by Lithuanians, Italians, Irish, and Jews,
whose presence gave the city's docks the appearance of a veritable
melting pot alongside ethnically homogeneous Boston and New York.
But it was the port's racial makeup, where blacks constituted fully 40
percent of the workforce, that was most telling. Among comparable
North Atlantic ports, only Baltimore—not coincidentally the other
late unionizer—came close to Philadelphia's racial mix.[10]

The diversity of Philadelphia's labor force was not only a partial
consequence of earlier union failures but also a contributing cause,
for it allowed agile shipowners to play off one group against another.
When the Poles, for example, complained that blacks were getting
easier jobs or being assigned to handle less offensive cargoes, the
employers obligingly inverted the status hierarchy by temporarily
placing African Americans on the bottom—until such time that they,
too, complained, prompting a reshuffling of the deck. By keeping
intergroup tensions at a high yet manageable level, the constant
churning of ethnic and racial groups effectively kept the longshoremen divided and docile.[11]

Roots of Unionization

Surveying the port of Philadelphia early in 1913, there was little to
suggest that the docks would become a hotbed of unionism by year's
end. From all appearances the open shop seemed fully in keeping
with the recent history of union failure, employer resistance, and labor
force balkanization. Organizing prospects were so bleak, in fact, that
when the IWW "invaded" Philadelphia in the spring to launch a citywide recruiting campaign, the longshoremen were not even included
in their plans. And for good reason. Having previously failed to rouse
the lethargic dockworkers through fiery soapbox agitation, the Wobblies dismissed them as hopeless.[12]

But despair soon gave way to anger as conditions on the docks
worsened. Unconstrained by union protection, stevedoring operators,
who subcontracted with local shippers to load and unload their vessels, began to bear down on the men, driving them long and hard.
The customary ten-hour shift was, as an employer later conceded,
"really thirteen or fourteen hours on the job" after taking into account
time for hiring and meals. With travel time added, the work "day"

extended well into the night. "We have worked until we are all worked down," as one veteran longshoreman put it. "Many times I have been so tired I could hardly get home. Sometimes the [street]cars pass[ed] my home, and I was so tired I was asleep."[13]

Although the ten-hour day was the rule, stretches as long as fifty hours or more were not uncommon. "Before the I.W.W.," recalled longshoreman Charles Carter, a former slave, "you knowed when you start to work but you never knowed when you was going to stop. You could go in from one hour to fifty and over. Only have time to run out and get a little morsel to eat and slide back, and work as long as the boss wanted you to work." Some bosses, it seems, never wanted to stop. John ("Jack") Walsh, an IWW veteran who helped to organize the docks, told a federal judge in 1918 of one gang that was forced to work 110 consecutive hours without rest. Two of the men, Walsh reported, were "carried up dead in the tugs and a few more of them, they ain't able to walk yet."[14]

What made the long hours so dangerous were the extraordinary physical demands of the job itself. Cargo-handling methods were still quite primitive before World War I. The few "labor-saving" technologies then in existence were developed with particular commodities in mind, such as elevators for storing grain, extractors for loading coal, pumps for discharging oil and molasses, and conveyor belts for handling sugar. Otherwise, the men relied on brute force, carrying everything from two-hundred-pound sacks of potatoes to five-hundred-pound slabs of bacon on their muscular shoulders, or else wrestling with handheld dollies laden with even heavier loads.[15] Transporting such cargoes fifty feet or more from the wharf to the ship's hold while negotiating treacherous gangplanks and congested work areas required not only enormous strength but also constant vigilance to avoid serious injury. The physical and mental fatigue that normally set in after a full ten-hour shift placed anyone working longer hours at considerable risk to life and limb.

Such risks came with the job, as work often continued around the clock until a ship was dispatched. When the port was busy a shift might last twenty-four hours or more. At quitting time, Walsh recalled, "the boss would order the men back again, and he would tell you if you would not come back, 'You don't need to look for work there any more.' "[16] Nor was this an idle threat. Under the port's casual system of employment in which labor was handpicked as needed for each new job, failure to curry favor with the hiring boss was tantamount to being blacklisted and eventually driven from the industry. The resulting heavy dependence on employer favoritism, coupled with the chronic economic uncertainty of longshore work, imposed sufficient labor discipline to keep most men on the job for as long as needed, subject to miserable conditions, earning as little as twenty cents an hour.[17]

After suffering in silence for so many years, the longshoremen finally found their voice. In the spring of 1913 Wobbly leaders in Philadelphia received word that the port's dockworkers were interested in organizing, possibly under their banner. The request from the waterfront came as quite a surprise, even to the normally unflappable Wobblies. Local leaders were admittedly "at a loss" to explain the sudden interest in the IWW since, by their own reckoning, "few if any" longshoremen "understood the principles of industrialism or the form of the organization." Whatever their doubts at the time, the Wobblies immediately sent a local organizer, Edward Lewis, down to the docks to sign up the anticipated flood of new recruits. But after canvassing the waterfront, Lewis came back empty-handed, unable to find even a single supporter. Just as the Wobblies were about to give up on the mercurial dockworkers, however, they came through. Following a meeting of striking sugar workers, a small group of longshoremen who were in attendance approached the stage to ask Wobbly veteran George Speed for assistance in organizing the waterfront. In agreeing to help, Speed laid the foundations for what would become one of the most durable associations in IWW history.[18]

Speed met with the longshoremen the following morning at IWW headquarters, where they hammered out three principal demands. At the top of the list was money, with the longshoremen seeking to increase the hourly wage from the current "sliding scale" of twenty to twenty-five cents to a uniform rate of thirty-five cents for all categories of day work. A second demand calling for overtime pay, although nominally focused on wages, was really about limiting the length of the working day. Recognizing that they were in no position to refuse work beyond ten hours, the longshoremen sought to make "overtime" less attractive to their employers by demanding time and a half after 6:00 P.M. and double time for Sundays and holidays. The last demand was for union recognition, not of the IWW, but of a "standing committee" of dockworkers.[19]

The demands galvanized the longshoremen. On May 13, without waiting for a response from the stevedores, the men began leaving their jobs. After three days more than two thousand longshoremen were out, stranding twenty vessels along a twenty-mile stretch of the Delaware River. Other ships, particularly those on tight schedules, were forced to sail without their full complement of passengers or cargo. As activity ground to a halt, several large shipping lines rerouted their vessels to nearby ports, discharging cargo in Baltimore and New York for eventual shipment by rail to Philadelphia. In response the strikers fired off telegrams to longshoremen in other cities pleading for solidarity and asking them not to service any vessel that had been diverted from Philadelphia. With their flanks covered, both sides dug in for what one local newspaper described as "a fight to the finish."[20]

On Strike with the Wobblies

The leadership of the walkout was still unresolved. Although the Wobblies claimed to be in charge, only a minority of strikers actually belonged to the IWW. The vast majority were uncommitted. With the rank and file up for grabs, the ILA sent organizers down to the docks in an effort to wrest control of the walkout from the IWW. But the strikers, mindful of the ILA's history of nonsupport, were openly hostile, up to the point of reportedly threatening federation organizers with bodily harm.[21]

The Wobblies moved with uncharacteristic caution to fill the leadership vacuum. Avoiding any hint of radicalism, they stuck close to the original demands, promoting them in the language of fairness, not revolution. "We have come here to get a square deal for your working men," organizer Edward Lewis explained at one of the first strike meetings. "And we will continue your fight until we get what is your right share." The time for talking was over, he continued. "We are strong enough to do anything. . . . Our great power lies in being able to sit with our hands folded and do nothing. And then everything is at a standstill."[22]

Lewis's advocacy of direct action was well tailored to the economics of commercial shipping. Stiff competition and narrow profit margins compelled shipowners to keep labor on a tight leash to minimize operating costs. While ships were at sea, work discipline was maintained through an archaic system of maritime codes and practices that subjected the crew to corporal punishment, arrest, and even imprisonment for acts of insubordination. On reaching port, however, the tables were suddenly turned against employers by the economic necessity of getting vessels discharged and reloaded as rapidly as possible and on their way to the next destination. When faced with a spontaneous job action on the docks, time-conscious shippers often found it less costly to yield to union demands than to "wait out" a strike and risk paying additional wharf rental charges and expensive late fees once their cargoes arrived overdue at the next location.[23]

Lewis's advice to the longshoremen to simply sit with "hands folded and do nothing" resonated with their daily experience of power dynamics at the point of production. Solidarity, while essential, was not enough: to fully realize their disruptive potential, the dockworkers also needed the freedom to take collective action when relations of force were most favorable. Lengthy time contracts of the kind pursued by the ILA, which included strict prohibitions against "unauthorized" work stoppages, were of little value to the longshoremen whose power resided in the ability to strike at a moment's notice, whenever the shipowners were most economically vulnerable. Lewis's insistence on direct action, backed by the IWW's refusal to sign contracts, found a most receptive audience on the docks.[24]

The Wobblies' seeming obsession with direct action went hand in hand with a logic of collective action that relied on labor solidarity, rather than contracts, as the basis of economic power. Aggressively confronting what had long been the Achilles' heel of unionism in Philadelphia—persistent ethnic tensions—strike leaders made it a point to have each nationality represented on all decision-making bodies, including, most important, the fifteen-member negotiating committee. This model of "collective leadership," patterned after the recently successful IWW strike of textile workers in Lawrence, Massachusetts, helped to unify the port's 1,700 white longshoremen.[25] But the walkout's success depended on winning over the remaining 1,300 African-American dockworkers. Without them, the strike stood no chance.

Reaching out to the port's black longshoremen, the Wobblies couched their appeal in the race-neutral terms of class solidarity, failing to mention racial victimization as a possible concern of African Americans. In suppressing race, the Wobblies were guided by their ideological privileging of class with its attendant commitment to color-blind organizing. Unlike many AFL unions, including the ILA, which tolerated and in some cases sponsored separate locals for blacks and whites, the IWW promoted integrated, biracial unionism as a matter of principle.[26] The Wobblies' inclusiveness, backed by constitutional guarantees that "no working man or woman shall be excluded . . . because of creed or color," left a generally positive impression on Philadelphia's sizable African-American religious community, with some of its most outspoken religious leaders warmly embracing the IWW.[27]

Early in the walkout the African Methodist Episcopal Church in Philadelphia came out in support of the Wobblies. "The IWW at least protects the colored man," declared one minister, "which is more than I can say for the laws of this country." Nor was he alone in his views. An influential black Protestant minister took the stage at an IWW meeting a few weeks later to lash out at the "moral skunks" who inhabited the police department and city hall and to offer his support for the Wobblies. "The I.W.W. doesn't care for laws, if by breaking laws they can get righteousness," he said. "History shows that the great martyrs broke the laws of the church and now we erect memorials to them." He then went on to commend the IWW because "it believes in the colored man."[28]

Putting their beliefs into practice on the docks, the Wobblies openly and aggressively recruited black longshoremen into their newly chartered Local 8 of the Marine Transport Workers' Industrial Union, an IWW affiliate. Such overt displays of "race mixing" were a clear violation of contemporary social norms, even in northern liberal strongholds like Philadelphia. Indeed, the "city of brotherly love" was anything but loving in its treatment of African-American workers, fewer than two hundred of whom had managed to break the AFL's color barrier as members of the unionized skilled trades. Local 8's outstretched arms offered a sharp contrast to what one scholar described as "the hostile or indifferent treatment of Negroes" at the hands of the city's mainstream labor movement.[29] "The IWW was the only union," recalled James Fair, a veteran longshoreman, "accepting black workers freely. They advocated just one thing—solidarity. . . . That sank in with a lot of us." Hundreds of longshoremen, black as well as white, poured into Local 8 over the next few days.[30]

Local 8's emergence elicited a predictable response from local shipowners, who vowed to fight as long and as hard as necessary to keep the IWW off the docks. Privately, they were counting on an early victory. Frederick W. Taylor, representing four of the port's larger shipping lines, dismissed the IWW as "a business proposition" whose main function was to collect dues while offering "nothing in return except empty promises which cannot be filled." Counting on the historical lack of solidarity on the docks, Taylor was confident that the better-paid longshoremen would not "unite with all kinds of labor for a uniform rate of pay." When the men came to their senses, Taylor wrote reassuringly, the Wobblies would "silently slip away with the cash" and the waterfront would return to normal.[31]

As the walkout entered its second week with no end in sight, it was Taylor who came to his senses. Although still promising victory, he now realized that the stevedores had a real fight on their hands. To combat the growing strength of the IWW, Taylor convinced the port's employers to create "an independent nucleus of power" on the docks by establishing nonunion beachheads on several piers. From these staging areas, skeleton crews were put to work under constant police protection.[32] The labor performed by the strikebreakers, Taylor admitted in confidence, "was extremely slow and unsatisfactory." Still, he insisted, their presence was "absolutely necessary to prove that the power over the work was retained by the Steamship Companies."[33]

What had been an orderly and peaceful walkout was suddenly transformed by the introduction of strikebreakers. The calm was shattered late in the afternoon on May 21, when about fifty strikebreakers, heading home after work, were confronted by a larger group of pickets. The men began arguing, then fighting, freely exchanging blows with fists, clubs, and lead pipes. Close to one thousand residents of the surrounding neighborhood flowed into the streets, turning an otherwise minor confrontation into a full-scale riot. The police arrived but, according to press accounts, "were powerless. The crowd filled the street and the pavements and many of them took sides with the strikers. Bricks and bottles were hurled from windows and alleys." Five men, all of them strikers, were taken into custody, and many more were injured. A few hours later, in apparently unrelated incidents, two men suspected of strikebreaking were beaten by roving bands of pickets.[34]

The local press used the rioting as an occasion for Wobbly-bashing. Philadelphia's leading daily newspaper, the *Public Ledger*, baring its editorial fangs, denounced the recent clash as a "desperate campaign against the basic institutions of civilization." The IWW's "hysterical followers" had no real interest in the "unmolten mass" of immigrants, who were "like putty in their hands." The recent outbreak of violence on the waterfront was entirely consistent with the Wobblies' use of "destruction, intimidation, murder or anything else in order to bully society into acceptance of a half-baked theory which would upset all standards that have been constructed by centuries of human effort and social endeavor." Lest there be any doubt as to the proper course of action, the *Public Ledger* called on an aroused public to face the IWW "peril . . . squarely and courageously. There is no place in America for it. It must be driven out, exiled, exterminated."[35]

Faced with escalating attacks in the media and on the picket lines, Local 8's leaders convened an emergency mass meeting at which they urged the men "to remain firm and not be discouraged." Promising to raise bail for anyone arrested, union officers threatened to respond in kind to all future acts of violence directed against the longshore-men. "If the police are looking for trouble they will get it," declared one strike activist. "This town has never seen an I.W.W. strike. We go in to win. If we cannot do it peacefully, then we do it otherwise."[36]

The waterfront remained tense. Union carpenters, who had been building dining facilities for the strikebreakers, walked off the job in a show of solidarity. Members of other marine trades stopped re-porting for work. As cargo handling slowed to a crawl, even Taylor, writing in confidence, had to admit that their strikebreaking efforts were largely symbolic, amounting to little more than "putting up a bold front." With his own credibility now on the line, Taylor extended an olive branch to the strikers, inviting three former employees into his office to discuss the impasse. He argued that a ten-cent hourly increase was not really in the men's best interest because it would end up diverting shipping from Philadelphia to Baltimore, Montreal, and other low-wage ports. In a spirit of compromise, Taylor proposed a five-cent increase to thirty cents per hour for straight time—the prevailing rate in Boston, Montreal, and most other competing ports. Taylor reluctantly agreed to the overtime demands but ruled out union recognition. As a gesture of reconciliation, he promised not to retaliate against any strikers and to make jobs available for all former employees who had walked out.[37]

The men took Taylor's offer back to the membership for

consideration. That evening the longshoremen voted to accept the proposal. On learning of the settlement the strikebreakers called a job action of their own, apparently fearful of reprisals from unionists. The employers wasted no time in firing the ringleaders while allowing the others to stay on until the regular longshoremen returned to claim their former jobs.[38]

The Wobblies under Attack

The walkout produced no clear winner. Although the shipowners succeeded in shaving a nickel off the original wage demand, the men won a uniform rate of thirty cents an hour, thus doing away with the highly unpopular "sliding scale." Of the two remaining demands, the longshoremen secured the ten-hour day but failed to win union recognition. Both sides claimed victory, but neither the Wobblies nor the shipowners were satisfied with the outcome.[39]

Dissension arose first among the employers. Shortly after the men returned to work, the port's leading shipping interests sat down together for the first time since the walkout to discuss the terms of the recent settlement. Taylor, its principal architect, was called on to defend his actions, particularly concession of the ten-hour day. Describing the ensuing discussion as "not harmonious," Taylor was besieged from all sides, after which his motion to ratify overtime pay failed to secure a second. Leading the opposition was a representative from the stridently antiunion International Mercantile Marine Company, who offered an alternative motion allowing each operator to independently set wage rates for evenings, Sundays, and holidays.[40] In casting the lone dissenting vote, Taylor warned his fellow shipowners that any failure to honor their verbal agreement would "have the effect of maintaining the I.W.W. in the field." But no one else in the room seemed to take the IWW threat seriously. Fully aware of past failures to unionize the port, the employers dismissed the Wobblies as "a huge joke," giving them at most three months on the docks.[41]

For a while it appeared that the shipowners might be right. In early June the city's newspapers, again led by the *Public Ledger*, began cranking up the propaganda machine, running highly sensationalized front-page stories of local IWW activity. Under lurid headlines warning of an "IWW invasion," readers learned that an "army of unrest" was stalking Philadelphia, "agitating and coercing thousands of men and women to forsake their labor and to join their ranks." The next installment, focusing on IWW losses, reviewed a recently aborted strike of street cleaners led by the Wobblies. Using this incident to compare the "relative merits" of the IWW and the AFL, the *Public Ledger* opined that many disillusioned street cleaners "expressed their sorrow at having abandoned the latter organization."[42]

Riding this latest wave of anti-Wobbly sentiment, the ILA dispatched its own army of organizers to the docks, thus locking horns with the IWW for a second time in as many months. Unlike the first encounter, however, the Wobblies already had a substantial following on the docks, with about half of the port's thirty-five hundred longshoremen enrolled in Local 8. ILA organizers, still fuming over their earlier defeat, pulled out all stops. Working every possible angle, they approached leaders of the rival MTW and offered them salaried positions with the AFL if they would swing their members into the ILA. When the Wobblies refused to take the bait, ILA officials embarked on another, more desperate fishing expedition, this time accusing Local 8 of financial improprieties and demanding a full accounting of all union funds. Local newspapers obligingly picked up the story, but it died for lack of evidence.[43]

ILA organizers were also slugging it out in the trenches. Charging the Wobblies with everything from promoting anarchy to mismanaging the recent walkout, their efforts finally paid off when the smaller of two branches making up Local 8 declared its independence from the national IWW and refused to purchase monthly dues stamps. It is not clear what prompted such drastic action. National IWW leader Joseph Ettor, who was brought in to straighten out the wayward longshoremen, later observed that he had "no complaint . . . after what was dealt out to them." Their criticism of the IWW, he concluded, was "justified" by the actions of certain local "spokesmen for the IWW"—presumably a reference to Edward Lewis, who had been expelled from another IWW local shortly before the walkout. Wobbly misleadership, coupled with unrelenting ILA attacks, finally took its toll on the two hundred or so members of Local 8's branch 2. In early June, shortly after returning to work, they voted 100 to 30 to switch allegiance from the MTW to the ILA.[44]

But the ILA's election victory proved hollow, despite effusive praise from the commercial press and promises of support from local stevedores. By the end of the summer, after nearly three months of campaigning, the struggling AFL local had fewer than five hundred dues-paying members. In a move seemingly calculated to give the appearance of momentum, local ILA charters were issued for Port Richmond and South Philadelphia.[45] All that was missing was the longshoremen. "The situation in Philadelphia," acknowledged William Hembosy, ILA district officer, "is very slow in maturing in our favor. Our only obstacle is the poisoned minds of both the Polish and Lithuanians."[46]

Hembosy's failure to even mention the more numerous African-American longshoremen is hard to figure. It may have reflected racist thinking of the sort common to many AFL leaders at the time who refused to see black workers as anything other than rate-busters or potential strikebreakers. But that was not, generally speaking, true of the ILA, whose officers knew black longshoremen, particularly in the Gulf ports, as solid and reliable unionists. Whatever their personal views on race relations, men like Hembosy could simply not afford to ignore black workers in ports where they composed a substantial part of the labor force. That he did so in reporting on the obstacles facing the ILA in Philadelphia suggests that African-American dock-workers may have been more supportive than either Poles or Lithuanians.[47]

White ethnics, in any case, became the principal target of ILA organizers. Hoping to counter the Wobblies' influence with Poles and Lithuanians in particular, Hembosy requested literature in their native languages. "The IWWs," he complained, "have kept singing into the ears of these men that the A.F. of L. officials sell their organization out to the highest bidder, also that they take all the money in their treasury. . . . [T]hey have got to the point that they believe it to such an extent that anything that has the name Federation in it must be of such a character that no honest man would have anything to do with it."[48] In branding AFL officials as sellouts, IWW leaders drew a clear line of demarcation between Local 8, a "real union" committed to solidarity and rank-and-file militancy, and the ILA, which, in Wobbly vernacular, was all "fake and foney," just another "job trust" led by "labor fakirs" intent on making "bum deals" with the shipowners.

While this discourse on union legitimacy spoke to many of the longshoremen's concerns, its silences told an even more important story. Noticeably absent was any reference to the one issue that the media, union leaders, and most contemporary observers regarded as *the* defining difference between the IWW and the AFL: their sharply contrasting political orientations. Except for occasional charges of disloyalty directed at the IWW, which failed to move the longshoremen, the interunion battle for supremacy on the docks was surprisingly free of ideological warfare. Indeed, none of the surviving documents from this period even mentioned the ILA's conservatism, much less its support for capitalism. Nor were the IWW's revolutionary convictions explicitly discussed in any of its propaganda aimed at the longshoremen. Instead, Local 8 portrayed itself as honest and accountable, and as a product of both, responsibly militant.

Industrial Syndicalism in Action

Local 8's lack of revolutionary fervor did not go unnoticed by the national organization. Speaking before the eighth annual IWW convention in the fall of 1913, general organizer George Speed, who had been instrumental in pulling the longshoremen together only a few months earlier, went on at some length about "the deplorable state of affairs in Philadelphia." Ripping into Edward Lewis and others for failing "to enlighten or instruct in any way on the aims and objects of Industrial Organization," Speed charged them with "bull dozing" and "brow-beating" their followers. Not appreciating the importance of indoctrinating the rank and file, all that Local 8's opportunistic leaders "looked for was just numbers" of new recruits.[49]

Speed's indictment would resurface with serious consequences in a few years, but for now, Local 8, finding itself embroiled in guerrilla warfare on the docks, enjoyed immunity from such charges. Since returning to work following the May walkout, the longshoremen and shipowners had been going at it on a regular basis, mostly minor skirmishes over hiring and the contested ten-hour day. Noting "considerable dissatisfaction and discontent" among the men, wary employers reported in late June "a great increase . . . in the number of longshoremen wearing the I.W.W. buttons."[50] Much more than a symbol of organizational loyalty, the button had become a powerful weapon in the men's struggle to control the job. In the absence of union recognition, Local 8's survival depended on cornering the local labor market. This was accomplished by pressuring the port's stevedores, under threat of a renewed strike, to hire only those men displaying current buttons, which were issued at the beginning of each month on receipt of fifty cents in dues. Where this practice was adopted, as it was on most piers, membership in the MTW became a condition of employment, thereby securing the union's presence on the docks.[51]

Job control in the hands of the Wobblies was unlike anything ever fashioned by the rival ILA. Consistent with the AFL's business syndicalism, the ILA established itself in other ports by essentially giving up the right to strike during the life of the contract in exchange for preferential employment of its members. Direct action thus became a weapon of last resort for protecting the ILA's job territory—not, as with the Wobblies, an ongoing and vital practice for sustaining workers' collective control over hiring. And once codified in writing, the ILA's continued access to the job depended on restricting its membership to a small and regularly employable segment of the dockside labor force—not, as with the Wobblies, whose job control was maintained by keeping the rank and file in an aroused state of mobilization and combat readiness.[52]

Local 8's success in establishing job control without the usual encumbrances of membership exclusiveness, high dues, or restrictive contracts made it—for a time at least—the darling of national IWW leaders, who pointed to the "Philadelphia model" as a solution to the perennial problem of building a union movement that was capable of protecting its members without succumbing to the sins of the AFL.[53] Not surprisingly, waterfront employers took a decidedly different view of the IWW button, seeing it as undermining labor discipline and vowing to banish it from the waterfront. Leading the charge once again was the International Mercantile Marine Company. When its hiring stevedore fired five men after they refused to remove their union buttons, the entire force of almost three hundred quit work, paralyzing the company's operations. Other companies followed suit, leading to a rash of job actions. Although the longshoremen were still no match for the powerful and determined International Mercantile Marine, the port's two largest stevedores caved in almost immediately, establishing the union button on all but a handful of the city's piers. If, as Speed charged, Local 8 had failed to educate its members in the theory of revolution, its campaign of direct action provided the port's untutored longshoremen with a practical and compelling lesson in industrial syndicalism.[54]

Local 8's industrial syndicalism also found expression in its solidaristic organizational principles. The strikers' original demand for a single, uniform rate of pay was aimed not only at doing away with the unpopular "sliding scale" but also at placing the entire waterfront labor force—from the lowliest waterboy to the most skilled winch driver—on the same economic plane. Such leveling seemed positively irrational to employers, who regarded the longshoremen as "fools" for allying with the likes of "water-tenders, oilers, cooks and waiters."[55] Fools or not, the men held their ground. When the shipowners finally agreed to a universal wage of thirty cents per hour, it applied to everyone on the organized docks. In later years other ports around the country would introduce plans for equalizing earnings within particular maritime occupations, but nothing so inclusive as the universal wage was ever adopted outside of Philadelphia.[56]

Equality and solidarity also guided Local 8's approach to race relations. The remarkable interracial unity displayed during the May walkout was put to the test after the men returned to work. No longer held together by a unifying opposition, conflict turned inward as old schisms reappeared. In a bold move intended to bridge the racial gap, Local 8 inaugurated a policy of rotating the union's top elected positions between black and white officers. One month an African American served as president assisted by a white vice president; the next month this pattern was reversed. Local 8's bylaws further stipulated that at least one of its two secretaries, who directed the union's daily activities, was to be a black member in good standing. As the only integrated union in the country with rotating biracial leadership, Local 8 represented, according to the *Messenger*, a radical black monthly, "the vanguard of American labor."[57]

Much of the impetus behind Local 8's progressive racial policies came from its indigenous black leadership, particularly Benjamin Fletcher. Born and raised in Philadelphia, Fletcher first came in contact with the IWW in 1911 on the city's docks where he was working as a longshoreman.[58] The following year, while the Lawrence textile strike dragged on, a steady stream of IWW partisans—most notably Elizabeth Gurley Flynn, whose fiery oratory earned her the nickname "Rebel Girl," and Patrick Quinlan, a hotheaded Irishman who later turned up on the payroll of the ILA—passed through Philadelphia, occasionally stopping long enough to address the longshoremen.[59] Although these periodic agitational efforts failed to produce permanent organization on the docks, the Wobblies' message of militant interracial unionism appealed to Fletcher, who joined the IWW in 1911, becoming the corresponding secretary for Local 57, a "mixed" local made up of workers employed in various industries throughout the city.[60]

Fletcher's recruitment was a real coup for the IWW. Jack Lever, a longshoreman who worked alongside Fletcher in the early days, remembered him simply as "one of the best organizers [he] knew." Articulate, charismatic, and indefatigable, Fletcher had few peers. "He has been of more service to the masses of the plain Negro people than all the wind jamming Negro leaders in the United States," observed the *Messenger* in 1919. With a "vision far beyond that of almost any Negro leader" in America, Fletcher was praised as that rare trade unionist "who fights for the great masses to lessen their hours of work, to increase their wages, to decrease their high cost of living, to make life more livable for the toiling black workers." In more contemporary terms, James Fair, an African American who joined Local 8 in 1917, described Fletcher many years later as "something like a Martin Luther King," who instead of championing civil rights "turned to organized labor and improving our standards of living."[61]

Fletcher was surrounded by a strong supporting cast of black activists on the waterfront. Local 8's policy of rotation in office generated a large pool of experienced African-American leaders who, along with Fletcher, were often at the center of the union's ongoing factional struggles. Unlike Fletcher, however, who remained a Wobbly until his death in 1949, the second tier of black cadre—led by Glenn Perrymore, Alonzo Richards, Charles Carter, Dan Jones, and Joseph White—had a more complicated, at times strained, relationship with the IWW.

Local 8's white leaders, although fully supporting interracial unionism, were more suspect as organizers. Edward Lewis, the main spokesman during the strike, was apparently torn between his two great loves: the IWW and alcohol. When sober, he was a real asset; when not, he was unreliable and ineffective. George Speed, from the national headquarters, was a much more dynamic leader, whose extensive organizational experience was put to good use in the early days leading up to the walkout. But his incessant revolutionary posturing alienated longshoremen and hard-core Wobblies alike. By the time he left town that summer, Speed was, in his own words, "hated possibly as well as any man could be." When Lewis dropped out of sight a short time later, Local 8 found extremely capable replacements for both men, turning to veteran Wobblies John Walsh, an experienced dockworker, Walter Nef, an itinerant IWW organizer, and Ed Doree, a former hard-rock miner.[62]

Invigorated by the infusion of new blood, Local 8 refused to rest until it controlled not just the docks but also, as Walsh insisted, every "transport worker aboard ship, truck, railroad, or street car." The first in line were the harbor boatmen, who affiliated with Local 8 as branch 4 following a successful strike for higher wages. Next came the seamen. Led by Genaro Pazos, a marine fireman and avowed syndicalist, the port's two hundred or so Spanish-speaking sailors gravitated to Local 8 as a temporary base of operations before eventually striking out on their own as Local 100 of the MTW. By the middle of 1914, with the city's streetcar workers reportedly "on track for the I.W.W. special," the Wobblies' syndicalist goal of "One Big Union" for all of Philadelphia's transport workers seemed within reach.[63]

Flushed with success, Local 8 declared May 16—the first anniversary of its founding—a nonworking holiday on the waterfront. On the eve of the walkout the stevedores announced that anyone failing to report for work in the morning would be subject to immediate discharge. Despite such threats, more than two thousand longshoremen, many of them defiantly waving small Local 8 pennants, assembled the next morning to mark the union's first year of existence. Accompanied by three bands, the interracial, multiethnic crowd paraded along the waterfront, through neighboring working-class districts en route to a city park, where they were regaled by several speakers, black as well as white, in English and in Polish, on the importance of solidarity, organization, and job control.[64]

Returning to work the next day, many longshoremen felt "they had won a great victory," having completely tied up the port for the second time in as many years. "Now that they have had a taste of power," observed Wobbly partisan John McKelvey, "they are more than ever convinced of the necessity of organizing all those employed in any capacity on the waterfront."[65] The longshoremen put their convictions into practice a few weeks later when a vessel docked at one of the port's few unorganized piers. Unable to secure enough nonunion workers, the stevedore hired members of Local 8 to fill out his crew. After getting on the job, however, the union men refused to work alongside "scabs." A picket line was formed and loading ceased.

Another ship, docking at the same pier a few hours later, was similarly stranded, forcing its captain, in desperation, to push back from the wharf and set sail—only to try his luck at another unorganized pier, five miles downriver, where he again met a large crowd of angry longshoremen. Loading finally got under way the next morning, with an all-union crew. "We are fast reaching the point," declared McKelvey, "where we will be the master of the port."[66]

A Fragile Solidarity

In little more than a year Local 8 had turned the longshoremen's world upside down, transforming them from timid and defenseless "wage slaves" into self-confident, even cocky, "masters of the port." The first of the year found the men, still intoxicated by their newfound sense of power, demanding a twofold increase in wages. When the employers balked, more than three thousand members of Local 8 walked off the job on the morning of January 27, 1915, effectively closing the port. The strike was settled by nightfall after most shipping lines agreed to a ten-cent increase, advancing the basic hourly rate to forty cents, sixty cents for overtime, and eighty cents for Sundays and holidays.[67]

The lone holdout among the waterfront employers was Charles M. Taylor, head stevedore for the antiunion coal wharves at Port Richmond, a few miles north of the city. Refusing to negotiate, Taylor locked out Local 8, notifying its members that their services were no longer required. Using nonunion labor furnished by like-minded employers, Taylor continued operations through mid-February, when Local 8, hard-pressed by the seasonal slump in shipping activity, finally threw in the towel and ordered the strikers back to work under the old wage scale. Having beaten back the wage demand, a defiant Taylor ordered all returning employees to surrender their IWW buttons before reporting for work. Other employers, taking advantage of the unusually sharp economic downturn, followed Taylor's lead until the union's control over hiring was broken throughout the port. Unable to provide any semblance of job security, Local 8 lost its hold over the longshoremen, most of whom stopped paying dues or attending meetings.[68]

The resuscitation of East Coast shipping later that year breathed new life into the skeletal remains of Local 8. Early in 1916 the Wobblies led a walkout against the Southern Steamship Company, returning to work a short time later as "union men, proudly wearing the I.W.W. work button." Their success triggered similar actions on other piers until Local 8 had been restored to its former self, complete with job control. In April, after ignoring the Philadelphia waterfront for over a year, *Industrial Solidarity* reported that Local 8 was back in business with more than three thousand members.[69]

With the docks once again secure, Wobbly organizers turned their attention to other harbor workers, inducing the port's "coal heavers," who load coal onto ships, to join the MTW. The seamen began making headway with the marine firemen, and in the spring a new branch of Local 8, representing the port's lighterboat captains, was formed. Topping off a most successful recruiting campaign, a group of dockside lumber handlers, previously affiliated with the ILA, voted by a two to one margin to throw their lot in with the rejuvenated Wobbly local. Philadelphia's marine workers, as MTW leader John Walsh reported in May, were "on the map for industrial unionism."[70]

Also on the map were the waterfront employers, who had no intention of turning the port over to the IWW, or any other union, without a fight. In June the Southern Steamship line shaved a nickel off the going pay rates for dock work, then threatened to move their entire operation to New York if the men resisted. Three hundred longshoremen, representing almost the entire crew, promptly walked out, throwing up a picket line around the Southern line for the second time in recent months. But this time the employers were ready. With the appearance of the first picket, they converted one of the struck piers into "an emergency camp" capable of accommodating as many as two hundred strikebreakers, who were lured "with food of excellent quality, soft, springy cots to sleep on and clean sheets three times a week."[71]

The strike remained orderly and peaceful for the first few weeks. But beneath the surface calm, pressure was slowly building. The lid finally blew off in early July, when Thomas Kenney, a Wobbly and ardent strike supporter, was shot through the heart and killed by Warner Maddox, an African-American cook who was serving the strikebreakers. In his defense, Maddox claimed that he was besieged by strikers while on his way home from work. Fleeing on foot, he and a friend sought refuge from his angry pursuers in a public washroom, from which he fired into the crowd outside, fatally wounding Kenney.

The police arrived and rescued the barricaded Maddox, who, along with two other cooks, both African Americans, was taken into custody and charged with inciting to riot.[72]

The waterfront exploded in violence the following day when Glenn Perrymore, a black strike leader, confronted "a colored detective disguised as a scab," asking him what he was doing on the docks. But, according to an eyewitness, "instead of showing his shield, he answered it was none of Perrymore's business, and pulled his gun. Perrymore grappled with him. He emptied his gun of five shots; while the rest of the police and detectives started in, Perrymore was hit on the head with a blackjack five times."[73]

What the press described as a "short but spirited" fight ensued. Several shots were fired. One picket was hit in the leg, and another miraculously escaped with only a minor flesh wound when a bullet fired at close range glanced off a metal spectacles case that he carried in his breast pocket. Casualties from two days of fighting exacted a heavy toll: five strikers were hospitalized with severe injuries, one was "killed outright," and the seemingly invincible Local 8—its ranks shattered—tasted defeat for the first time.[74]

The Southern line's victory was a real setback for the union and, in its racial fallout, a harbinger of things to come. Although the strikebreakers were never identified, it was hardly a coincidence that everyone who was mistaken for them, including cooks and detectives, was black, whereas all of the known strikers—with the notable exception of Perrymore—apparently were white. Such racial polarization was the extreme, as there were many African Americans who walked picket lines and whites who crossed them. But just as there was no denying the strength of Local 8's color-blind traditions, it was no longer possible to look beyond the increasingly racialized character of class conflict on the waterfront.

Even if the class-centric Wobblies had wanted to ignore the growing salience of race, rival AFL leaders would not let them. Speaking before an audience of the port's offshore workers in May, an official with the AFL's International Seamen's Union proudly declared, as part of his recruiting pitch to the predominantly white sailors, that he would "not sign any 'niggers' in his union." Walsh, representing the IWW, took the stage and left no doubt where his organization stood. "This fellow," he responded, "wears a number 2 hat; if brains were radium, he would not bring the price of a cigarette." But the seamen's separatist vision, however opaque to Walsh and his fellow Wobblies, clearly projected the growing distrust and solidifying racial identities animating at least some maritime workers, black as well as white.[75]

Race and class loyalties collided a few months later during a strike of the port's sugar workers. On January 31, 1917, two thousand un-skilled laborers employed in the dockside refineries walked off the job after employers rejected their demands for a ten-hour day, over-time pay, and a modest increase in the hourly rate. Eventually turning to the IWW for leadership, the sugar strikers—mostly Polish and Lithuanian like the port's white longshoremen—called on and re-ceived immediate assistance from Local 8. Presenting no demands of their own, fifteen hundred longshoremen walked out in support of the sugar workers, sacrificing their own incomes and quite possibly their jobs. "It was a wonderful and inspiring picture of class solidar-ity," observed Ed Doree, a Wobbly spokesman for Local 8.[76]

The walkout remained peaceful until several hundred strikebreak-ers—African Americans recruited from outside Philadelphia, proba-bly from the South—were put to work in mid-February. A few days later a small but vocal group of women, identified as wives of strikers, assembled in front of the sugar refineries in a desperate attempt to appeal to the strikebreakers. "Don't take the bread from our babies," mothers shouted, holding their infants and small children aloft for all to see. Cries of "We are starving" and "We want our husbands to get their jobs back and to give us food" echoed from the noisy and spirited protesters. As the strikebreakers began pouring out onto the streets after the shift change, the women, in close pursuit, showered them with pepper, then pelted them with rocks and bricks. Their husbands, now converging on the fleeing strikebreakers, angrily cursed them as they were whisked away in company vans.[77] When the women, having been told to "quit annoying the negroes and go home," refused police orders to disperse, "Hell broke loose," according to one eyewitness. "Without a moment's warning police, by the hundred, came in from all sides, on foot, on horseback and in patrol wagons, shooting and clubbing. It was a massacre. The workers had no chance. They began to fall." When it was over, one striker, a prominent activist and Wob-bly, lay dead, with scores of men and women injured, including sev-eral police who suffered cuts and lacerations from flying projectiles.[78]

Violent clashes between strikebreakers and sugar workers contin-ued sporadically for the next several weeks until the walkout was called off in April. It was the IWW's second major setback on the waterfront in less than six months; and in both cases—first the Southern line and now the sugar trust—the employers' use of black strikebreakers had proven decisive. Although the Wobblies did their best to mask the underlying racial dynamics of each defeat, it became a major motif in strike coverage provided by the local press, which, in failing to distinguish "strikebreaker" from "Negro," routinely treated the two as synonymous.[79] For the diverse membership of Local 8, torn between the IWW's unifying doctrine of class struggle and their own recent experiences of racial discord, solidarity remained a desirable yet elusive goal.

Conclusion

Philadelphia's longshoremen accomplished nothing short of an organizational revolution on the docks before World War I. The city's waterfront, long known as the most secure open-shop port on the North Atlantic, was dramatically transformed during the spring of 1913 into a hotbed of unionism—and not just any unionism, but a particularly aggressive species of industrial syndicalism cultivated by its IWW leaders.

Local 8's inclusiveness enabled the port's dockworkers to overcome their long history of division and disorganization. Whatever the merits of the ILA's more restricted model—and there were plenty of longshoremen in Boston and elsewhere who swore by it—racially segregated craft unionism was a recipe for failure on Philadelphia's heterogeneous waterfront. By bringing the entire dockside labor force under the same organizational umbrella, Local 8 was able to establish a viable portwide presence for contesting the shipowners' ability to whipsaw blacks against whites, Poles against Italians, even one gang against another. Interracial industrial unionism thus emerged as a sound, if unstable, strategy for leveling the field of combat, and its continued viability depended on little else.

Local 8's reliance on direct action also complemented the longshoremen's "situational power" at the point of production. In refusing to sign contracts, the men were free to take collective action whenever the shipowners, facing tight deadlines, were most vulnerable to economic pressure. Of course, the lack of a contract was something of a double-edged sword. While freeing the longshoremen to press the class struggle, it also left them exposed to hostile employers who were under no contractual obligation to negotiate—as, for example, during the winter of 1915, when a determined Charles Taylor turned a routine walkout into a fight to the finish that left Local 8 in ruins. If this experience taught the longshoremen a painful lesson about the limits of direct action, it did nothing to shake the Wobblies' belief that contracts had to be avoided at all costs. Like most elements of Wobbly faith, however, the dockworkers were converts in name only. They supported direct action and opposed contracts up to the point that doing so increased their economic clout on the job.

Local 8 also addressed the chronic insecurity of waterfront employment in ways that capitalized on the longshoremen's disruptive capacities. Without overturning the traditional casual system of hiring, the Wobblies managed to tilt the balance of power decisively toward their members by compelling stevedores, under threat of renewed strike activity, to hire only those men wearing a current union button. Through its innovative system of job control, Local 8 demonstrated the possibility of building a mass organization that effectively advanced its members' interests without resorting to exorbitant dues, arbitrary skill qualifications, or any of the other restrictionist practices customarily employed by craft unions to limit members and corner the labor market.

Local 8's IWW leaders did not stumble on the importance of job control by themselves. They also had the rank and file, vociferous and independent at times, to remind them of their mission. Whenever the Wobblies strayed too far from the membership, the longshoremen simply withheld their support—whether it took the form of repudiating hard-liner George Speed as he prattled on about revolution, or briefly abandoning Local 8 after it lost job control in the winter of 1915. Through sustained contact with the longshoremen, Local 8's IWW leaders gradually came to internalize their pure and simple syndicalism. "We function as a job organization," declared a Wobbly spokesman following Local 8's first anniversary celebration in May 1914, "and have no time to split hairs" over abstract ideological questions. "Job control is the thing."[80]

But Local 8's job control, like most other aspects of its industrial syndicalism, differed in important ways from that of the rival ILA, whose practice of business syndicalism outside of Philadelphia led to a much more limited mobilization of dockworkers around their immediate job territory in defense of the contract. In contrast, Local 8 claimed as its jurisdiction the entire waterfront and everyone employed there, whose control over the job depended, not on a piece of paper, but on the collective organizational capacities of the workers themselves.

Chapter Three

Wobblies under Siege

Philadelphia's IWW leaders succeeded where most of their comrades failed because they remained in touch with the pure and simple syndicalism of the rank and file. So long as the dockworkers were able to pursue their own brand of militant industrial unionism, Local 8 was secure. Its chief rival, the ILA, wedded to its trademark business syndicalism of craftism, contracts, and conciliation, failed to generate much of a following among the longshoremen. Launched with high expectations in 1913, the ILA's organizing campaign never really got on track, as neither of its two locals, representing South Philadelphia and Port Richmond, lasted more than a year. By 1915 the Wobblies had the city's docks all to themselves.[1]

But the ILA did not roll over. It came storming back after World War I and eventually wrested control of the waterfront from the IWW. The ILA's victory, which seemed so improbable only a few years earlier, was set in motion by changing relations of force that isolated, weakened, and ultimately destroyed Local 8. Facing growing wartime opposition from various agencies of the federal government, the embattled Wobbly local found no peace in postwar America. State repression deprived the longshoremen of their most experienced leaders when in 1917 Walsh, Nef, Doree, and Fletcher were arrested and subsequently imprisoned on charges of threatening national security. With Local 8 still reeling, the federal government and local shipowners turned up the heat, working closely with one another in support of the ILA at the expense of the Wobblies. As ILA leaders seized the offensive, Local 8 came under attack from a most unlikely source—its own national organization, which suspended the longshoremen in 1920, allegedly for failing to uphold the IWW's revolutionary principles.

With all of these forces arrayed against them, the Wobblies some-how managed to hold on, although their grip was loosening, partic-ularly over Local 8's most recent African-American recruits. A resur-gent white racism that was sweeping many parts of the country, including Philadelphia, fueled the growth of black racial conscious-ness on the docks. Seeking to capitalize on rising tensions between black and white longshoremen, ILA organizers went after the port's increasingly restive African Americans, chartering a separate all-black local in 1919. But the tenacious Wobblies held on, retaining both job control and most of their followers.

Even after receiving massive and timely support from employers and government agencies alike, the ILA's newly fortified leaders were still unable to dislodge Local 8 until they, too, embraced many of the same organizational practices of industrial syndicalism by erasing the color line, installing a racially balanced union leadership, and coming to rely more heavily on the disruptive capacities of the rank and file. In 1926 the transformed ILA, now fully integrated and led by former Wobblies, won portwide recognition from the shipowners by taking direct action on the job in defense of their work button—just as the longshoremen had done years earlier as members of Local 8.

In telling the story of organizational succession on the Philadelphia waterfront, this chapter rewrites the familiar script in which proletarian conservatism is cast in a starring role as the villainous adversary of early-twentieth-century class formation. Far from a simple morality play cel-ebrating a triumphant "bourgeois" ideology, the struggle on the docks came down to a contest of wills, decided much more by relations of force than by the force of ideas. That Local 8 held on as long as it did was mainly due to the widespread appeal of its industrial syndicalism among the longshoremen, few of whom would have anything to do with the business syndicalist ILA until it essentially remade itself in the im-age of the IWW. Although the Wobblies' revolutionary vision died with them, important parts of their industrial syndicalism lived on for a time, finding a comfortable, if unlikely, home inside the ILA.

The War at Home

America's entry into World War I brought momentary peace and prosperity to the Philadelphia docks. Shipping activity along the Del-aware River, which had already increased dramatically in response to the growing allied demand for war materials, reached a frenetic pace following President Woodrow Wilson's formal declaration of war in the spring of 1917. As production of military hardware swung into high gear, the waterfront became congested with cargo destined for the European theater. Working around the clock, the labor force was stretched to the breaking point.

Wartime labor scarcity placed the MTW in a commanding position. Even the navy, whose port surveillance officers characterized Local 8 as "extremely dangerous," was forced to hire its members exclusively on civilian loading operations. There was simply no getting around the feisty Wobbly union. The "labor market in Philadelphia is controlled by the Marine Transport Workers Local 8," reported the navy as part of a confidential investigation into "Bolsheviki" influences within the maritime industry. "It is an extremely powerful organization locally" that "absolutely controls the labor along the waterfront."[2] When the first members of Local 8 reported for work at the navy yard, they were ordered, at the point of drawn bayonets, to relinquish their IWW work buttons. The longshoremen refused. After a brief standoff, they were put to work under the watchful eye of naval intelligence officers.[3]

Local 8 was not alone in benefiting from the overheated war economy. MTW branches in other North Atlantic ports, particularly New York and Boston, also reported progress in their escalating efforts to dislodge the ILA. In Baltimore, where the ILA maintained separate locals for whites and blacks, roving organizers Fletcher, Walsh, and Jack Lever built a significant following among the port's African-American longshoremen, more than a thousand of whom joined the MTW after a strike in the spring of 1917. The port's stevedores, wary of the Wobbly presence in nearby Philadelphia, worked hand in glove with AFL officials, at one point deducting union initiation fees and dues from the men's weekly pay envelopes and then forwarding the proceeds directly to the ILA. Still, Nef reported in April, Baltimore's longshoremen, roughly two-thirds of whom were African American, "are sticking to the I.W.W., and as things are going it will not be long until the I.W.W. will have all the workers and the I.L.A. will have nothing but the contract."[4]

While wartime labor markets offered generally favorable conditions for union growth, the proliferation of "no strike" agreements signed by many AFL unions, coupled with a growing federal bureaucracy of mediation and conciliation services, threatened to deprive the long-shoremen of their principal weapon, direct action.[5] Mindful of the rising patriotic tide sweeping the country, the dockworkers were not about to take on the U.S. government, but neither were they willing to meekly surrender the right to strike. On May 15, 1917, the fourth anniversary of Local 8's founding, the Wobblies called a general strike, shutting down twelve miles of waterfront along the Delaware River. Led by three bands, the longshoremen, marching five abreast, paraded through the waterfront district. Coming on the heels of the racially divisive walkout against the sugar trust, "it was certainly good to see," noted one observer, "the members marching up the street with heads erect. . . . American, Polish, Lithuanian, Belgian and col-ored men in the same line voicing exactly the spirit of the I.W.W."[6]

This same spirit moved the federal government to act. Jack McDevitt, an experienced FBI undercover operative, was assigned full-time to Philadelphia, with orders to monitor the activities of the port's longshoremen. On September 5, as part of a coordinated raid on IWW headquarters across the country, agents with the Justice Department descended on Local 8, seeking evidence of a national conspiracy to strike and disrupt the war effort. In a futile search for anything incriminating, detectives ransacked the office, confiscating or destroying all membership records, account books, correspon-dence, literature, office supplies, and the only working typewriter. Returning to the crippled union hall a few months later to finish the job, agents arrested Local 8's most prominent Wobbly leaders—Fletcher, Nef, Doree, and Walsh—taking them into custody for trial in Chicago, where they were charged with violating the recently en-acted Espionage Act, interfering with the constitutional rights of em-ployers, and conspiring to strike, among other offenses.[7]

The four defendants went on trial in April. While Fletcher did not testify on his own behalf, Nef, Doree, and Walsh did, freely admitting that the Wobblies controlled the Philadelphia waterfront. All three vigorously denied allegations that they were part of a wider conspiracy to undermine the war effort by sabotaging loading operations on the North Atlantic. Despite the port's exemplary record of efficiency dur-ing the war and the lack of evidence that the defendants did or said anything to impede shipping, all four were convicted in September 1918, sentenced to a minimum of ten years in Leavenworth Federal Penitentiary, and fined several thousand dollars each.[8]

In 1922 a government pardon attorney assigned to review the case would write of his "considerable difficulty in ascertaining just what these Philadelphia defendants did that constituted the offense of which they were convicted." Their real "crime" was being effective leaders of the IWW, as a Justice Department attorney implied in arguing at the time against Fletcher's release. Fletcher, he wrote, "was a Negro who had great influence with the colored stevedores, dock workers, firemen, and sailors, and materially assisted in building up the Marine Transport Union which at the time of the indictment had become so strong that it practically controlled all shipping on the Atlantic Coast." On that basis, and seemingly little else, Fletcher and the other Philadelphia defendants were remanded to Leavenworth, where—except for a brief taste of freedom in 1920 while released on bail—they remained until 1922, when President Warren G. Harding issued conditional pardons.[9]

The lengthy incarceration of Philadelphia's Wobbly leaders dealt a serious blow to Local 8, as all four men were sorely missed, particularly Fletcher and Nef. "With them gone," James Fair recalled, "activities gradually ceased here in Philadelphia. . . . We had several other organizers come along to do what they could do, but the odds were against us."[10] Local 8's leadership passed into the less capable hands of William ("Dan") Jones, an African American, and Joseph Green, who was white. Reviewing Jones's performance in office, an informant for the War Department characterized him as "more conservative" than his predecessor, Ben Fletcher. Jones and Green proved to be competent but uninspiring caretakers, lacking both the vision and the intellectual depth of the men they had replaced. After completing his first year in office, Green stepped down amid allegations of financial improprieties. His successor, Paul ("Polly") Baker, seized the reins of local leadership and never let go.[11]

Weakened by government repression and festering internal dissension over union finances, Local 8 seemed ripe for the picking. Laying plans for what they hoped would be a bountiful harvest, ILA strategists hired Patrick Quinlan, a former Wobbly who had long-standing contacts with many of the port's black longshoremen, to lead the next phase of their campaign.[12] Quinlan, who had been "born again" as an organizer for the AFL, began by proselytizing local religious leaders, urging them to "instruct their people not to join the I.W.W." Acting on the recommendation of FBI agent McDevitt, the Justice

Department dutifully advised its Philadelphia office to contact "the Polish Priests of the city and take them into our confidence as suggested by the representative of the American Federation of Labor."[13] But the clergy, however supportive, lacked organizational muscle; so Quinlan turned to the powerful Teamsters Union, whose leaders politely begged off.[14]

Quinlan knew he was in for a fight when, shortly after arriving in Philadelphia, he was tracked down and severely beaten by his former IWW comrades. He eventually recovered, but the campaign he led did not. After three full months of intense organizing, Quinlan had only managed to line up thirty-seven supporters. He noted "some discontent over the mismanagement" of Local 8's funds but confessed to "making little or no headway against the I.W.W." Offering his "services in another field," Quinlan concluded that his presence in Philadelphia had become counterproductive. "My work here has spurred the I.W.W. officials to greater activity," he reported in April 1918. "They are spending large sums of money now and have all their officials 'on the street' hustling. They have posted [leafleted] their members not to talk to me. . . . On the whole the injunction is obeyed. Now and then I get talking to them when there is no official around, and they admit things are by no means all right but they say the I.W.W. made good on the river front."[15]

So long as the Wobblies "made good" by controlling the job, Quinlan had nothing to offer the rank and file except the same tired denunciations of Bolshevism and anarchy, which, as in the past, failed to move the longshoremen—with one notable exception. In May Charles Cole, Local 8's African-American secretary, resigned his post in a patriotic huff, telling undercover agent McDevitt that "he did not want to have any further connection with an organization that was being criticized as much as the I.W.W." Lining up with the ILA's Quinlan, Cole reasoned that "something must be wrong" with the IWW "if the Senate of the U.S. saw fit to pass laws to put this organization out of business." Although other longshoremen no doubt felt the pull of wartime patriotism, it was not enough to pry them away from Local 8.[16]

As the ILA's campaign faltered, the U.S. Shipping Board, the principal wartime agency charged with regulating labor relations in the maritime industry, offered to recognize the MTW as the port's exclusive bargaining agent. It was a remarkable overture, and a clear mea-

sure of Local 8's power, that the Shipping Board was forced to recognize the Wobbly union while another branch of the federal
government, the Justice Department, was actively prosecuting its
leaders. Not quite sure what to make of the offer, Philadelphia's IWW
leaders brought it before the General Executive Board (GEB) in Chicago, which bristled at the government's insistence that Local 8 select
a single representative to serve on the National Adjustment Commission with full authority to negotiate wages and conditions. After
condemning the proposal as "autocracy and a violation of IWW principles," the GEB reluctantly gave its consent, provided that Local 8's
representative was elected by the entire membership, remained at all
times "under their instruction and supervision," and was subject to
recall. On agreeing to these terms, the Philadelphia longshoremen
were formally recognized by the Shipping Board. In October Local
8's basic hourly wage rate was advanced from forty to sixty-five
cents—the first substantial pay increase won without a fight. The
Wobblies had truly arrived.[17]

No Peace for Local 8

The signing of the armistice one month later transformed the Philadelphia waterfront into a veritable battle zone. With the precipitous
drop-off in transatlantic shipping, the swollen dockside labor force
was thrown into a desperate scramble for work that reopened Local
8's recently healed racial wounds. An undercover operative working
with the Office of Naval Intelligence observed a growing "undercur-
rent" of resentment directed primarily at younger Poles for putting
in overtime and depriving others, particularly African Americans, of
work opportunities. "A bad feeling is slowly developing between these
two elements," it was reported, because of the sudden scarcity of
work.[18]

The relative oversupply of labor was not helped by the added presence of several hundred African Americans who landed on the Philadelphia waterfront during the war. Swept up by the "great migration" from the South, many black workers arrived on the city's docks
directly from similar employment in New Orleans, Mobile, and other
eastern Gulf ports. Other migrants followed a more circuitous route,
making their way onto the docks in the final months of the war after
being discharged from southeastern Pennsylvania's once-booming

steel mills, shipyards, and construction sites.[19] Fed by this stream of
new arrivals, Local 8 grew dramatically, initiating sixty to seventy men
every week. Heavy wartime recruiting of African Americans tipped
Local 8's racial balance, and blacks outnumbered whites by war's
end.[20]

Few wartime recruits were schooled in Local 8's industrial syndicalism. Experienced longshoremen from the Gulf Coast knew unions,
if at all, only as economically weak, segregated bodies affiliated with
the ILA, while black migrants from the rural South typically had no
previous contact with organized labor, except perhaps as victims of
craft union exclusion. Knowing little of Local 8's history, and even
less of the IWW, their primary loyalty was to the job, not to the
union.[21]

Partially offsetting the wartime influx of "job-conscious" southern
blacks was a smaller but highly vocal group of IWW stalwarts who
began showing up on the Philadelphia waterfront in the spring of
1919. Coming mostly from the port of Seattle, where they recently
had been screened off the docks in the early stages of an employer
offensive against the MTW, the western Wobblies wasted no time in
openly criticizing Local 8's leaders for not doing more to distribute
the available work.[22] Caught in the crossfire between the growing
supply of longshoremen and the ever-shrinking demand for their services, Local 8's embattled leaders quietly raised the initiation fee from
$2.50 to $25.00 in an effort to dry out the already-saturated labor
market. But there was no turning off the spigot, as wave upon wave
of displaced war workers, many of them African Americans, continued
to spill onto the docks, with most finding irregular employment in the
nonunion coastwise shipping trade. By the spring of 1920, with more
than seven thousand men roaming the Philadelphia waterfront in
search of work, the employers held all the cards.[23]

Also playing into the shipowners' hands was Local 8's growing organizational isolation, as MTW locals elsewhere on the North Atlantic
fell one after another before the advancing ILA. In New York the
Wobblies were driven off the docks by red-baiting ILA officials following an unsuccessful wildcat strike in the fall of 1919.[24] In Boston
and Newport News, where viable MTW locals had sprung up during
the early phases of the war, the ILA regained control after being
formally designated by the Shipping Board as each port's sole bargaining agent. And in Baltimore the once-formidable MTW longshore

local, with some fourteen hundred African-American members at its height, was eventually undermined by a combination of employer blacklisting, virulent race-baiting, and strong government backing for the ILA. With the ILA closing in on all sides, Local 8 was now completely on its own.[25]

No longer able to count on sympathetic job action elsewhere in the event of a local walkout, Philadelphia's longshoremen were compelled to coordinate their efforts more closely with marine workers in neighboring ports. The Wobblies saw their opening in the spring of 1920 when coastal cargo handlers in New York and Boston defied their ILA leaders and walked off the job to protest a wage cut. With coastwise traffic tied up along the Atlantic seaboard, Local 8's nearly four thousand deep-sea longshoremen walked out on May 26, demanding an increase in wages from eighty cents to $1.00 an hour. Bolstered by the refusal of the port's marine firemen to supply steam for running "scab winches," more than one thousand longshoremen employed in the coastwise shipping trade streamed into Local 8 by nightfall. The next day the strike was tight as a drum, as nothing moved across the docks. Taking advantage of a specially reduced $1.25 initiation fee, unorganized cargo handlers kept pouring into Local 8 until its membership reached almost eight thousand. Represented by the Wobblies, the coastwise strikers demanded an equivalent 25 percent increase in their basic hourly rate, from sixty-five cents to eighty cents.[26]

The work stoppage could not have come at a worse time as far as the city's commercial interests were concerned. With more than 150 vessels already in port waiting to be serviced and another 117 freighters on their way to Philadelphia after being rerouted from strike-ridden New York, the walkout was a most "unfortunate occurrence," observed the municipal director of wharves, docks, and ferries. "Never before in the history of Philadelphia," he added, "has the port enjoyed such prosperity as it had up until the strike was called."[27]

Local shipowners took immediate steps to end the walkout. Barely one week into the strike they organized a free taxi service, with regular stops at employment agencies throughout the city, to transport strikebreakers to the docks. When the "scab cabs" failed to provide enough replacements, the stevedores turned to their former employees, sending all four thousand members of Local 8 a letter ordering them to report immediately for work on the grounds that their wage demand

and ensuing walkout were both in violation of the union's "ironclad agreement" with the Shipping Board.[28]

Local 8, responding in its next strike bulletin, flatly denied the existence of any such written agreement. In keeping with IWW principles, union leaders insisted that they had "never signed an agreement with anyone for any period of time." Offering a $10,000 reward to anyone producing an agreement, the Wobblies dared the employers to prove them wrong. "Come, Mr. Boss," they taunted, "and show us that agreement. We are, indeed, surprised to learn that we possess such a thing as an agreement." If, as seems almost certain, Local 8's representative to the National Adjustment Commission agreed on basic terms and conditions with the Shipping Board, it was apparently never formalized beyond a verbal understanding, as nothing in writing was ever found.[29]

The disputed status of the agreement was symptomatic of the growing distrust between the longshoremen and their employers. With recriminations flying in all directions, both sides readied themselves for a fight to the finish. Local 8 marshaled its forces, calling both the grain ceilers and the sugar house workers out on strike. In retaliation the shipowners asked the federal government to intervene, ostensibly to prevent cargoes of raw sugar and unprocessed flour from spoiling.[30] But Shipping Board officials, honoring their official position of neutrality in labor disputes, refused to act, prompting individual stevedores to approach the union for help. When a request to load flour for "the starving people in Belgium" was brought up on the floor of a union meeting, Local 8 leaders urged the men to "let it perish," according to agent McDevitt, who was in attendance that evening. "It don't belong to us," McDevitt recorded in his notes. "It belongs to the bosses. If the bosses want it unloaded, let them pay $1.00 per hour."[31]

Shipowners stranded with perishable commodities were prepared to pay whatever it took to unload. When a cargo of bananas arrived in the port, members of Local 8 were hired, at the desired rate of $1 an hour, to unload the ripening fruit. But as work got under way, the men discovered several strikebreakers on the job. A fight broke out, the police were called in, and the union members walked off the job, demanding their pay and the immediate discharge of all strikebreakers.[32] Clearly, the strike was no longer about money, if it ever was. As the longshoremen would demonstrate repeatedly over the next few weeks, no amount of money was enough for them to betray their commitment to labor solidarity. When the strikers were asked to unload four thousand crates of lemons at $1 an hour, they voted unanimously not to break ranks. When first Poles and then African Americans were promised preferential employment if they returned to work, both groups refused—as did the Italians, who were at one point offered $1.20 an hour, or twenty cents *more* than the union was demanding.[33]

Such solidarity was possible as long as the union was winning. Then, on June 4, the Shipping Board finally broke its silence. It issued a public statement condemning the longshoremen's demands as "unjustified and arbitrary," adding that their actions were in sharp contrast to the "patriotic attitude" displayed by offshore marine workers whose AFL leaders recently signed a one-year agreement renewing their current wage rates. Throwing the full moral and material weight of the federal government against Local 8, the Shipping Board instructed its local agents to refuse any wage increase while admonishing the port's commercial operators not to cave in. With momentum slipping away from the union, the men's resolve weakened, and small contingents of strikers began to drift back to work.[34]

Violence was not far behind. On June 7 nearly one thousand strikers battled police in what local newspapers described as a "riotous scene in which revolvers were fired . . . and clubs used freely" by both sides. The trouble started that morning after a group of three hundred African-American longshoremen, splitting off from the larger crowd, tried to halt loading operations on one of the city-owned piers. Outnumbered police called for reinforcements. As the strikers surged forward, a phalanx of fifty mounted officers, riding ten abreast, charged into the crowd. With guns drawn the police "rode rough shod over the fighting longshoremen," who, bloodied and beaten, ran for safety. Having failed in their show of force, strike activists began bickering among themselves, with blacks and whites reportedly accusing one another of prolonging the walkout.[35]

The next outbreak of violence, on June 9, brought racial tensions more clearly into view. While on their way home from work that evening, three African-American strikebreakers ran into a group of pickets. All three men had apparently been drinking, and one, Louis Townsend, was armed with a loaded revolver. After forcing his way past the pickets, Townsend "went mad," as one eyewitness described it, pulling his gun, wheeling around, and firing indiscriminately into the crowd. With enraged union men in hot pursuit, Townsend, joined by his two companions, ran down the main waterfront artery, "shooting at everyone in sight," injuring two small children and an elderly bystander before fatally wounding Stanley Darylak, a Polish striker.[36] Although the Wobblies once again did their best to play down the racial angle, Townsend's subsequent arrest for murder undermined the already-sagging morale of many black longshoremen. "I talked with several negroes," agent J.K., an undercover Shipping Board operative, reported a few days later, and "individually they are ready to go back to work."[37]

After five weeks of almost continuous rioting, the longshoremen returned to work on July 7, under the former wage scale. The "winners," Philadelphia's shipping interests, lost an estimated $50 million in delays and lost trade due to the strike. The human costs were also staggering: five killed, including one small child and two innocent bystanders, more than two hundred seriously injured, and scores arrested and imprisoned. But the big losers were the longshoremen, who not only lost some $2 million in wages but also, more important, the crucial contest of wills.[38]

Even in defeat the longshoremen could take some measure of comfort knowing that the recent strike was not entirely of their own making. Having begun in New York and Boston, the walkout was, in a sense, forced on Local 8 as the cost of its growing organizational isolation following the postwar collapse of sympathetic MTW branches in neighboring ports. Facing a highly unfavorable labor market, Philadelphia's longshoremen struck when they did to capitalize on the coastwide shutdown and the resulting inability of local shipowners to reroute cargoes. If this otherwise sound strategy failed, it was because the union's inexperienced leaders grossly underestimated the hostility of the federal government and the waterfront employers. They were about to make the same mistake with their own national organization.

The Wobblies Self-Destruct

Local 8 now found itself treated like a spurned lover. The wartime honeymoon with the Shipping Board was definitely over. Waterfront employers and port officials began to speak openly and with increasing bitterness about their rocky seven-year relationship with the "I Won't Work" longshoremen. Yet, when divorce proceedings were initiated later that year against Local 8, it was the national officers of the IWW—not the federal government or the employers—who filed papers.

On August 5 an unnamed AFL source from Philadelphia cabled the head of the Soviet Embassy in New York that Local 8 was loading the *Westmount*, an American steamer, with a shipment of shrapnel bound for General Peter Wrangel's anti-Bolshevik forces operating in the Crimea. The Soviet ambassador immediately contacted James Scott, national secretary-treasurer of the MTW, threatening to expose the "traitorous" actions of the Wobbly longshoremen. Scott rounded up his supporters on the IWW's General Executive Board and headed for Philadelphia. At a hastily called "rump meeting" of Local 8, he lashed out at the port's dockworkers, calling them, as one participant recalled, "scabs and traitors and every conceivable form of mean and dirty things." Scott was followed to the platform by two GEB members, who summarily ordered the longshoremen to stop all work on the *Westmount*. The sixty men in attendance agreed to take the matter up at their next regularly scheduled union meeting in four days.[39]

Local 8's Wobbly leaders, including the four Leavenworth defendants who recently had been released on bail pending appeals, supported the substance if not the tone of Scott's remarks. Business agent Polly Baker, accompanied by Ben Fletcher, visited the *Westmount*, trying to persuade the men not to handle munitions. But loading continued, mostly at the hands of young Poles and African Americans who had been recruited during the recent strike.[40] "Scores of them," charged two veterans of Local 8, are "breaking down every principle and rule established by the union." Convicted union leaders John Walsh and Walter Nef spoke out against the loading but were powerless to stop it. A more determined Ed Doree, fresh from Leavenworth, vowed to bring his home local up on charges if the men persisted.[41]

The rank and file, however, showed little interest in the whole affair. Only two hundred bothered to attend the next regular union meeting set aside to discuss the *Westmount* controversy. Taking the floor, Scott gave a repeat performance, hurling one accusation after another at the longshoremen and vowing to "expel [them] all tomorrow" if munitions were still being loaded. But the men were not about to be stampeded. With many newer members dragging their feet, the union voted to defer any action until hearing from the GEB. The longshoremen did not have long to wait. The next day, just as Scott had promised, they were expelled.[42]

The suspension order signed by the GEB made Scott's earlier invective seem mild by comparison. Local 8's "misguided longshoremen," it read, "have betrayed the International Labor Movement." Having committed "high treason against their class," Philadelphia's seven thousand dockworkers are a "disgrace" not only to the IWW but also to "the basic principles of World Revolution." Suspension "was the only course open," insisted the *Fellow Worker,* a New York–based IWW publication. "As a class-conscious organization we had to deal with these traitors uncompromisingly. They have dragged our name in filth. We must purge ourselves of this terrible stain."[43]

Much more than a routine house cleaning, Local 8's suspension fit neatly into several oppositional agendas. Rival unionists had perhaps the most to gain. Although the ILA was never directly implicated, the loading scandal was brought to light by an unnamed AFL source in Philadelphia with enough knowledge of the waterfront to identify the *Westmount,* its cargo of shrapnel, and its final destination. Even if the ILA was not involved, which seems highly improbable, the federation's sudden concern for the welfare of the new Soviet regime was hard to square with its earlier condemnations of Bolshevism. But AFL leaders were nothing if not practical. Weighing their hatred of communism against their desire to isolate and weaken Local 8, they eagerly jumped on the pro-Soviet bandwagon as a way of discrediting the IWW.[44]

Even among "fellow workers" the suspension campaign was not always motivated by the highest of principles. For Scott and other elected officers in the New York headquarters of the MTW, Local 8 threatened not only the "world revolution" but their own jobs as well. With some seven thousand dues-paying members, the Philadelphia longshoremen had more than enough votes to decide any election of officers to the national MTW. If, however, Local 8 was suspended, its members would no longer be in good standing and none of their votes would count. Scott was evidently aware of this contingency, as revealed in a personal letter intercepted by agent McDevitt.[45] Whether he also knew that Fletcher intended to challenge him in the upcoming MTW election is unclear. In any case, shortly after Scott engineered Local 8's expulsion, Fletcher publicly announced his candidacy for secretary-treasurer of the MTW—the salaried position currently occupied by Scott. When the ballots were counted, Fletcher came out on top, but he was denied his seat after the votes from Philadelphia were invalidated.[46]

Local 8's suspension also played into the hands of rival factions within the IWW's national office, which was then sharply divided over their stance toward Bolshevik Russia. Earlier in the year the Moscow-leaning GEB had announced its strong support for the Third International, stopping just short of urging formal affiliation with its trade union arm, the Red International of Labor Unions. While many Wobbly activists were willing to give the fledgling workers' state a chance to prove itself, others saw the Soviet regime as more of the same old "political bunk" and campaigned vigorously against affiliation.[47] Partly through such efforts, the IWW's mood toward Moscow soured, capped by the election of a new, more independent board that summer. But before the new officers were installed, the current pro-Soviet GEB seized on the *Westmount* incident as an example of what was wrong with the syndicalist IWW, urging, as its parting shot, "the United Communist Party . . . to help build up a Revolutionary Organization that will make forever impossible a repetition of the dastardly action of the Philadelphia longshoremen."[48]

While rival ILA leaders, politically vulnerable MTW officers, and insurgent Communists each had an interest in seeing Local 8 suspended, the longshoremen did not make it easy. At their next weekly union meeting, on August 17, they voted unanimously "not to load any munitions in the Port of Philadelphia" and to immediately expel any member found doing so. But the GEB was still not satisfied. Egged on by Scott, pro-Communist board members demanded a thorough investigation of Local 8 to determine if it was in strict compliance with the policies of the IWW "in every particular"—knowing full well that the union's recently enacted $25 initiation fee violated the constitution.[49]

The GEB's unrelenting persecution of Local 8 was too much for many hard-core Wobblies, including the newly installed board chairman, Roy Brown. "I am having the time of my life," he confided to Nef, "running the gauntlet of abuse from this bunch of fanatics." Even the outgoing board chairman, the ultrarevolutionary George Speed, who had been run out of Philadelphia years earlier, felt

compelled to offer his apologies to the longshoremen for the "griev-
ous mistake" of suspending them.[50] With Local 8's fate being fought
out in the pages of *Solidarity*, participants on both sides soon lost
sight of the *Westmount*, still berthed in Philadelphia with its deadly
shipment of munitions. On August 30, as the partially loaded vessel
was preparing to quietly slip out of port, agents from the U.S. Treasury Department suddenly appeared and ordered the longshoremen
to discharge its cargo. Although government officials refused to comment, press reports indicated that the *Westmount* was now believed
to be a "blockade runner," destined not for Wrangel's forces but for
the Soviet army by way of the Black Sea.[51]

The longshoremen's patience was wearing thin. Fully one month
had elapsed since promising not to load war materials, the *Westmount*—whatever its destination—never set sail, and yet they were
still suspended. "If the board continues to stand pat," a Wobbly loy-
alist wrote confidentially, "it will be impossible to reorganize these
men into the IWW again, and such action as this has got the active
members disgusted and are ready to give up their [union] cards. I
myself am included."[52] Hoping to capitalize on these sentiments, a
leaflet, unsigned but bearing the marks of the rival ILA, appeared on
the docks. Directed at "colored members who have lately joined the
local," it attacked Local 8 for tolerating speed-ups, abusive foremen,
and racial discrimination in hiring and job assignments. The Wobblies, dismissing the circular as "a piece of camouflage" for organizing
a separate local of black workers, called for unity. "If we ever permit
ourselves to become divided," they argued, "we are bound to be defeated"—certainly a familiar message but one that must have rung a
bit hollow at the time coming from a union that had itself recently
"become divided" from its own national organization.[53]

Suspended Again

With the munitions incident resolved, national IWW leaders lifted
the suspension order in October, just in time to shift their attack to
constitutional grounds, citing the longshoremen for numerous violations of IWW bylaws and giving them until December 1 to comply
or face suspension for a second time. Many of the specific complaints
concerning financial transactions with the central office arose from
simple misunderstandings and were easily cleared up. But not so with

Local 8's $25 initiation charge, which openly violated the IWW's universal $2 entrance fee. The ensuing debate over membership policies struck at the heart of Wobbly unionism, consuming the national organization in a heated, often bitter, controversy over its methods and objectives.

What had begun a few years earlier as the much-celebrated "Philadelphia model" had now become the equally infamous "Philadelphia controversy." Representing the GEB, Chairman Brown took a firm line, excoriating the longshoremen for practicing what he termed "the A.F. of L. kind of job control" that relies on high initiation fees to pay business agents who then police the contract. "If the right sort of education had been given the membership," he argued, "by now they would have understood that real job control, as the I.W.W. understands it, is not accomplished by the dictation of salaried business agents, who dicker with the boss stevedore. I.W.W. control is the kind that is maintained by the *members on the job,*" relying on direct action to win conditions. "If," Brown continued, "every member would refuse to work alongside a man who did not have the button, there would be no reason for maintaining business agents."[54]

Local 8 replied through a four-page "open letter to the membership," written by Ed Doree, that was reprinted in *Solidarity* and distributed to the leaders of the major industrial unions. Unless the GEB yields, Doree began, "a month from now, the Philadelphia M.T.W. will have passed out of existence, either as part of the I.W.W. or else as a 'shop control' organization." While freely admitting that the $25 fee violated the IWW constitution, Doree argued for greater flexibility so as to avoid any "straight-jacketing of experiments." When, as in this particular case, "the constitution proves not a protector but destroyer of some object for which we are fighting," he wrote, "[we must] either experiment or pass out of existence." Recalling that many of the IWW's most successful organizational innovations over the years had to also overcome similar constitutional objections, Doree asked, "How many 'irrefutable arguments' and 'basic principles' have we already thrown into the waste-paper basket?"[55]

Doree then took aim at the GEB's AFL-baiting. "The A.F. of L. has high dues, we hear. The I.W.W. low fees. Who," he asked, "has the members?" Not the IWW with its low fee and still lower membership but rather the AFL whose "prohibitive large fees," Doree dryly noted, "seem to have allowed about four to five million members to filter into its ranks." It is true that "the A.F. of L. is conservative and the bosses don't fight it as they do the I.W.W." But, he added, "the bosses are at this moment giving the A.F. of L. a real battle— and the A.F. of L. hangs on—on to no great ideal, no great philoso- phy—hangs on to shop control." For Doree, it all boiled down to a simple aphorism: "Because the A.F. of L. tries to protect the job, members stick to it; because the I.W.W. does not, members do not stick."[56]

On the Philadelphia waterfront, Doree continued, "we now have seven members to every job." Such a huge surplus, as the AFL has shown, is inimical to effective job control. But the federation's solu- tions of erecting insurmountable financial barriers or "closing the books" are not the only answers. Instead, Doree proposed establish- ing "reasonable safeguards around our already existing unions" by charging a high enough entrance fee to discourage "every Tom, Dick and Harry" from simply paying the union $2 for the privilege of work- ing. An initiation fee of $25 was enough to keep "floaters" and other casual workers away from the waterfront, he contended, without be- ing "prohibitive" for the average working longshoreman making nearly $9 a day.[57]

The alternative of low fees had been tried and, according to Doree, failed. During the recent strike the union brought in more than five thousand members under a specially reduced initiation fee of $1.25. When the men returned to work, the new recruits bypassed the cen- tralized hiring locations where the union had traditionally enforced its closed shop and reported directly to the docks, often without their union buttons. For two months, as the "union scabs" were hiring off the docks, Local 8 lost its coveted job control and conditions suffered. "We are just now beginning to get back some of the many things these new members robbed us of," Doree wrote in December. "It was this job-hungry, non-principled bunch of low-fee artists who gave us hell. They always do."[58]

In the end Doree and Brown were not that far apart. Both rec- ognized the importance of job control and the role of direct action in maintaining it. And both swore allegiance to the IWW's syndicalist vision of a worker-run society. The question dividing them was how to get there. While Brown followed the path of "accepted I.W.W. doctrine," Doree allowed himself to be guided by "practical experi- ence."[59] Indeed, Doree had little patience for what he called "fancy blue-prints" of the future, none of which were possible, he argued, without first securing job control in the present. Attention should be focused on how best to retain, not hypothetically administer, shop control. "It's the story of the hare-stew once more: 'To have hare-stew, first catch the hare.' "[60]

Not everyone shared Doree's culinary expertise, however. Focusing on the finished "stew," a group of doctrinaire Wobblies, taking on Doree in the pages of *Solidarity*, began by reaffirming the IWW's "ultimate aim" of running industry. "Until then," they insisted, "there can be no such thing as shop or job control." So long as the "exploiter" owns the job and is free to "close it down any time he wants to," workers' control is meaningless. Urging the board to resolve the dispute "without sacrificing a single principle," they called on the longshoremen to "either abide by the constitution . . . or be expelled."[61]

Most of those who wrote to *Solidarity* responded in a more constructive vein, seeking to delineate the fine line between Local 8's practice of "shop control" and what several writers characterized as a "job trust." If longshoremen follow Doree's advice, one reader warned, "we shall be on the high road to job trustism, jurisdictional fights, 'inner circles,' jealously guarding the big treasuries, corruption, graft and all the other 'beauties' of a decadent job trust craft system."[62] Others expressed similarly dire yet vague warnings, with one reader detecting "the aristocratic spirit of the A.F. of L." in Doree's position. Even some of Doree's erstwhile supporters were put off by his "apparent reactionary attitude."[63]

The only letters openly supporting Doree's position came from readers who identified themselves as marine workers. In Philadelphia, an unnamed dockworker observed, the coastwise men "have had a chance to join many times. If they were content to work for small wages and make no effort to help themselves, you would penalize the men who have joined and allow these spineless workers to join just when it pleased them to do so. There is too much of the 'ideal' in that stuff." The IWW can set whatever abstract principles it likes, but "if the rules of the organization are too rigid to meet conditions, self-interest will demand that the rules be broken." Local 8's decision to raise the initiation fee was a case in point. The whole controversy, he wrote, was cooked up by "the brainstorms"—apparently a reference to the Communists—who are "going to educate (heavy on education) the I.W.W. and the workers in general in old Doc. Marx."[64]

The clashing views of Wobbly unionism that appeared in the pages of *Solidarity* reflected the broad appeal of the IWW's industrial syndicalism, encompassing as it did both revolutionary ideologues and militant pragmatists who, despite their strategic differences, embraced the same organizational logic of worker self-activity, labor solidarity, and unrestricted direct action. With each side claiming to represent the "true" spirit of the IWW, neither was willing to compromise, leaving the GEB no choice but to suspend Local 8 in early December. Fellow marine workers were aghast. At an emergency meeting held a few days later, port delegates from MTW locals across the country adopted a strongly worded statement calling for immediate reinstatement of Philadelphia's longshoremen. Pointing out that the ILA was "as always, on the lookout for an opportunity to break up Local 8," they pleaded with the GEB to prevent "theoretical bigotry" and constitutional "technicalities" from prevailing "over the real concrete interests of thousands of workingmen."[65] But the theorists and the constitutionalists refused to back down. At the next IWW convention, in the spring of 1921, after two full days of discussion devoted to the "Philadelphia controversy," the delegates voted 774 to 96 against reinstating the longshoremen. Local 8's organizational isolation was now complete.[66]

"Race-Firstism" and the ILA's Emergence

The Wobblies' latest setback provided an opening for ILA Local 1116, founded in the fall of 1919, to capitalize on the growing unrest among the port's five thousand African-American cargo handlers. Though apparently not formally chartered as a separate "colored" local, the ILA's newest outpost was widely seen as such, with a leadership and following that were from its inception overwhelmingly, if not entirely, black.[67] Local 1116's initial recruiting pleas, aimed at the large number of casual men employed in coastwise shipping, fell on deaf ears. But with the racialization and subsequent failure of the 1920 strike, followed by Local 8's suspension and deepening organizational isolation, many black dockworkers were finally listening. By July 1921 Local 1116 had more than a thousand members. An undercover operative, noting the growing "number of colored longshoremen . . . leaving the IWW" for the ILA, wrote of Local 8's imminent demise.[68]

The Wobblies fought back, summarily expelling twenty-five to thirty African Americans for fraternizing with the ILA. Manuel Watts, one of those purged, approached the FBI in August to register his concerns. With three supporters at his side, including Glenn Perrymore, one of the heroes of the 1916 strike, Watts reportedly characterized Local 8 as "practically an outlaw organization" operating outside the IWW and without a valid charter. He "pulled out," according to a local FBI agent, after becoming disenchanted with "the I.W.W. programme" and the confrontational "tactics" of its leaders. This was clearly the story that the bureau wanted to hear. That it was, at best, an incomplete account is suggested by Watts's strong desire at the time to be reinstated. Whatever he may have thought of the IWW program and tactics, Watts and the others, stripped of their union buttons, were unable to find work anywhere on the docks.[69]

The contest between Locals 8 and 1116 illustrated Doree's earlier claim that workers would "stick" to whatever union controlled the job. None of this was news to the ILA, whose leaders, working through international president T. V. O'Connor, prevailed on one of the port's largest employers to hire a gang of ILA men to round out his regular Wobbly crew. This arrangement lasted all of four hours, after which the ILA gang was dismissed, leaving the Wobblies to finish the job.[70] Being completely frozen out of the hiring process, the ILA's appeal was primarily limited to newer workers, particularly coastwise men without an established claim on the waterfront. Regular deepwater longshoremen and Local 8 veterans like Watts and Perrymore, while conspicuous among the ILA's earliest leaders, represented a small fraction of its twelve hundred members.[71]

In the absence of effective job control Local 1116 held onto its membership through its racial exclusiveness. For the large number of African Americans confined to the unorganized coastwise trade, Locals 8 and 1116 were, for all practical purposes, indistinguishable, except for the color of their membership. Although neither union could promise them steady work, the all-black ILA at least offered a more socially secure environment, free not only from possible white domination but also, more realistically, from the prospect of recurrent racial conflict over jobs and union policy. More experienced dockworkers from the South were also drawn to the ILA. Like its "colored" counterparts found in many of the larger Gulf Coast ports, Local 1116 provided a safe haven through its racial separatism, being both comfortably familiar and a proven means for parceling out jobs between the races. Still others, following Charles Cole's lead in 1918, were eventually driven from Local 8, and into the waiting arms of the ILA, by the pervasive climate of fear in postwar America—whether it was the fear of being associated with any form of radicalism at a time of Palmer raids, alien deportations, and general repression of the left or simply the fear that Local 8, isolated and swimming against the prevailing political currents, was about to go under.[72]

The ILA's recruiting efforts fortuitously coincided with the resurgence of black racial identity sweeping the country during the early 1920s. As articulated by Jamaica-born Marcus Garvey, a charismatic proponent of Pan-Africanism, doctrines of separatism and "race-firstism" developed large followings throughout the rural South and in many northern cities with sizable African-American populations. In Philadelphia, widely recognized as "one of the most powerful strongholds of Garveyism in the United States," Garvey's United Negro Improvement Association (UNIA) was a force to be reckoned with. The Quaker City was home to the Baptist minister J. W. H. Eason, who in August 1920 was chosen to head the American branch of the UNIA, thus freeing Garvey to become self-styled "Provisional President" of the African continent.[73] At its height the local chapter was capable of turning out as many as five thousand enthusiastic supporters to hear promises of a brighter future in a new Ethiopia populated by American blacks. "Our ship is at sea," Garvey told an overflow crowd in Philadelphia's Olympia Theatre, "and sailing toward the port of destiny."[74]

Garvey's ship, unlike his Ethiopian empire, was more than a mere figment of his imagination. In addition to his other duties, Garvey served as president of the Black Star Line, a three-vessel shipping operation wholly funded and staffed by the UNIA. Launched in 1919 as a vehicle for raising capital and, ultimately, conveying his followers back to Africa, the struggling line soon fell on hard times.[75] Still, its thousands of shareholders, many of them small-time investors, refused to bail out. When the Yarmouth, the flagship of the Black Star Line, docked for the first time in Philadelphia on May 8, 1920, some three thousand shareholders "thronged the pier" and, according to the Public Ledger, "cheered lustily" the arrival of the aging British freighter. While unloading baggage for its fifty-three black passengers and greeting its all-black crew, the port's African-American longshoremen—poised to begin their ill-fated walkout later that month—saw up close the viability of racial separatism.[76]

Race-firstism gradually found its way into Local 8. In the summer of 1921, with Pan-Africanist sentiments on the rise both nationally and in the City of Brotherly Love, the *Messenger* sent a reporter to Philadelphia to cover the developing separatist campaign on the docks. "Strange to say," observed the anti-Garveyite monthly, "this move came from alleged intelligent Negroes outside of the union, who have heretofore cried down the white union workers on the grounds that they excluded Negroes from their unions." When the prospect of a separate local for blacks was raised at the next meeting of Local 8, the six hundred longshoremen in attendance would have none of it. "White workers were as violent as the Negroes in condemning this idea of segregation," according to the *Messenger*. "All over the hall murmurs were heard, 'I'll be damned if I'll stand for anybody to break up this organization,' 'It's the bosses trying to divide us,' 'We've been together this long and we will be together on.' "[77]

Not all of Local 8's three thousand members were as well versed in the principles of class solidarity. So union leaders began a regular educational forum aimed at shoring up their black membership. Week after week invited lecturers railed against what the *Messenger* described as "alleged Negro leaders masquerading in the guise of race loyalty" and their allies "preaching the nefarious and dangerous doctrine of race segregation." The ILA, as the "self-appointed . . . saviors of the Negro workers," came in for special attack. Local 1116 was charged with fomenting racial "discord and dissention" on the waterfront. "By keeping the workers divided" along racial lines, one speaker argued, the ILA was really "serving the interests of the Stevedores and Shipping Interests." If some African Americans were taken in by Local 1116's "sugar-coated" promises, the *Messenger* wrote reassuringly, "the militant, class-conscious and intelligent Negro workers" knew better, greeting the ILA with "curses instead of blessings."[78]

Local 8's black supporters, while including "class-conscious" militants, generally consisted of regularly employed deepwater longshoremen who had benefited most from the union's racially egalitarian policies. Older black workers told the *Messenger* of times past "when a colored man could not walk along the water-front, so high was the feeling running between the races. But, now all races work on the

water-front."[79] And they did so—like everything else in Local 8—not
in isolation from one another but in close and often intimate contact,
with white and black longshoremen laboring side by side. "When we
worked," James Fair recalled, "we worked on the docks together, we
worked on the wharves together, and we worked in the hold together." Although racial discrimination in hiring and job assignments
was not unheard of during the Wobblies' reign, it was, by all accounts,
the exception rather than the rule. Having so thoroughly routed "the
Southern bugaboo" of interracial contact, the *Messenger* concluded
that "no finer spirit of brotherhood can be found anywhere" than on
the Philadelphia docks.[80]

But Local 8's "spirit of brotherhood," premised on the inclusiveness of class, was to that extent incapable of appreciating the exclusiveness of race. Precisely because the Wobblies were so color blind
in their administration of the union, they were unable to see, much
less understand, the attractiveness of racial separatism to many African Americans, whose identities and interests were shaped by experiences both on the job and off.[81] Local 8, even at its best, was no
more than an isolated island within an increasingly turbulent sea of
racial hatred and bigotry sweeping across the country.

In the wake of postwar reaction, the rising tide of white-on-black
violence engulfed one city after another. Philadelphia, although
spared the explosive rioting that rocked Chicago, St. Louis, and Tulsa,
was no exception.[82] Beginning in the spring of 1919, rioting broke out
between whites and blacks, concentrated in the contested residential
zones bordering the city's emerging urban ghettos. In May white residents of a predominantly Irish neighborhood stoned the house of a
recently arrived black family, whose occupants in turn fired on the
crowd, injuring three men and triggering what the press described as
"a riot in the streets."[83] Later that summer a "free for all fight"
erupted on the edge of town when a twelve-year-old white boy was
hit in the mouth by a black carnival attendant after the youngster was
caught sneaking into one of the exhibits. A small group of white men
who saw the incident rounded up "reinforcements" and came after
the attendant and his fellow African-American carnival workers, who
engaged in a violent pitched battle using razors, knives, stones, and
sticks as weapons. More than one hundred police were required to
restore order. Eight men—all African Americans—were arrested.[84]

Racial tensions were briefly driven from public view to the privacy of city hall, as black community leaders quietly brought their concerns before the mayor and the city council.[85] Unresponsive government leaders saw violence spill back out onto the streets in the spring of 1921 following an otherwise routine interracial altercation. When the city's augmented riot squad arrived at the uptown location, they found fifty whites and blacks battling in the streets, with one white man, critically shot, lying in a pool of blood. Wading into the angry crowd, police went after several black men, who gamely fought back. Two African-American suspects, identified by members of the white mob, were taken into custody and charged with aggravated assault.[86]

Rising racial tensions, both on the job and off, played into the hands of the all-black ILA, as Local 1116 kept nibbling away at Local 8's membership. By the fall of 1921, faced with rising levels of unemployment and ILA agitation, Local 8 rejoined the IWW in a desperate search for organizational allies. Reducing their initiation fee to the constitutionally mandated limit of $2, the port's deepwater longshoremen, after a year's hiatus, became Wobblies once again.[87]

Black and White, Disunite

Affiliation with the national organization provided Local 8 with psychic comfort but little else. Without viable MTW unions operating on the docks outside of Philadelphia, the port's shipowners remained free to reroute cargo and import strikebreakers in the event of a local work stoppage. The longshoremen, whether or not members of the national IWW, were still on their own, as unprotected as ever from the razor-sharp teeth of the employers' whipsaw.

With the expiration of the current "agreement" on October 1, 1922, Local 8 demanded a reduction in the length of the working day from nine to eight hours. Seeking to revive the eight-hour day, one of the casualties of the failed 1920 walkout, the union proposed limiting straight time from 8:00 A.M. to 4:00 P.M. When the employers balked, the men took matters into their own hands. Reporting for work as usual at 7:00 A.M., they stood by idly for the first hour, refusing to begin until being assured of receiving the overtime rate of $1 an hour. Some of the smaller stevedoring firms immediately caved in and began paying overtime from 7:00 A.M. The larger operators, however, remained intransigent, repudiating not only the men's demand but their union as well, declaring that they "would no longer deal with the I.W.W. or its affiliated organization." Embracing the open shop, an employer spokesman announced their intentions to "treat with the men as individuals and if they refuse to work on our terms shall have others take their places."[88]

The longshoremen, recalling the debacle of 1920, responded cautiously. When a motion was made to authorize a portwide strike on October 14, only twenty-four votes out of several hundred cast were in favor. "We are not looking for a fight and we shall not start it," Polly Baker assured the nervous citizens of Philadelphia. The shipowners "will come to us," another union leader told the men. "We won't have to go to them. Just let the work accumulate," he implored, "[and] the Boss Stevedores will come down off their high perch." Refusing to make the first move, the union declared its members "locked out."[89]

Presenting the dispute as a lockout, rather than a strike, was more than a slick public relations move. It also prevented an open break within the union's own ranks, which were already fractured along racial lines. "There is considerable dissatisfaction among various gangs of Stevedores[,] principally the negro element," reported an undercover operative with the Shipping Board, identified as "agent #10." Many blacks, he explained, "feel they will lose more money than they can make up on strike." Noting renewed ILA attempts "to break up the solid front of Stevedores," agent #10 wrote that "the attitude is plainly for a split."[90]

That a split did not occur at this time was largely attributable to the efforts of Alonzo Richards, chairman of the lockout committee. As an original member of the union, Richards had seen it all, including the rival ILA, which he led briefly. After finding the "the methods and tactics used by the AFL . . . too tame for the longshoremen to get any results," he returned to Local 8 in time to assume leadership of the lockout.[91] Richards was a popular leader among both races. "[He] makes a good speech . . . despite the fact he is colored," observed a second informant, agent #2. "The workers listen to him with rapt attention." Taking the stage at a union rally in the early days of the lockout, Richards tried to reach the men through the same language of fairness that had launched their struggle in 1913. According to the notes of agent #2, Richards said, "We have never had a square deal from the Bosses. We work hard and our work is dangerous as every one knows. We should have fought for an eight hour day and had it long before this. Nearly every other class of men have it and why shouldn't we?"[92]

While some men later confided to agent #10 that their current wage rates, even without overtime, were more than fair for the kind of unskilled labor they performed, most longshoremen felt a sense of moral obligation to the Wobblies for all that they had accomplished. The dockworkers, wrote agent #10, "fully realize they owe the radical organization an obligation, as it is through this union that the stevedores receive the high rate of pay and they know if it were not for the radical methods of the Union in the 'One Big Union Idea,' the stevedores would likely be doing 10 hours work for $4.00 a day." Whenever the men appear to weaken in their resolve, agent #10 noted, they are at once reminded that their advantageous conditions were achieved "through the Union and its strong Union direct action methods."[93]

With Local 8's ranks holding tight, the ILA resorted to its own version of direct action—in support of the shipowners. Newly elected ILA international president Anthony Chlopeck, after conferring with Philadelphia's employers, offered to supply as many "replacement" workers as needed from neighboring ports. As the lockout spread, idling five thousand workers and stranding thirty vessels, more than five hundred longshoremen, members of the New York ILA, were put to work under police protection.[94] Local 8 countered the ILA's strikebreaking efforts by distributing ten thousand leaflets, written in English and Italian, along the New York waterfront, explaining the lockout and asking for the men's support. With recruiting stalled, Chlopeck turned to his predecessor, T. V. O'Connor, who had recently been appointed vice president of the Shipping Board. In flagrant violation of the Shipping Board's official policy of neutrality in labor disputes, O'Connor immediately dispatched a government vessel to Philadelphia to house and feed strikebreakers.[95]

The shipowners, led by the virulently antiunion United American Line, also turned up the heat, issuing a warning to "avoid Philadelphia for the present and route . . . shipments via Baltimore and New York."[96] With their jobs fast disappearing to strikebreakers or ILA men in other ports, Local 8 members began drifting back to work. Seeking authorization to put up picket lines around the offending piers, Baker urged the longshoremen to support a selective strike. The longshoremen voted largely along racial lines; the black majority turned down his request.[97] Local 8, observed agent #2, was "like a house divided," with many members no longer paying dues, tempers flaring, and fistfights breaking out on the floor of the union hall. As Richards began speaking out against any escalation of the conflict, Baker became increasingly isolated. "Many of the negro longshore-men are anxious to depose him," agent #2 reported a few days later.[98]

With Local 8 wracked by internal dissension and barely limping along, the employers moved in for the kill. In advertisements in several local newspapers, they announced the formation of a "Long-shoremen's Employment Bureau" through which prospective workers could apply for jobs on the docks. The creation of the bureau amounted to an open declaration of war, Baker insisted, as he pleaded with the men to retaliate by calling a general strike. But again they refused.[99] George Speed, who was in town helping out, was characteristically blunt: either declare a strike, he told the men, "or put your button in your pocket, get on the docks and throw the scabs overboard." Still no action. Exasperated, Speed dashed off a letter to the national office in Chicago characterizing the situation in Philadelphia as "practically hopeless."[100]

Local 8's leaders, agent #2 wrote, were "in a state of gloom," caught "between the fires" of warring racial factions. "Many of the negro stevedores want to get back to work," observed agent #10, convinced that the dispute was unwinnable.[101] As cargo began to move freely across the docks, union leaders returned to the membership with their earlier proposal for selective picketing. The outcome was the same: most of the whites, joined this time by fourteen blacks, supported picketing, but they were voted down by the African-American majority, many of whom began returning to work. Although Local 8 maintained a brave front, issuing regular "strike news bulletins" in the days that followed, most men had abandoned the struggle long before it was officially called off on November 18.[102]

The longshoremen found conditions on the docks very different from the way they had left them. Like the aftermath of the 1920 strike, they returned to find the employers in charge of hiring. "The bosses pick and hire leaders," observed a veteran organizer, with the result that "gangs of favorites, gangs of negroes, or whole gangs of whites" predominate along the formerly integrated waterfront. The Wobblies, having lost control over hiring, were powerless to impose their vision of labor unity on an increasingly racialized labor force.[103]

The Final Battle

Local 8 was in ruins. Philadelphia, the country's third busiest port behind New York and New Orleans, was once again an open shop, as the formerly ubiquitous union button was nowhere to be seen. In its place the men were now required to carry a work permit issued by the shipowner's employment bureau. Modeled after the "Seattle Plan," which featured a centralized registration and hiring system designed to identify "undesirables," the bureau's principal function was to "stabilize" the labor force by weeding out union activists, scores of whom were blacklisted and eventually driven from the docks. Some managed to find employment aboard ship; others, like Polly Baker, went to work in the dockside sugar refineries.[104]

The longshoremen who continued to work on the waterfront did so under worsening conditions. Besides being required to report for work at the original 7:00 A.M. starting time, they were forced to stand "around in the cold for hours waiting to be hired." Stevedores also regularly "chiseled" the men out of their wages by starting work early and quitting late. The roughly sixty cents that were "stolen" daily from each dockworker lined the pockets of their greedy "gang bosses and slave drivers." Once the defiant "masters of the port," the longshoremen had been reduced to defenseless slaves forced to "pay the drivers to drive them."[105]

With Local 8 seemingly unable to put its own house in order, national MTW officers sent in a wrecking crew, led by Earl Yeager. Described by a government informant as "the biggest agitator the whites have and a vicious fighter," Yeager was closely allied with the ascendant pro-Communist faction of the IWW that still had it in for the longshoremen.[106] At the union's regularly scheduled business meeting in early January 1923, Yeager, flashing credentials from the MTW main office, demanded the floor. Reviving an old vendetta, he accused the longshoremen of withholding dues from the national organization and demanded their charter, seal, and all stationery. Union leaders refused. The next day a leaflet appeared, signed by Yeager's IWW clique, warning the port's dockworkers about "fakirs" masquerading as Wobblies and announcing the opening of a new MTW hall, located several blocks away from Local 8's headquarters. For the next few months the longshoremen had not one but two Wobbly locals claiming to represent them.[107]

The stalemate was finally broken in spring 1923 when Ben Fletcher reluctantly led his followers out of the IWW. Looking back over the past ten years of affiliation with the Wobblies, Fletcher acknowledged the "more than 500" members who had been "arrested upholding the principles of the organization" as well as those who paid even more dearly, with life and limb.[108] "The history of the Philadelphia Longshoremen's connection with the I.W.W. is one of unswerving loyalty to its fundamental principles," he insisted. But the national organization's continuing "interference in local affairs," its lack of material support during the last two major strikes, and its preoccupation with collecting dues at the expense of organizing other ports left them "no other course of action." With that, the independent Philadelphia Longshoremen's Union was born.[109]

Fletcher's independent union maintained a low membership and an even lower profile during its brief existence, occasionally popping up in the pages of *Solidarity* as an object of ridicule. "How foolish it was," observed a supporter of Yeager's newly chartered MTW local, "for some small independent union of the workers to try to fight the One Big Union of the Bosses." But the same was true of the official MTW union, whose following was, if anything, even smaller, with fewer than fifty paid-up members.[110] Although Fletcher's union was probably not much larger, it was at least representative of the workforce, attracting longshoremen of both races. In contrast, most, if not all, of Yeager's followers were white.[111]

The racial polarization on the docks was but a microcosm of the growing tensions between white and black Philadelphians that exploded on the city's streets that summer. Rioting broke out in mid-July when several black men responded to two admittedly "abusive" white children by pushing them into the street. A "general fight ensued," after which six African Americans were taken into custody alongside a dozen whites who were held as witnesses.[112] Sporadic clashes continued throughout the month, and the first week of August was marked by what the press described as a "succession of race disturbances" that sent several black men to the hospital. Philadelphia's long, hot summer of 1923 culminated in early September with an attempted lynching in a busy downtown section of the city that was narrowly averted by the police.[113]

With racial tensions still running high, the ILA launched a major recruiting drive in the spring of 1924. Warning blacks that they would "be taken advantage of" in an integrated setting, ILA organizers held out vague promises of preferential treatment in Local 1116's segregated atmosphere. In the absence of job control, however, the ILA's racial separatism was scarcely any more attractive than the Wobblies' interracial unionism. "The I.L.A. has nothing to offer," observed the *Marine Worker*, national organ of the MTW. "Philadelphia with an open shop and no organization has the same wages and better working conditions than New York, Baltimore or Boston with I.L.A. control."[114]

All three unions—the independent, the MTW, and the ILA—were now on a collision course. Early in 1925, with the ILA campaign shifting into high gear, Fletcher brought his remaining followers back into the MTW, thus redrawing the original battle lines between the IWW and the AFL. Joining Fletcher were several familiar faces, including George Speed and former Local 8 officer Polly Baker. The reconstituted Wobbly local began to hold weekly mass meetings in March.[115] There was certainly lots to talk about. "In the past two years," wrote Wobbly organizer Claude Erwin, "up-to-date machinery, ships, and rigging have increased handling capacity of cargo until one man does as much as five did previously and on some cargo as much as twelve men formerly handled." Although wages were the same as in 1923, the added demands placed on each worker meant, as Erwin put it, that "he is only able to make about one-fifth per week of what he made under I.W.W. union conditions."[116]

The speed-up and low wages, coupled with discriminatory hiring practices by employers, provided favorable conditions for Wobbly recruiters. With former Local 8 members leading the way, the MTW was back on its feet by April, holding its first regular business meeting in more than two years. Following a rousing speech by Fletcher, who reportedly "held the audience spell bound for over an hour," more than one hundred men signed up. "Even the old-time members had to congratulate him," commented *Solidarity*, "for the fine impressive talk he made."[117] Over the next few days, nearly one thousand IWW work buttons were distributed along the waterfront to dues-paying members and supporters alike, creating "a sensation among both the men and the bosses." As the longshoremen continued to line up to pay dues, the employers maintained an eerie silence. "To date," the western-based *Industrial Worker* reported on April 5, "very little opposition has been reported by the boss stevedores."[118] The next day, however, the powerful Jarka Stevedoring Company—apparently acting on orders from O'Connor of the Shipping Board—dismissed several gangs for refusing to remove their IWW work buttons. At an emergency union meeting with five hundred members present, the men voted to set up picket lines around all Jarka piers. Later that same evening most of the company's white gang bosses walked out in sympathy with nearly three hundred strikers, leaving behind only three African-American gang bosses to supervise a skeleton crew of strikebreakers.[119]

Faced with a resurgent MTW, Local 1116 mobilized its members, hundreds of whom were escorted by a heavily armed police convoy from their union hall down to the waterfront, past Wobbly pickets and onto the piers. A week later Wobbly leaders, charging the ILA with "deliberate and open scabbing," called off the strike. But the battle was far from over.[120] Now it was Local 1116's turn to prove itself. Joseph Ryan, ILA international vice president in charge of the North Atlantic district, was brought to town. At the next union meeting Ryan outlined his plan for organizing the port of Philadelphia. Appropriating Local 8's two key demands from 1922, Ryan called for a reduction in the workday from nine to eight hours and a uniform starting time of 8:00 A.M. Striking an uncharacteristically militant pose, the ILA chieftain then threatened to shut down the port if their demands were not met by May 1.[121]

The ILA's strike deadline conveniently coincided with a previously announced work stoppage that had been called by the MTW in honor of May Day. But in late April Wobbly leaders abruptly canceled their plans, fearing that a walkout on May 1 would only strengthen the ILA's bargaining position with the port's stevedores.[122] The arrival of May Day—a time normally reserved for celebrating working-class unity—found Philadelphia's dockworkers more divided than ever, with the Wobblies busily at work as hundreds of ILA men stood by in disbelief.

If many longshoremen were confounded by the IWW's actions, readers of *Solidarity* were even more so. Under the headline "I.L.A. Scheme to use I.W.W.," organizer Claude Erwin tried his best to put a positive spin on the Wobblies' descent into strikebreaking. Local 1116's job action was not really a walkout, Erwin insisted. ILA members, borrowing a page from Local 8's 1922 playbook, merely "stood by" when called on to begin work at 7:00 A.M. The entire performance was staged to secure a contract, nothing more. By 9:00 A.M. Ryan was reportedly making the rounds among the shipowners, telling them that, in the event of a possible IWW strike on May 15 to commemorate the founding of Local 8, the ILA would furnish men to all stevedores with whom they had a contract. "There may have been a time," Erwin wrote, "when workers and even members of the I.W.W. could have been bamboozled by these tactics, but that time is past." The longshoremen were wise to the ILA's "scheming pie cards" whose efforts were directed at undermining, not the bosses, but the IWW.[123]

Ryan's promise of industrial peace was not worth the cost of a contract to the port's antiunion shipowners. But he did secure a commitment from the Shipping Board to guarantee preferential employment for ILA members while their union's wage and hour demands were under review.[124] With job control finally within its grasp, Local 1116 began reaching out to the port's regularly employed deepwater longshoremen, including many whites. By July, following the Shipping Board's approval of the eight-hour day, the ILA's hold was tighter than ever. Local 1116's dues-paying membership stood at 2,500, with an additional 250 men enrolled in the ILA's newly chartered "Polish and Irish local."[125]

The organizational rivalry between the MTW and the ILA had taken some truly bizarre turns over the years. Whatever "fundamental principles" had been at stake in the beginning seemed largely irrelevant now that Ryan was promoting direct action to win the eight-hour day and the Wobblies were willing to strikebreak on May Day. Disillusioned and discouraged, the men were "apathetic," Erwin wrote. "You can talk with them, and can't get an argument. They all admit that they got conditions under the I.W.W. banner, and that they need the organization back. They also say they are ready to come back when the rest are, but will not make the start as individuals."[126]

Many Wobblies gave up on their organization altogether. Former Local 8 leader Polly Baker gradually came to the realization that an isolated local of the MTW could never hope to be effective surrounded as it was by a hostile, increasingly entrenched ILA. Although Baker still "favored the IWW idea," the disappearance of Wobbly sympathizers in neighboring ports made his continued allegiance to the MTW impractical. As he told Fred Thompson of the IWW several years later, the men took the employers seriously when they

threatened to destroy the MTW's last outpost by diverting shipments
to "friendly" ILA ports outside of Philadelphia. Nor was this an idle
threat. Between 1923 and 1926, the last years of the MTW's existence,
the volume of foreign cargo passing through the port of Philadelphia
fell by more than 25 percent, for a net loss of more than 1.7 million
cargo tons. At the same time, New York, Newport News, Norfolk,
and Baltimore, the four closest deepwater ports—all within four hundred nautical miles of Philadelphia and all under contract with the
ILA—increased their foreign shipments by 2.4 million cargo tons.
With cargoes, and jobs, following the ILA, Philadelphia's dockworkers
did likewise. "The longshoremen," Baker recalled in 1934, "wanted
to keep their jobs" above all else.[127]

Baker was no exception. Reading the handwriting on the wall, he
accepted an offer from Ryan to become head ILA organizer for Philadelphia in June 1926. "I went right to it," he later wrote, stopping
first at Local 1116's headquarters. What he found was not really a
union "but a social club," as veteran longshoreman James Moocke
put it years later. "They had no contracts or nothin' at the time." And
they were not likely to get much more without support from the port's
nearly two thousand white dockworkers.[128]

Baker began, as the IWW had before him, by tackling the "race
question." Making contact with former Wobblies Glenn Perrymore,
Alonzo Richards, and Dan Jones and other ILA leaders, he put forward what had become a familiar syndicalist vision on the Philadelphia waterfront: one big union representing all of the port's longshoremen. Baker's proposal met with mixed reactions. Abraham
Moses, one of Local 1116's founders, recalled that some of his fellow
African Americans feared "colored executives [wouldn't] have a
chance" in an integrated union. But such separatist concerns paled
alongside the increasingly oppressive working conditions imposed on
longshoremen of both races. By August, after three intense months
of agitation, Baker "succeeded in breaking the race question" with
the election of a slate of white union officers to serve alongside Local
1116's present leaders. Continuing another popular Local 8 tradition,
the ILA committed itself to maintaining a racially balanced leadership, retaining the offices of president and secretary for blacks while
reserving vice president and financial secretary for whites.[129]

The decimated MTW local died a quiet death a few weeks later.
But the Wobblies' industrial syndicalism lived on through the meta-

morphosed ILA, now fully integrated and led almost exclusively by former IWW activists. In October, after the shipowners refused to recognize the ILA, union leaders responded like any self-respecting Wobblies, by taking direct action. Once again emulating Local 8, they distributed some two thousand ILA work buttons throughout the port as a way of forcing recognition. When that failed, the union called a portwide strike. As in past walkouts, O'Connor from the Shipping Board intervened, but this time he sided with the ILA-led longshore-men. Together with Ryan, O'Connor prevailed on the shipowners to not only recognize the union but to concede the eight-hour day as well. Once "the 8 hour day went into effect," Ryan later recalled, "the rest of the job was easy." By the end of the year, almost all of the port's longshoremen had joined the ILA, thus bringing to a successful conclusion its decade-long struggle for supremacy on the Philadelphia waterfront.[130]

Conclusion

The ILA's victory on the Philadelphia docks may come as no surprise to most students of organized labor. Given what many observers re-gard as the special "fit" between America's "job-conscious" working class and the AFL's unique brand of unionism, it could hardly have been otherwise. It follows that Local 8's defeat was less noteworthy in and of itself than the fact that it took the rival ILA more than a decade to accomplish what was supposedly inevitable.

But a close examination of the struggle for union supremacy on the Philadelphia waterfront suggests that the outcome was hardly in-evitable. When free to choose between the IWW and the AFL, the longshoremen sided repeatedly with the Wobblies. Their unswerving loyalty over more than a decade did not, however, rest on the IWW's radical preamble, its trenchant critique of capitalism, or its belief in revolutionary action. None of that mattered very much to the rank and file, as the Wobblies learned to their dismay. "I have talked with the old members and ex-members" of Local 8, wrote veteran IWW organizer Claude Erwin in 1925, "and with only an occasional excep-tion, I find that after all these years they do not know a thing about the I.W.W." Even Wobbly loyalists like Ben Fletcher conceded years later that few dockworkers of either race "possessed the idealism of the IWW."[131]

If few longshoremen were moved by the IWW's idealism, and fewer still cared about its ultimate goals, most found compelling its organizational logic of industrial syndicalism. Significantly, the rival ILA was unable to compete until it, too, adopted many of the key elements of Wobbly unionism, including not only Local 8's popular wage and hour demands from 1922 but also its interracialism and direct action, along with many of its former leaders. By 1926, then, the two organizations had become almost indistinguishable, just as the longshoremen were approaching a critical fork in the historical road. Had they been free to act solely on their preferences at the time, it seems likely that the Wobblies, as the prime movers of unionization, would have triumphed as they had so many times in the past. But the dockworkers were not choosing in a vacuum. Indeed, in a very real sense they were no longer choosing at all, as the IWW option had been largely foreclosed by changing relations of force on the docks.

Government repression of the Wobblies during World War I deprived Local 8 of its most capable leaders at precisely the time when they were most needed. Facing the difficult postwar adjustment, the longshoremen were without experienced leadership and under increasing attack from all sides. Federal undercover agents, sounding out the union for possible weak spots, worked closely with local shipowners and ILA leaders to discredit and weaken Local 8. Willfully violating the government's official policy of neutrality in cases of rival unionism, the Shipping Board sided openly and consistently with opponents of Local 8, whether it involved publicly condemning the union's actions, sheltering strikebreakers, or granting favorable terms to ILA negotiators.

Still, Philadelphia's Wobblies might have survived the state's onslaught had it not been for the sectarian and ultimately self-destructive policies carried out by their own national leaders. Not once but twice the longshoremen were charged with ideological shortcomings and suspended. On both occasions the timing could not have been worse, with the first suspension coming on the heels of the failed 1920 strike and the second one taking effect as the ILA's postwar offensive was getting under way. A third suspension was only narrowly averted in 1923 when the port's dockworkers, facing yet another round of accusations, withdrew from the IWW. In truth, the longshoremen did not so much turn on the Wobblies as the Wobblies turned on them. Veteran Local 8 leader John Walsh admitted as much at the IWW's national convention later that year. "We have lost the longshoremen," he concluded, "more through our fault than theirs."[132]

If IWW misleadership was partly to blame for Local 8's demise, the historical conjuncture of postwar America must also bear some share of the responsibility. Committed to their color-blind principles of class solidarity, the Wobblies found themselves swimming against the rising tide of racial separatism that was sweeping the country. The rival ILA, capitalizing on the upsurge in black racial identity—a product of both resurgent white racism and its ideological reaction in the form of Garveyism—built a significant following on the docks by reconstituting itself as an all-black local. Set against a backdrop of rising economic competition on the docks and a chilling climate of racial distrust, the Wobblies' pleas for solidarity fell on deaf ears.

The ILA's victory over the IWW, in short, depended on a confluence of forces over which neither party had much control. At no time was the outcome anywhere near certain, much less inevitable. The Wobblies never backed down, kept pushing forward, and retained their base of support on the docks; and, had it not been for the ILA's stunning self-transformation coupled with a particularly lethal combination of state repression, IWW sectarianism, employer discrimination, and resurgent racial consciousness, Local 8 may very well have held on to influence the character of longshore unionism throughout the tumultuous 1930s.

Whether the constellation of forces that sunk Local 8 were fortuitous or endemic to the American class experience is open to debate. It is clear, however, that the ILA's victory was not the inevitable product of failed working-class consciousness. On the contrary, the longshoremen's workplace aspirations remained remarkably stable as they made their way from the IWW to the AFL. It was the ILA and, to some extent, Local 8 that were forced to change in response to the pure and simple syndicalism of the rank and file.

Chapter Four

Serving Up Industrial
Syndicalism on the Streets
of New York

New York's culinary workers turned to the Wobblies for leadership in the course of a bitterly contested citywide strike that broke out in the winter of 1913. Ill conceived and poorly timed, the walkout's fate was sealed with the defection of its original leadership and the loss of public support. The indomitable IWW entered the fray despite the impossible odds and knowing full well that victory was most likely beyond its reach. When the strike was called off weeks later, the Wobblies were already gone, vanishing almost as suddenly as they had appeared only a few short months earlier.

The Wobblies' lack of staying power came as no surprise to the rival AFL union, whose leader dismissed them as a "celluloid fronted bunch of REDS" hopelessly out of touch with "the best of the conservative men working" in New York.[1] Much the same explanation for the Wobblies' failure was offered years later by two industry insiders who were, in fact, reds: Jay Rubin and Martin J. Obermeirer, both members of the Communist party and leaders among the city's hotel and cafeteria workers. Writing in 1943, Rubin and Obermeirer attributed the national IWW's "swift rise and swifter disintegration" to "the inability of its leadership to gauge accurately the attitude of the average worker." As they argued in *Growth of a Union*, one of the few book-length studies of culinary unionism, "the American worker was not ready to admit an irreconcilable difference between employer and employee when the I.W.W. burst upon the country with its emphasis on direct action" and its view of signed agreements "as not only valueless but positively anti-labor. . . . Such conceptions were radical departures for the worker and they startled him."[2]

Yet, in New York City alone, more than six thousand of these supposedly "startled" workers—four times the number then enrolled in the rival AFL union—were comfortable enough with the Wobblies to follow them into battle in the winter of 1913. If, as Rubin and Obermeirer contend, most American workers "shied away" from the IWW's class conflict rhetoric, its emphasis on direct action, and its rejection of contracts, the city's hotel and restaurant workers were not among them.[3] Indeed, it was precisely these "radical departures" in mobilizing strategies that drew the unorganized wait staff, cooks, and kitchen workers to industrial syndicalism in New York.

This chapter examines the sources of industrial syndicalism among the city's hotel and restaurant workers, focusing on the succession of organizational forms and corresponding repertoires of collective action that culminated in the IWW's brief but telling ascendancy in 1913. For much of the previous three decades unionization followed a generally zigzagging path, vacillating between strategies of inclusion and exclusion, professionalism and proletarianism, and contractualism and direct action. As "service" workers, those who waited on the public were unable to simply follow the ready-made blueprints for union building that had been drawn up with craftsmen and other manual laborers in mind. So the culinary workers were forced to learn by doing, guided mostly by their own experiences on the job.

The city's first culinary union was launched in the 1880s by a small group of German waiters, early followers of the Knights of Labor before turning to the Socialists. But the ideologically advanced waiters lacked the disruptive capacities to sustain their expansive vision of unionism in the face of escalating attacks by employers and entrenched craft unionists. Being both economically vulnerable and isolated from the unorganized yet more strategically located food preparation staff of cooks, chefs, and other kitchen workers, the vanguard waiters retreated to the practice of business syndicalism, finding refuge behind the exclusionary walls of the AFL.

Few of the city's culinary workers followed the German waiters into the AFL. Instead, most of those employed in the larger kitchens and dining rooms, including the vast majority of immigrant waiters, pressed forward in search of a more open and aggressive organizational form. With the formation of the International Hotel Workers'

Union in 1911, thousands of New York hotel and restaurant workers were introduced to a peculiar blend of unionism, at once more inclusive than the AFL yet abandoning its focus on production in favor of remedial action through the courts. In the absence of meaningful protection on the job, however, rank-and-file culinary workers were forced to take matters into their own hands, initiating direct action that ultimately led to the citywide walkout in 1913 during which the IWW rose to prominence.

However brief the Wobblies' reign, they were not merely some historical "accident" whose leaders just happened to be in the right place at the right time. Much more than a chance encounter on the streets of New York, the mass of unskilled culinary workers were drawn to an organizational logic of industrial syndicalism as the product of nearly three decades of class struggle from which they drew clear and enduring lessons about the advantages of labor solidarity, mass mobilization, and unrestricted direct action.

Occupational Subcultures

What made turn-of-the-century New York City a center of culture and nightlife also made it a prime target for culinary unionism. Boasting an incomparable menu of nightly entertainment, eating and drinking establishments, and first-class accommodations, the "city that never sleeps" was always open for business, providing all these services for its many customers as well as jobs for the thousands of workers who made it all possible. Whether mixing drinks, making up beds, or preparing and serving food, bartenders, hotel keepers, and restaurant workers were a vital part of the local "service" economy. Although precious few of their pampered customers took notice, the plight of culinary workers did not escape the attention of hungry union organizers whose appetites were whetted by the city's large and highly concentrated workforce.

But organizing New York's polyglot labor force would not be easy. Like other less skilled trades at the time, culinary workers were an ethnically diverse lot, having been assembled from successive waves of European immigration. Out of the city's roughly forty-two thousand hotel and restaurant workers enumerated by the U.S. Census in 1910, fewer than one-fifth were native-born whites; and of these, nearly two-thirds were of foreign or mixed parentage. The vast majority, almost three-fourths, were foreign-born, with fewer than one in ten classified as nonwhite, mostly African American.[4]

The immigrant origins of the workforce were re-created over time by informal hiring practices that allocated jobs on the basis of nationality, eventually transforming the culinary workers from a largely undifferentiated immigrant mass into a honeycomb of ethnically based occupational enclaves. Cooks in the largest hotels were typically of German extraction, whereas Greeks were found in the kitchens of small cafés and neighborhood diners. The French waited tables in the larger restaurants or, if experienced, pursued the higher culinary arts as skilled pastry chefs. Some Italians became bakers specializing in bread, but most sought work in the hotel industry, where they predominated as waiters, busboys, and kitchen helpers. Southern and Eastern Europeans also found employment in the hotels, working mostly as laundresses, scrub women, and maids. Jews were hired exclusively in kosher bakeries or waited tables in smaller restaurants and delicatessens. The Irish tended bar and sometimes waitressed. African Americans normally waited on black customers or cleaned rooms in some of the city's most exclusive hotels.[5]

These complex patterns of labor market segmentation intersected the main occupational fault lines running between those who prepared food and those who served it. The kitchen staff, consisting of cooks, chefs, and their helpers, were the shock troops of industrial syndicalism, ready to strike at a moment's notice. In contrast, waiters and waitresses, though often among the first to unionize, assumed a more cautious stance, timing and measuring their collective action with greater care.

Cooks, chefs, and kitchen helpers were drawn to industrial syndicalism by their heightened disruptive potential. As food preparers, located far upstream in the production process, they occupied a most strategic position from which to disrupt the flow of business. "You cooks are the engineers of our industry," as one of their own explained. "When you stop, everything stops and every worker in the industry has to stop. If you don't prepare the food the waiters won't have any to serve, and the guest not being able to get his meals, will leave the house and so put the rest of the hotel workers, as bellboys, porters, maids, etc., out of work. Everything depends on you."[6]

But perhaps the most dependent of all were the employers. The limited supply of experienced cooks and pastry chefs, coupled with the high demand for their services, placed the kitchen staff in a commanding position, enabling them to flex their economic muscle with less chance of retaliation. Restaurateurs, fearful of antagonizing their "culinary artists," were openly conciliatory, tolerating infractions that if committed by other workers resulted in immediate dismissal or heavy fines. Cooks and chefs took notice of their additional leverage and were seldom shy about using it.[7]

The fluctuating pace of kitchen work underscored the efficacy of direct action. During busy mealtimes, with full pots and pans cooking on the stove and hungry customers waiting to be fed, kitchen managers were at the mercy of their workers. Much like the longshore industry, a fast turnaround time in the kitchen was necessary for economic survival. Repeated delays could just as surely sink a restaurant as a ship, ruining expensive food and angering customers who, as one militant cook explained, "would hardly risk getting indigestion and other stomach troubles, or being poisoned," by improperly prepared food. Between meals, when the demand for services slacked off, the balance of power tilted back toward employers. But even then the reluctance of most kitchen managers to retaliate against their highly prized cooks and temperamental chefs left restaurateurs relatively defenseless.[8]

Compared to the rebellious kitchen workers, the wait staff appeared outwardly more compliant. Many observers tried to account for these different occupational subcultures in terms of ethnicity, tracing the combativeness of cooks and chefs to their earlier indoctrination under the German and French labor movements, in contrast to the more conservative rural origins of many waiters and waitresses. Ethnic influences, however, were hardly this simple. Most Germans, it is true, were solid unionists; but some, like cooks, were leading militants while others, particularly waiters, lagged much farther behind. Likewise, French culinary workers often found themselves torn by competing loyalties rooted in syndicalism and craft professionalism. More perplexing still were the Italian hotel workers, whose ranks furnished some of the most militant unionists as well as many strikebreakers. Without entirely denying the influence of ethnic identities, they were at best weak predictors of collective action among New York's culinary workers.[9]

What the prevailing theories of ethnicity could not explain, gender might, leading other observers to focus on the "femininity" of the wait staff. Waiters, it was argued, were a self-selected group, lacking many of the "masculine" traits commonly associated with more defiant workers. Refined, cultured, and meticulously groomed, waiters were presumably the antithesis of the sturdy, roguish labor militant, and thus as a group temperamentally unsuited for industrial combat. In the case of waitresses, it was routinely assumed that, as members of the "fairer sex," they were beyond the pale of unionism.[10]

It goes without saying that waiters were not miners, that serving food was nothing like digging coal—or, for that matter, loading ships. Waiting tables was not for everyone; it appealed to a rather select group of men. But if waiters did not fit the gendered image of the quintessential proletarian rogue, they responded much like other men to the masculinist discourse of their male union leaders. Waiters were not simply told to stand up to their employers but to "stand tall, be men"—messages that reinforced a firm masculine identity. A case in point was the brief but telling controversy that erupted when restaurant and hotel proprietors, seeking to create a more manicured image for their help, refused to hire waiters who wore glasses or mustaches. Union leaders promptly denounced both restrictions but were clearly most upset by the mustache ban, which they saw as an assault on their masculinity. "In the old days," recalled a veteran waiter, "a moustache was a sign of manhood. But now the moustache is barred to us because the employers prefer that the waiters should seem servile." Equating servility with a lack of manhood, waiters wanted no part of either one.[11]

Waitresses, of course, inhabited a very different world in which their "femininity" was often used as a ploy to extract larger gratuities from a mostly male clientele. Such displays of sexuality, however, were purely tactical and in no way incompatible with support for unionization. Indeed, many waitresses turned to unions to protect themselves, as women, from the routine abuses they endured at the hands of their more aggressive, groping customers. Loretta Szeliga, for example, became active in the union during the 1930s after seeing so many of her sisters forced into compromising relationships by "the boss" who, as she recalled years later, "does not see why he cannot use the waitresses' bod[ies] for other purposes than waiting on the table." When Szeliga refused to let customers fondle and caress her, the owner, a friend of hers, begged her to quit, which she did. For Szeliga and countless other waitpersons, male and female alike, the "femininity" of the profession was seldom an obstacle to organizing.[12]

The moderation of the wait staff thus depended less on who they were than on where they were located in the process of production. Positioned far downstream from the source of food preparation, waiters and waitresses lacked the strategic location of the kitchen staff. Although their labor was arguably an essential part of a pleasant dining experience, business was certainly possible without them. When temporarily shorthanded, other restaurant workers, such as busboys or dishwashers, could be pressed into waiting tables; and in the event of a walkout or job action, even customers could be prevailed on to serve their own food. "The waiters alone don't count," admitted a waiter of many years experience. "Alone they are of no more importance than are the porters, bellboys, housemen or the female employees. They all can be replaced and their work performed by unskilled persons. Not so with the cooks." Lacking the disruptive capacities of the kitchen staff and being so easily replaced, waiters and waitresses were seriously disadvantaged in any protracted contest with management.[13]

This sense of powerlessness was reinforced by the tipping system, which, as a veteran waiter complained, left him "hang[ing] upon the benevolence and charity [of his customers] for his daily bread." "Unless the customer tips," he explained matter-of-factly, "the waiter will starve."[14] Waitresses were no less destitute. A survey of more than one thousand women restaurant workers conducted in 1915 by the New York City Health Department found that close to 90 percent earned less than $9 a week in wages and were therefore "obliged to depend upon tips to make enough to live on." Even with free meals and tips added, one-third were still receiving less than $10 a week, the minimum amount on which a single woman could live independently in New York City.[15]

The necessity of earning good tips often came at the psychological expense of the wait staff. "The average waiter never gets so used to insult that it fails to reach him," confessed a waiter of many years. "It hurts just as much when he is fifty as it did when he was twenty. . . . When without reason or justification he hears himself abused when he knows he has done his best, the sting is there no matter how old he may be."[16] The tipping system also fueled intense competition, compelling waitpersons to outdo one another in an effort to provide the extra service and special attention that might earn an additional nickel or dime in gratuities. Being so heavily dependent on tips makes waiters "most conservative," observed one union leader. "He is a small business man gambling daily upon the extent of his earnings and gets accustomed to rely upon his individual action."[17]

Still, waiters and waitresses were capable of collectively striking back, provided the timing was right. Like the kitchen staff, their power crested during busy mealtimes when a sudden and unannounced walkout was most costly to employers. Job actions that extended beyond a single meal, however, rarely met with success because of the ready availability of replacement labor. This unique economic niche—combining a weak strategic location, dependency on the customer, and short-lived disruptive power—inclined waiters and waitresses toward a more measured industrial strategy of spontaneous direct action followed by momentary retreat.

In this way distinct patterns of mobilization and collective action took hold among kitchen workers and waitpersons. Rooted in industry economics, these occupational subcultures were less a result of individual demographic characteristics—whether nationality, ethnicity, or gender—than of collective organizational capacities growing largely out of the production process itself. The kitchen staff's advantageous strategic position, heightened disruptive potential, and relative job security sustained their combativeness, just as the absence of such conditions among waitpersons, coupled with their dependence on the economic generosity of customers, supported a more guarded stance. Guided by these alternative organizational road maps, New York's culinary workers followed their own circuitous path to industrial syndicalism before World War I.

The Rise of Unionization

The visionary Knights of Labor brought their crusade against "wage slavery" to New York's culinary workers in 1885 with the establishment of local assembly number 8742, also known as the German Waiters Union. True to the Knights' inclusive model of unionism, the city's bakers and cooks were issued charters the following year, only to disappear within a few months. Local 8742 hung on a bit longer before dwindling to a mere ten members. Subsequent efforts to revive the struggling waiters' local came to naught.[18]

When Local 8742 permanently closed its doors in 1888, New York's culinary workers turned cautiously toward the American Federation of Labor, then the only game in town. Only a few months earlier the federation had established its first beachhead in the city, chartering Local 281 of the recently organized Waiters Union. Significantly, many of its members, most of whom were German Jews, had been affiliated with the Knights. While their reasons for leaving were never made public, workers who dispensed alcohol as part of their job, whether as bartenders or waiters, were made most unwelcome by the Knights' strenuous opposition to the liquor industry. In Local 281 New York's waiters found a new home, as did the city's bartenders on receiving their own charter a few months later.[19]

Local 281 carried into the present the lessons of its past. Inspired by the Knights' solidarity, it spearheaded efforts to organize the nation's catering workers. In 1891, while still struggling to establish itself, Local 281 called for a national convention of culinary trades. Meeting that spring in New York City, the assembled delegates, representing some four hundred fifty waiters and bartenders from Manhattan, Brooklyn, and New Jersey, drafted a union constitution and bylaws that were submitted to the AFL along with an application for a national charter. When a charter was issued a few days later for the Waiters and Bartenders National Union, New York's waiters, in recognition of their pioneering role, were honored as Local 1.[20]

The newly formed waiters' and bartenders' union held its first annual convention the following winter in New York. With Julius Leckel, a firebrand waiter representing Local 1, presiding, "the socialist spirit was unmistakably present," recalled one of the participants. Leckel and his Socialist comrades were committed to the union as "a matter of principle and did most of the organizing." The three-day conference, termed "The Waiters Parliament" by the local press, embraced the Socialist vision of its leaders and endorsed a resolution "that all wealth is produced by the workers, and that the workingman does not get his share of the wealth he produces." Moved by a growing spirit of solidarity, the delegates agreed to expand the name of their organization to the more inclusive Hotel and Restaurant Employees National Alliance, or HRE.[21]

As the HRE began its ambitious westward expansion, Local 1's influence waned. Increasingly, its Socialist founders appeared out of sync with their own national organization. Local 1's status reached a new low at the 1898 convention when its two delegates were suspended and replaced after they accused international president William Pomeroy, an ambitious Chicago politician, of stacking the convention with his cronies. Although the charges against Pomeroy were later sustained, New York's waiters fell further out of step with the union's top leadership, who pegged their future on organizing the bartenders. With "union beer" the new rallying cry of culinary unionism, Local 1's pleas for solidarity fell silent.[22]

The growing sectionalism that threatened to consume the national organization eventually devoured New York. In 1903 Local 1 became embroiled in what was to be the first of many jurisdictional disputes, this time with waiters' Local 3, its recently chartered crosstown rival. After failing to resolve their differences, HRE international president Bob Callahan stepped in, determined that the city's workers were "impossible" to organize, and then abruptly suspended Local 1. When the suspension order was lifted four years later, culinary unionism in New York was in shambles, with fewer than two thousand members. Except for bartenders, the city was virtually unorganized: waiters' Local 1 claimed about six hundred members, but none of the cooks and hardly any hotel workers were unionized.[23]

With their backs against the wall, the waiters once again stepped forward, taking the organizational lead. Only this time they set out in a different direction. Still besieged by rival HRE locals and facing determined employer opposition, the waiters turned to a more defensive strategy of job control unionism. In 1909 Local 1 raised its initiation fee from $15 to $65, effectively "closing the books" by limiting membership to those already on the union rolls.[24] New York's waiters, once the vanguard of worker solidarity, were now trailing their own national organization on the road to business syndicalism— a destination that left behind the vast majority of the city's less skilled culinary workers.

The resulting organizational vacuum was soon filled by the International Hotel Workers Union (IHWU). Founded in 1911, the IHWU was created in the image of its maker, Joseph Vehling, an industrious German immigrant whose meteoric career took him from being an entry-level cook right out of school to assistant manager in one of

Europe's leading hotels at the tender age of twenty-three. Vehling's personal success closely informed his "uplift" vision of unionism. Writing in the first issue of *International Hotel Worker*, the union's monthly newsletter, Vehling promised "to uplift this marvelously manysided and complicated trade to the common standard of every good and decent profession in public life." His goal was to see the culinary business "recognized as a fullfledged profession among the other professions and arts and industries of the nations."[25]

The new union took its professionalizing mission seriously. Guided by its leader's "indestructible idealism," the IHWU promised to restore dignity to all hotel employees by promoting the culinary arts rather than industrial warfare. "I am far from looking for trouble," Vehling declared, seeking to distance himself and his organization from the more confrontational methods of direct actionists. "I do not intend to rouse dissatisfaction, nor fan hatred and to stir up the malcontents. . . . I have no intentions of that kind. I bear no malice towards anybody."[26]

Vehling reserved his anger for the "degrading" conditions of work that threatened to reduce one of the world's most intellectually demanding trades to "mere stupid drudgery." Vowing to "do away with everything harmful to the health, the intellectual welfare and civic responsibility of the hotel employee," he advocated a shorter workweek, higher pay, and an end to tipping. Consistent with his professionalism, Vehling sought relief through third-party intervention. Rejecting direct action in favor of litigation, the IHWU flooded the municipal courts with lawsuits aimed at unscrupulous proprietors and headwaiters who tried to take advantage of their help. Judicial remedies were usually forthcoming in the form of back wages or reinstatement.[27]

Although Vehling's efforts did little to elevate the status of the profession, the union's rising visibility heightened the level of AFL activity. Condemning the independent IHWU as "dual unionism," HRE leaders countered with their own hotel organizing campaign. With powerful Local 1 serving as a beachhead, the international issued a new charter, Local 5, for enrolling hotel waiters. Joseph Elster, an experienced waiter and union activist, was engaged to lead the organizing drive. In many ways Elster was a natural for the job. Recognized as "an eloquent speaker and tireless organizer," he already had a sizable following among hotel workers. In other respects, however, Elster was a high-risk candidate. Never having been a member of the AFL's inner sanctum, he owed his primary allegiance to the rank and file, not his sponsoring organization. Only weeks before signing on with the HRE, Elster had appeared on the same stage alongside Vehling, warmly praising his efforts and agreeing to serve in a temporary capacity as business representative for the IHWU. Such flagrant disregard for organizational loyalty no doubt troubled Elster's new employers, but they agreed to give him a try.[28]

Elster received enthusiastic backing from the HRE's international headquarters, which, in the face of the IHWU's growing presence in the field, pulled out all stops. Late in 1911 the union's General Executive Board allocated a special appropriation for the hotel campaign, assigned an experienced team of paid organizers, and even allowed Local 5 to set its initiation fee at an inviting $5, well below the going rate. But, after a promising start, Elster's efforts bogged down in fierce jurisdictional warfare. Dismayed by the "absence of practical cooperation" among its locals, the HRE's General Executive Board sent international president Jere Sullivan to New York to get the stalled hotel drive moving once again. Sullivan, a bartender by trade, had little understanding of the hotel industry and even less patience for dealing with the city's warring culinary locals. New York, he concluded, was "unorganizable."[29]

Elster, now more determined than ever, kept plugging away throughout the winter of 1912, eventually picking up enough steam to overcome the bureaucratic inertia and destructive in-fighting of his parent organization. By March Local 5 had enrolled almost one hundred dues-paying members. With the hotel drive finally shifting into high gear, Elster came out publicly against HRE officials, condemning them for neglecting the mass of less skilled culinary workers. As relations continued to deteriorate, an open break seemed unavoidable. In early May Elster led several hundred of his followers into the rival IHWU.[30]

If Vehling appeared less than appreciative, it was because he faced a growing insurgent movement inside his own ranks. Only a few weeks earlier, the membership had voted by a slim majority to participate in the annual May Day parade. Some fifty workers, representing the union's activist core, marched as a unit under the IHWU banner. A few days later, on May 5, when one of the marchers, a waiter at the Belmont Hotel, showed up late for work, he was told to report to the maitre d', Victor Pearl, who asked whether he had attended the parade. After answering truthfully, the waiter was fired. The next morning another waiter, also a May Day participant, was dismissed after admitting under Pearl's vigorous interrogation that he belonged to the union. When a group of irate workers from the Belmont appeared before the IHWU's executive board to request strike authorization, the usually articulate Vehling was at a loss for words.[31]

Direct Action Comes to the Hotel Industry

The demand for direct action emanating from the rank and file caught Vehling and other officers off guard. Despite their best efforts to redirect the men's anger away from the dining room to the more familiar environs of the courtroom, the culinary workers remained intently focused on the point of production. Facing a groundswell of opposition, IHWU officials reluctantly shelved their plans for further legal action. On May 7 union leaders formally authorized a strike against the Belmont, strategically timing the walkout to coincide with the busy dinner hour when it would be most effective. The following evening at exactly 7:15 union stewards in each of the hotel's three dining rooms sounded a shrill whistle, announcing the walkout. As four hundred guests looked on in utter amazement, the waiters calmly set down their trays and, with characteristic courtesy, apologized for their actions. "Pardon me," one waiter was overheard saying to his party, "but I beg to inform you that there is a waiters' union now, and by that whistle which you have just heard we have been ordered to strike." Nearly one hundred waiters, more than half the force, then quietly filed out, exchanging their menus for picket signs.[32]

From their temporary strike headquarters across the street from the Belmont, the waiters demanded Pearl's "immediate and unconditional" discharge. When the hotel manager refused, they expanded their protest from Pearl himself to the system of industrial despotism he represented. In their indictments of "Pearlism," strikers told of being arbitrarily discharged, required to work sixteen- to eighteen-hour shifts without any days off, and forced to eat tasteless, unhealthy food on the run. But the most common complaint targeted Pearl's voracious system of fines, which regularly consumed up to half their salary, leaving waiters with an average of $12 in wages at the end of a month.[33] During a typical one-week period before the walkout, the Belmont's fine book totaled forty pages of assessments for "lax service." Included among the nearly five hundred separate infractions were such offenses as failing to place a napkin on the table (25 cents), wearing a food-stained uniform (25 cents per stain), dropping a spoon (50 cents), smiling in the dining room ($1), speaking to co-workers ($1), and drinking discarded coffee in the pantry ($3), which included additional fines ($1) levied against two co-workers who failed to stop the coffee drinker.[34]

Challenging the basis of Pearl's authority, the waiters called for scrapping the system of fines, reinstating all strikers and May Day participants, and subjecting future disciplinary action to independent review. Edward Fogg, manager of the Belmont, rejected the demands, defiantly announcing, "The inconvenience caused by the strike . . . was a thing of the past. We have filled the places of the men who went on strike, and all the trouble is ended."[35] But Fogg's assurances convinced no one, certainly not the Belmont's guests, whose mass exodus the following morning left one of the city's largest hotels "practically empty" by noon.[36]

Fanning out across Manhattan, strikers and their supporters distributed more than ten thousand handbills urging waiters, "Demand Your Rights. . . . BE A MAN." Appealing specifically to "extra waiters"—a classic reserve army that was called on to service unusually large banquets, or, as in this case, to replace strikers—the leaflet broadcast a recent union proposal to increase their nightly wage from $2 to $3. The message got through to waiters at the plush Waldorf-Astoria, where, as the first of two thousand guests began arriving that evening for a gala banquet, five hundred "extras" stopped work and demanded the $3 wage, which the beleaguered hotel manager immediately conceded. Pointing with evident pride to this latest job action, a striking waiter noted "how easy it is for us to make and enforce demands, if only the right moment is chosen, and if the workers act in concert."[37]

This lesson about direct action was not lost on the rank and file. The IHWU's decisive victory over the Waldorf-Astoria and the growing visibility of the Belmont walkout fueled a dramatic surge in membership. In little more than a week the union saw its ranks swell from a few hundred to nearly eight thousand. With the relatively powerless waiters making up almost three-fourths of its membership, union leaders turned their attention to the strategically located cooks. Calling them "the key to the situation," IHWU secretary Edward Blocklinger announced an ambitious campaign to enroll the city's ten thousand cooks.[38]

The union had no problem "arousing co-operation" from the cooks, who, as one chef reported, "have more to complain of than the waiters." They, too, worked long and hard, regularly putting in thirteen- and fourteen-hour shifts with no days off. Wages, having dropped 15 percent over the last ten years, were little compensation. While capable of earning as much as $100 per month in the finest kitchens, most cooks averaged about $50, with some earning as little as $35— out of which they paid for their own knives, cooking utensils, and uniforms, as well as any breakage. And because their work site, unlike the waiters', was typically hidden from the customer, their physical surroundings were worse still. Often located underground without sunlight or proper ventilation, the kitchen staff's work area was described by one observer as a "hell hole," crowded and hot, with scalding, leaky steam pipes overhead and cold, wet cement floors below.[39] Such conditions produced a high incidence of rheumatism and communicable diseases that eventually destroyed the health and character of many cooks. The "poor assistant cook or dishwasher" was easy to recognize, recalled a veteran chef, "because he looked so terrible usually. They would work until they could not stand up any longer, then go home, get drunk, sleep, fight with their wives, have kids and get drunk again. It was all work and sleep, drink and fight."[40]

While the cooks had ample reason to complain, they also had the disruptive capacity to act on their grievances, as they demonstrated with wicked effectiveness one evening at the posh Vanderbilt hotel. On May 15, at the peak of the dinner hour, a whistle was blown in the hotel's main dining room calling the waiters out on strike. In what was becoming a familiar scene to upscale New Yorkers, a few guests calmly served themselves while the rest waited for their food to come up from the kitchen. But this time there were no new orders on the way because several cooks had joined the walkout, effectively crippling the restaurant. As disgruntled diners headed for the exits, the hotel manager headed for the IHWU headquarters where he immediately granted the workers' demands, including union recognition, a six-day workweek, a pay increase, an end to all fines, and managerial review of all discharges.[41]

Holding up the Vanderbilt settlement as a model, the IHWU presented a similar proposal to the citywide Hotel Men's Association. The *New York Herald* described the union's demands as "involv[ing] radical changes," and an employer spokesman offered the opinion that "they will stand some revising." But with the union remaining firm, managers at the Gotham, Manhattan, and Astor hotels—hoping to avoid a repeat of the Waldorf-Astoria walkout—unilaterally granted the higher pay scale for extra waiters.[42] Following a week of fruitless negotiations, the employers' association abruptly broke off talks with the union. In retaliation, the Belmont's kitchen staff walked out, joining their fellow waiters. "We did this," union leader Blocklinger explained, "just as an object lesson to show what we can do in that branch of the hotel service in which the proprietors have said we are the weakest."[43]

Culinary workers, now moving together and capitalizing on the element of surprise, began picking off restaurants one by one. On May 27, in the middle of dinner, more than two hundred fifty workers—representing all of the waiters and most of the cooks—stormed out of the Knickerbocker hotel. The guests immediately followed, forcing the manager to close the dining and grill rooms. Strikers paraded triumphantly around the moribund hotel before marching off to union headquarters where organizer Elster reassured them that "the Knickerbocker died to-night." "There is many a hotel proprietor," he said ominously, "who will not do much sleeping to-night wondering if his turn will come to-morrow. And it will—that is, somebody's will—and keep a coming until the union's victory is complete."[44]

No idle threat, the IHWU struck again the following evening at the Holland House and Churchill's restaurant. Newspaper accounts reported that the union's "dragnet . . . swept those establishments practically bare of waiters and cooks. . . . The hotel was crippled so that it could make only a pretence of doing business, and the restaurant was closed tight as wax in five minutes." Jubilant strikers and their supporters poured into the streets, choking off traffic. Police charged the crowd repeatedly, flailing their clubs "without discrimination[,] and broken heads and bruised bodies attested the vigor of their activities." As the battle raged in the streets, from atop nearby hotel balconies "richly dressed women waved their handkerchiefs . . . and some of them drained their glasses to the mob."[45]

Strike fever spread rapidly, first to the Waldorf-Astoria and then to Breslin's and Rector's, two of mid-Manhattan's finer restaurants. The following evening, May 30, the union took aim at the city's largest hotels, hitting the Plaza, Astor, St. Regis, Gotham, Imperial, and Prince George, thereby adding 1,600 strikers that night alone. Within two days the ranks of striking culinary workers, now assembled from more than fifty restaurants and hotels, had grown to 6,000, with total union membership surging to 16,000.[46]

Employers, led by the Hotel Men's Association, marshaled their forces. Seeking to exploit the one chink in the union's armor—the relative ease of replacing waiters—they aggressively began to recruit strikebreakers. Many of the larger chain hotels imported experienced black waiters from their southern operations that were already winding down for the slow summer season.[47] Buoyed by their successful recruiting efforts, the chairman of the employers' association was "confident of victory." Dismissing as "impossible" the IHWU's demand for recognition, he threw down the gauntlet, vowing never "to submit to the dictation of any union."[48]

In declaring war on "any union," the hotel operators unwittingly fanned the flames of labor solidarity. Long-stalled and previously secretive negotiations between the IHWU and the HRE got moving once again. In early June an IHWU spokesman announced progress toward a possible merger with the AFL. As talks continued with the HRE, some six thousand strikers turned out to hear Big Bill Haywood of the IWW and Rose Pastor Stokes of the Socialist party. With little apparent regard for their divergent ideological agendas, the culinary workers welcomed allies from any quarter—whether craft unionists, Wobblies, or Socialists—so long as they supported the walkout.[49]

Union leaders rallied their troops around an expanding conception of professionalism that broadly defined their struggle as affirming the value and respectability of culinary labor. Status-conscious waiters, reminded of their skills, were urged to demand greater respect from their customers. As one striker put it, "The waiter is really the salesman of the hotel. He comes into direct contact with the guest and must not only present a good appearance, but must also be intelligent, and very often speak two or three languages." His voice breaking with emotion, he continued, "We have been damned, looked down upon and spurned. But we are skilled workers."[50]

The interwoven messages of skill and respectability directed at waiters were often counterposed to the pampered, unproductive lives of their employers. Denouncing all capitalists as "idlers," Rose Pastor Stokes portrayed labor and capital as separate nations. "There are no foreigners but the masters," she told an audience mostly composed of immigrant waiters and cooks. "We workers all belong to one land— the land of work. We are all one nation arrayed against another na- tion—the capitalist class. . . . How long will you tolerate idlers?" The Wobblies' Big Bill Haywood struck a similar note, describing wealthy diners as rich "tramps" who "render no more service to society than the hobo at the bottom of the social scale." The lowly waiter, he continued, may lack money but not power. Referring to an incident earlier that day when Judge Gary, a major investor in U.S. Steel, was refused service in a local restaurant, Haywood told the strikers, "You are bigger than the Steel trust. . . . You have demonstrated that Gary is small potatoes as compared with your union."[51]

But the union was still not big enough to corral its less disciplined members. Waiters, claiming their wives "ordered them to quit their foolishness," began drifting back to work.[52] Hoping to close the gen- der gap by force of example, union leaders called the hotel chamber- maids out on strike. But it was a case of too little too late. Having been largely ignored by the union up to that point, the chambermaids were understandably reluctant to throw their lot in with what was increasingly seen as a losing cause. With nowhere else to turn, IHWU officials appealed to the skilled trades—engineers, electricians, and stationary firemen—who occupied a small but strategic niche among hotel workers. Again the results were disappointing.[53]

In a last-ditch effort to hit employers where it hurt them most, the union launched a publicity campaign to scare off customers by ex- posing routine health code violations involving food preparation. Sworn testimony and affidavits were collected from countless kitchen workers who described in lurid detail the unsanitary, often illegal conditions hidden inside the "glittering jungle" of Manhattan's finer hotels and restaurants.[54] One of the most common health violations involved reusing partially consumed food and drink. Busboys admit- ted draining half-empty glasses of wine back into the bottle. Dish- washers told of being forced to scrape butter from dirty dishes, then wadding it into a ball by hand and presenting it to the cooks for use in food preparation. Waiters were reportedly instructed to salvage all uneaten food, which, when suitably "dressed up," was presented to the next customer. Serving spoiled and contaminated foods was also quite common. Sauces and soups were stored as inexpensively as possible, frequently in old, rusty tomato cans left to warm by the stove. "The tin cans," as one cook explained, "are terrible things. The cook is apt to cut his finger on the sharp edges; the blood runs into the food and that food is served to guests of the hotel." In the fashionable Mouquin restaurant, known to most cooks as the "rat house," rodent infestation was widespread. One chef told of finding a drowned rat in the soup. "The rat," he calmly reported, "was thrown away. The soup was served to the guests." Numerous cooks testified that they had been disciplined, even fired, for discarding spoiled meats or vegetables. Such dramatic accounts caught the public's eye—but not long enough to keep them away in sufficient numbers to salvage the walkout.[55]

By the middle of June IHWU leaders were ready to throw in the towel. At a mass meeting in Bryant Hall on June 21, the union's executive board endorsed the employers' latest offer to raise wages and improve conditions while refusing to recognize the union. When the rank and file balked, Rose Pastor Stokes resigned from the IHWU, citing her disagreement with "the great majority of strikers as to the wisest policies to pursue." Stokes's resignation deprived the walkout of one of its most colorful and articulate speakers, as well as its only proven fund-raiser. The strike dragged on a few more days before officially being called off on June 26, amid accusations of union misleadership.[56]

IHWU leaders pronounced the walkout a success, counting among its accomplishments some fifteen thousand new members, higher wages, better conditions, and greater "self-respect" for the city's waiters and cooks. "The dignity of this class of workers is now established," claimed the union's monthly newsletter. Coding their gains in exclusively masculine terms, it reported that the strikers "proved their manhood by risking their all and striking together as one man. . . . They have compelled the respect of both the employers and the public, and they will never forfeit it as long as the Union is virile, strong and on the level." Reflecting the new balance of power after the strike, many hotels abolished the hated system of fines that had provoked the original walkout at the Belmont, and a few restaurants and clubs even went so far as to openly discourage tipping in favor of a higher monthly wage. The union, its leaders insisted, had become a "Damocles sword over the heads of each and every" employer.[57]

But if some owners feared for their economic lives, rival unionists were not taken in by the IHWU's transparent swaggering. Writing in the July issue of the *Mixer and Server*, the HRE's monthly magazine, local organizer William Joyce described New York as "a good city to keep away from at this date." The "dual waiters' outfit," he wrote, "did more injury to the worker than it did good." Deriding the strike's "incompetent leadership," Joyce told how he had dogged IHWU officials during the walkout, appearing at all of their fund-raising events to speak out against dual unionism. He boasted of his success: only one AFL affiliate—maverick waiters' Local 1 of the HRE—contributed to the IHWU's strike fund.[58] Critics on the left, though less vocal, also chimed in. Coverage of the strike in *Solidarity*, the national IWW publication, praised the unity of the culinary workers but noted, in contrast to the claims of IHWU leaders, "the revolt is far from being general." In the waning days of the walkout, the IWW grew more critical. During the climactic mass meeting that ended the strike, several Wobblies took the stage at Bryant Hall and, turning to an agitated membership, accused their leaders of having "cold feet" for recommending a return to work.[59]

Continued sniping by rival unionists took a heavy psychological toll on the already battered rank and file, just as the IHWU's fragile industrial foundation began to crumble. In early July a leader of the German cooks charged that they had been used as "a cats' paw" by the waiters to further "their own selfish ends." In response union leaders pointed out that it was the cooks who, owing to their strategic advantages, secured all of their original demands, unlike the waiters, who won "only 75%" of theirs.[60] Besieged from without and riven by internal conflicts, the IHWU found itself at the mercy of vengeful hotel operators, whose constant encroachments threatened the union's recent gains. By the fall of 1912 the pages of the *International Hotel Worker* were taken up with stories of increasingly bold employer assaults: wages were slashed between 20 and 40 percent; working conditions and hours returned to prestrike levels; and the "abominable fine system" was reintroduced in some locations.[61]

From Professionalism
to Industrial Syndicalism

The latest employer offensive forced the retreating IHWU into a corner from which there was no easy escape. Finally shedding its remaining vestiges of professionalism, the IHWU came out fighting in the fall of 1912 with a freshly inked "progressive" constitution in hand which placed the union squarely on the path to industrial syndicalism. Declaring that "labor creates all wealth," the IHWU announced that its new goal was nothing less than "final emancipation" through "united action" against the employing class. In contrast to the business syndicalist HRE, the IHWU was organized industrially and guided by an inclusive vision of membership. To that end, the union opened its doors to noncitizens, fees were radically reduced to $1 for initiation and fifty cents for monthly dues, and all informal barriers "by reason of color, creed, sex or nationality" were lifted. Direct action, rather than Vehling's reliance on the courts, was the new weapon of choice. And the bane of syndicalist existence—the time contract—was expressly forbidden.[62]

The culinary workers waited patiently for the right moment to strike back. Having learned something about the importance of timing from last spring's walkout, they chose New Year's Eve—traditionally the busiest night of the year—to launch their own counteroffensive. Catching hotel and restaurant operators completely off guard, union leaders announced at 2:00 p.m. on December 31 that a strike would begin in five hours against all establishments found violating the terms of the recent settlement. While the element of surprise rendered employers momentarily defenseless, it also prevented the union from adequately mobilizing its membership. When the appointed hour arrived, only a handful of locations were struck. Yet, with cooks and kitchen helpers spearheading the walkout this time around, the affected employers were in a panic to settle. By nightfall thirteen houses had given in to the union's demands.[63]

When the morning newspapers declared the walkout "a fizzle," IHWU officials had a growing revolt on their hands. The flamboyant Elster, a convenient scapegoat, was promptly relieved of his duties. Walter Eggeman, an IWW sympathizer and strike activist, was placed in charge of the walkout. Under growing Wobbly influence, job action soon spread to the large hotels, where the union's guerrilla tactics were most effective. On successive evenings several hundred guests at the Waldorf-Astoria and Belmont hotels had their dinners disrupted by the shrill sound of a steward's whistle, calling the cooks and waiters out on strike.[64]

With the walkout back on track the union called its first mass meeting. Featured prominently among the speakers were IWW leaders Elizabeth Gurley Flynn and Arturo Giovannitti, both fresh from the highly publicized Lawrence textile strike. The local press, led by the *New York Times,* played up the IWW presence, intimating that the Wobblies were effectively running the strike. Rival union leaders agreed, publicly declaring, in the words of Jere Sullivan, that the walkout had been "turned over to . . . the espousers of sabotage, the advocates of force and turmoil, the I.W. of W."[65]

Consumed by their fears of "another Lawrence," the employers clamped down. At the Astor, where the wait staff was "forcibly kept from walking out," thirty workers "succeeded in escaping" when the signal was given. The two whistle-blowers, however, were less fortunate. They were seized by the hotel's security force, taken to the engine room in the basement, and, according to union sources, "beaten continuously" for over an hour. When news of the Astor incident reached the union, a large and angry crowd surged onto the streets, marched to the hotel, and demanded the immediate release of their "imprisoned" comrades. Projectiles were thrown, including a huge stone that crashed through a plate-glass window, narrowly missing several diners.[66]

A wave of violence washed across the hotel district, engulfing many strikers, whose bruised appearances provided "eloquent evidence of the brutality which [was] being exercised by the hotel detectives and plug-ugly guards." Describing the streets of Manhattan as a battle zone, a reporter for the Socialist *New York Call* wrote, "Here and there was a hotel striker with a smashed face or a bandaged head where a policeman's club or a thug's brass knuckles or blackjack had descended, while bruised eyes were comparatively abundant." Not that the workers were mere passive victims. Large armies of strikers gamely fought back, engaging, and in some cases routing, outmanned police, hotel security forces, and strikebreakers.[67]

Into this combustible situation stepped the Wobblies, whose dramatic entrance sparked a firestorm of protest. On January 10 IWW leader Joseph Ettor, in a much-anticipated address to the strikers, concluded on a rather unsettling note, at least to New York's wealthier class of diners. "If you are compelled to go back to work," he advised his audience, "go back with the determination to stick together and with your minds made up it is the unsafest proposition in the world for the capitalists to eat food prepared by members of your union."[68] The newspapers seized on Ettor's sensational threat as a means of discrediting both the strikers and their "anarchist" leaders. Hotel operators, championing the public's right to dine in safety, tried to have the Wobbly leader indicted for his comments.[69]

The controversy refused to subside, prompting Ettor's belated protest that he had been misquoted. Claiming his words had been "twisted," he professed his faith in peaceful tactics. Twisted or not, his advice was consistent with the IWW's views at the time on industrial sabotage. Indeed, on the day of Ettor's retraction, Giovannitti, his countryman and fellow Wobbly, was urging strikers to adulterate food with "harmless ingredients . . . such as a handful of salt in the soup, which would make it unpalatable without harming anybody but the proprietors."[70] Flynn, too, openly endorsed such forms of direct action. In a pamphlet on sabotage written later that year, she recounted an incident during the hotel strike that demonstrated the wisdom of Giovannitti's advice. One evening, Flynn recalled, she was asked to address an audience of "aristocratic women" on the causes of the walkout. While discussing at some length the deplorable working conditions, long hours, and low pay, her audience sat "stony-faced." But when she turned to the subject of unhealthy food, they suddenly came alive. "They only became interested," Flynn concluded, "when I began to talk about something that affected their own stomachs."[71]

Whatever Ettor intended, his comments about unsafe food alienated many middle-class diners whose support the strikers desperately needed. As growing numbers of customers marched defiantly through union picket lines, nervous IHWU officials began looking to bail out. On January 13 leadership of the walkout was assumed by a five-member committee, of which Wobbly leaders Flynn and Carlo Tresca were the most prominent. The IWW was now unambiguously in charge. Within hours the hotel operators issued a statement condemning "radical" strikers, said to consist of kitchen and pantry men and nonworkers. "This radical element," the employers charged, "are the kind of men who can be and are most easily influenced by the paid agitators and by men like Ettor."[72]

The Wobblies breathed new life into the walkout. By a nearly unanimous vote, some two thousand unionists, most of whom recently had been locked out by their employers, endorsed a general strike against the city's hotels and restaurants. Flynn, who was now almost single-handedly running the strike, set forth three demands: abolish the tipping system in favor of a $20 minimum weekly wage for waiters; establish a uniform eight-hour day for all; and outlaw private employment agencies, known as "vampires" to the culinary workers.[73] Aimed at empowering the tip-dependent waiters, unifying the kitchen and serving staffs around the goal of a standard working day, and gaining a greater measure of control over hiring, this latest round of demands went considerably beyond anything ever entertained by IHWU leaders in the spring walkout, just six months earlier. And, consistent with the IWW's practice of industrial syndicalism, union recognition—representing the centerpiece of the earlier IHWU program—was not even raised.

The three demands were placed before the entire membership for a vote. With approximately six thousand culinary workers in attendance, the motion passed overwhelmingly. Despite the strong show of hands, the call for a general strike fell on deaf ears. Except for the locked out hotel workers, who waged a desperate, at times violent battle against authorities and strikebreakers, culinary unionists failed to heed their leaders. Battle weary and facing a long, cold winter, they voted to return to work a few days later, on January 31.[74]

Critics on all sides of the walkout later agreed that "radical" influences were chiefly to blame for its failure. Certainly this was the message conveyed in the flurry of hostile editorials and news stories that appeared in the commercial press after the strike. The views of many observers were captured by HRE president Jere Sullivan in a private letter to Sam Gompers, written in early February. Any hope of unionizing New York's culinary workers was lost, he wrote, when the IHWU "slipped out of" its founder's hands. "The fellows that 'swiped the union' from Vahling [*sic*] . . . were all REDS . . . who gave them that class conscious stuff going and coming." Joseph Elster and others "with IWW leanings," Sullivan concluded, "succeeded in converting quite a number to their ideas."[75]

Yet the Wobblies—in this case as in so many others—were unable to translate the evident appeal of their ideas into an enduring organizational presence. IWW leaders accepted part of the blame for their failure, later conceding that they had been manipulated by IHWU officials who handed the reins over to the Wobblies only after the strike was petering out. As Flynn charged, she and her comrades were opportunistically employed "as official scapegoats" to absorb the costs of their inevitable defeat.[76]

IHWU officers denied all such allegations, arguing instead that most culinary workers were simply "not ready" to embrace the Wobblies' revolutionary vision. "We have found it a hard task to organize the workers of our industry," observed Frank Hinz, newly installed editor of the *International Hotel Worker*. "It is not an easy matter to make out of a crawling and cringing menial, who has been oppressed and morally prostituted by the tip-system for years and years, a class-conscious worker and a union man." "But," he added, referring specifically to the IWW's mission, "it is an absolutely impossible task to make of him right away a revolutionary, ready to fight for the emancipation of the entire class."[77]

Whereas the Wobblies appeared oblivious to political realities, the Socialists could think of little else. During the spring walkout, New York's large Socialist party left the strikers flapping in the breeze, blowing into and out of their lives with every change in the political winds sweeping across the city. "[When the Socialists ultimately] abandoned us," Hinz wrote, "the members of the IHWU came to realize that politics and political action may be all right outside of the unions, but that it has absolutely nothing to do with the internal affairs and the control of the policies of an economic organization." Without questioning the sincerity of local Socialist "politicians," Hinz left no room for them in the IHWU, insisting that "politicians and professional labor agitators must be kept out of [the] organization."[78]

Hinz reserved his most critical remarks, however, for the AFL, describing it as woefully "out of date" and "absolutely antagonistic to the progress of the working class." Citing the HRE's reliance on "arbitration, conciliation and agreements," he observed "that even the dullest of our members rebelled against the idea of affiliation with an organization under the control of the A.F. of L." "Conservative methods," he explained, "won't work with our union. . . . We were willing [during the first strike] to arbitrate and make agreements with the bosses. The latter either spurned us altogether or broke agreements as soon as they were made."[79]

The culinary workers thus needed to blaze their own trail, bypassing the illusory shortcuts promised by both "Socialist politicians" and the "fire-eating I.W.W." while simultaneously circumventing the many obstructions and detours created by the "reactionary A.F. of L." In the absence of an existing road map, Hinz argued, the only reliable means of navigation was to follow the familiar landmarks of direct action, mass mobilization, labor solidarity, and a rejection of contracts, which, like the points on a compass, promised to keep the rank and file headed in the right direction.[80]

Conclusion

New York's culinary workers found their way slowly but surely to industrial syndicalism after nearly thirty years of schooling in trade unionism. It was a practical lesson taught through their experiences on the job and reinforced by the distinctive occupational cultures within the industry, the changing relations of force between labor and capital, and the resulting elaboration of new organizational forms and repertoires of collective action that capitalized on the class capacities of unskilled hotel and restaurant workers.

The Knights of Labor were the first to instruct the city's culinary workers on the basics of labor solidarity. A small but powerful segment of waiters, inspired by the Knights' example, tried to carry forward their teachings with the formation of a new national organization encompassing all culinary trades, the HRE. But as the economically vulnerable waiters came increasingly under attack from sister AFL locals and resistive employers alike, they were forced to take up a more defensive position, eventually accepting the logic of business syndicalism in limiting union membership through high dues while also entering into restrictive contractual relations with many smaller firms.

The vast majority of unorganized culinary workers, having thus been excluded by the AFL, were introduced to unions through the efforts of the independent IHWU. Rejecting both the Knights' expansive solidarity and the HRE's incipient business syndicalism, the IHWU was guided initially by the professionalizing vision of its founder, who dangled before the rank and file the promise of occupational upgrading, judicial remedies, and piecemeal reforms. But with each new employer assault at the point of production, the union's legalistic defenses crumbled more and more, until, facing almost certain death, the IHWU reinvented itself as a self-described "progressive" industrial organization.

The transformed IHWU now embraced all of the key elements of industrial syndicalism: labor solidarity, mass mobilization, and unrestricted direct action. By the time the IWW appeared on the scene early in 1913, observed IHWU secretary Frank Hinz, "the principles, methods, and tactics of the two organizations were nearly identical."[81] Indeed, except for their more strident revolutionary posturing, the Wobblies were indistinguishable from the new-look IHWU, from their immediate demands and converging long-term visions to, more significantly, their common underlying logics of collective action. The Wobblies' industrial syndicalism was thus largely an extension of the IHWU's recent history of struggle and organizational transformation—and not, as many observers claimed, a "radical departure" that "startled" the "best of the conservative" rank and file, ultimately resulting in the IWW's untimely death.[82]

The IWW's sudden demise in New York was not the result of any fatal flaw in its logic of collective action but rather of the lethal credibility wounds its leaders sustained after assuming responsibility for a strike that was by all accounts unwinnable. In defeat the Wobblies had nothing to offer the rank and file: no past victories to build on, no promise of a continuing organizational presence, not even the kind of informal job control that enabled their "fellow workers" on the Philadelphia docks to withstand for many years a much longer string of organizational setbacks. Compared to Philadelphia, then, New York's Wobblies had it easy. They were spared massive government repression, never imprisoned or suspended from their own national organization. Nor did they face any of the divisive racial tensions that ultimately split the union in Philadelphia. And yet the IWW was more easily dislodged in New York, largely because it failed to provide credible leadership in a moment of crisis.

Where Wobbly leadership was not called into question, they made deep and lasting inroads among the city's culinary workers. Brooklyn's Italian bakers, for example, remained staunch supporters of the IWW long after the hotel and restaurant workers had fallen away. Organized late in 1913 by Joseph Ettor, they missed by several months the failed citywide strike and so had no reason to doubt the Wobblies' leadership abilities. Although only four hundred strong, the Italian bakers, under IWW leadership for more than seven years, won the highest wages in the industry, the shortest working day at seven and a half hours, the right to appoint their own foremen, and an end to all night work—all secured without a union contract and enforced solely by the organizational capacities of the rank and file.[83]

The success of the Italian bakers forcefully demonstrated what rival union leaders and employers feared most: the IWW's program of labor solidarity, mass mobilization, and unrestricted direct action offered perhaps the greatest promise for the long-suffering hotel and restaurant workers. While the Wobblies themselves might come and go, their practice of industrial syndicalism would continue to influence culinary unionism in the years ahead.

Chapter Five

"More Business Sense and Stability than the I.W.W."

Labor solidarity, mass mobilization, and unrestricted direct action were never the exclusive property of the IWW. Long after the Wobblies had disappeared from the field, the organizational logic of industrial syndicalism continued to influence the direction and content of American unionism, particularly in mass production industries that were still dominated by unskilled ethnic immigrants. In textiles, for example, the foreign-born workers who populated New England's mill towns following World War I were "not content with a purely craft and business union" like the AFL, noted a contemporary observer. Although often supportive of the Wobblies, "the foreigners actually want[ed] an organization that [would] have more business sense and stability than the I.W.W."[1]

Much the same concern animated New York's less skilled culinary workers, whose quest for a more organizationally sound expression of industrial syndicalism led them from one union to another over the next three decades. Coming out of the 1913 strike leaderless and dispirited, the rank and file struggled to find their bearings, finally doing so in 1916 with the formation of the International Federation of Workers in the Hotel and Restaurant Industry, a self-described "revolutionary syndicalist" organization. After leading some twenty thousand hotel and restaurant workers in a citywide strike, the International Federation was displaced in 1920 by the still more inclusive Amalgamated Food Workers Union. Aping the potent industrial syndicalism of its predecessor, the Amalgamated extended its reach into new areas of the industry, drawing cafeterias, lunchrooms, delicatessens, and bakeries into what was truly becoming the "One Big Union" of culinary workers envisioned years earlier by the Wobblies. But the aging Amalgamated, beaten down by the depression, lacked both the stamina and the inventiveness of its youth. Drawing its last breath in 1934 while leading thirty thousand culinary workers out on strike, the Amalgamated soon succumbed to the more aggressive Communist-led Food Workers Industrial Union, whose leaders, following a shift in the political winds, handed over the rank and file to the AFL.

This chapter locates the dynamics of organizational succession in New York in the workers' ongoing search for a stabler form of industrial syndicalism to counter growing resistance from employers and rival trade unionists alike. Embattled culinary workers fought back by embracing ever more inclusive institutional forms, relying on both the solidarity and the enhanced disruptive capacities of large numbers to fend off their smaller but generally better heeled challengers. As the ranks of industrial unionists swelled beyond the original nucleus of male cooks and hotel waiters, their capacity for collective action was sustained through a dense network of workplace committees and tighter forms of organizational discipline that kept the union's increasingly diverse membership in a perpetual state of combat readiness, poised to strike at a moment's notice.

New York's mobilized culinary workers were prepared to follow any leadership bold enough to engage the "class enemy" at the point of production. Whether commandeered by self-described syndicalists, amalgamationists, or Communists, their battle plans were drawn from a common repertoire of collective action, often wielding the familiar weapons of labor solidarity, mass mobilization, and unrestricted direct action. A very similar arsenal was eventually deployed by leaders of the AFL whose triumph in 1936 represented more of an affirmation than a rejection of the Wobblies' earlier industrial syndicalism.

Yet in some ways this was not the same industrial syndicalism that the IWW had introduced to the culinary workers more than a quarter of a century ago. With the formalization of collective bargaining in the 1930s, direct action was gradually restricted to fairly predictable intervals around the expiration of time contracts. Likewise, the once-expansive vision of industrial solidarity came to be more narrowly focused on the creation in 1938 of a citywide food workers' organization to coordinate, rather than dissolve, the multitude of AFL locals already in existence. If this was not quite what the Wobblies had in mind years earlier, the end result very nearly realized their goal of a single unified organization, encompassing all wage earners within the culinary industry and drawing its strength from the rank and file's disruptive capacity at the point of production. New York's unskilled food workers would have it no other way.

Filling the IWW Void

The culinary workers had barely returned to work following the January 1913 walkout when the AFL came after them. So as not to clash with the powerful waiters' Local 1, whose members were mostly drawn from smaller, neighborhood restaurants, HRE strategists charted a new waiters' union aimed at Manhattan's large hotel trade, the principal jurisdiction of the badly crippled IHWU. Known as the Cosmopolitan Hotel Waiters' Alliance, or Local 94 of the HRE, its recruiting efforts targeted the increasingly restive mass of foreign-speaking hotel waiters, many of them veterans of the recent strikes. The alliance's leading spokesman was none other than Joseph Elster, the former IHWU leader. Two other leaders from the recent walkouts—Patrick Quinlan, a renegade Wobbly who would later battle the longshoremen in Philadelphia, and William Thompson, a prominent officer in the IHWU—also swung their support to the alliance.[2]

But the alliance, hamstrung by the anti-immigrant sentiments of its parent organization, never got on track. While boasting of Local 94's new openness, organizer William Joyce maintained that he would not "accept the application of every Tom, Dick and Harry." In less polite terms, the union had no intention of enrolling the mass of "continental caterers," as international president Jere Sullivan pejoratively termed foreign-born hotel waiters. Writing in the *Mixer and Server*, he characterized them as "foreign lackeys" secured from the "foul spots on the earth" and tolerated for no good reason other than "their cheapness and lack of manhood." Immigrant hotel workers did not take kindly either to Sullivan's xenophobia or to his union. Local 94, with fewer than fifty members, was gone within the year.[3]

This latest recruiting failure was a bitter pill for HRE officials to swallow, especially considering that the alliance's main rival, the IHWU, had lost its hold over the city's culinary workers. Elster's departure, coupled with defections by Quinlan, Thompson, and others, left the IHWU without experienced leadership. Early in 1914, less than a year after initiating the largest strike in the history of New York's culinary industry, the IHWU suspended operations due to a lack of paid-up members.[4]

The city's once-vibrant mass movement of hotel and restaurant workers was now reduced to a scattering of HRE affiliates, led by durable Local 1, and the ever-present but organizationally weak IWW. While the craft unions began the slow task of rebuilding, the Wobblies kept the heat on the restaurateurs. Lacking an organized base within the industry, they turned to the unemployed, whose ranks had been recently swollen by blacklisted culinary and textile strikers. In one of the Wobblies' more creative applications of direct action, they printed and distributed one thousand authentic-looking tickets that read "Good for one meal. Charge to the Mayor's Committee on Unemployment." The Mayor's Committee, which had been created in response to the IWW's Unemployed Union, was billed by restaurants from all over the city for several days before the hoax was discovered. But by then, recalled one participant, "hundreds of hungry men were one or two meals to the good," ultimately at the expense of the restaurant owners.[5]

Using their Unemployed Union as a base of operations, the Wobblies extended their organizational efforts to the job, chartering a local branch of the Hotel and Restaurant Workers Industrial Union in the spring of 1915. The IWW largely ignored the waiters, instead appealing to immigrant kitchen workers employed "below the stairs" in the large hotels. At its founding meeting, attended by some two hundred followers, Elizabeth Gurley Flynn, Carlo Tresca, and other IWW activists called for an eight-hour day and the elimination of private employment agencies, threatening to shut down every hotel in the city if their demands were not met.[6]

When the increasingly intransigent employers rejected both demands a few months later, the strike was on, just as the Wobblies had promised—only the IWW union, having fallen on hard times, was nowhere to be seen. Instead the strike was initiated by HRE Local 1, whose leaders, invoking a proven syndicalist tactic, timed the walkout to begin on New Year's Day. Returning to work in early February, Local 1 secured much of what the Wobblies had originally demanded: the length of the working day was reduced from fifteen to ten hours, and private employment agencies were replaced with a union-

controlled hiring hall. But whereas the IWW union presented its demands on behalf of all culinary workers, Local 1's victory covered only
its current membership.[7]

Searching for an appropriate vessel to carry the benefits of direct
action to the mass of unorganized culinary workers, a group of former
Wobblies launched the International Federation of Workers in the
Hotel and Restaurant Industry (IFW) late in 1916. Soon renamed the
International Federation of Workers in the Hotel, Restaurant, Club
and Catering Industries—the first of several elongated titles designed
to reflect its ever more inclusive jurisdiction—the IFW was a model
of the "new unionism" in America, combining the organizational logic
of industrial syndicalism with military-like discipline.[8] Its constitution,
clearly drawing on the IWW for inspiration, urged workers to "com-
bine industrially on the economic field" where they could wage the
"class struggle" on their way to creating a "new social order" through
"the seizure of industry." But getting there would require a tight ship,
powered by a steady flow of dues and staffed by paid organizers. A
revolutionary union "without [a] system," IFW leaders declared, "is
like a steamship without a propeller."[9]

With experienced organizers at the helm, the IFW navigated its
way through a sea of unorganized culinary workers, building small
islands of unionization throughout the city. From these initial beachheads, the IFW recruited from the largest restaurants and hotels
where conditions, in the absence of union protection, had become
unbearable. Kitchen and dining staffs were again putting in fourteen-
and sixteen-hour days, seven days per week. Waiters, whose wages
had plummeted to around $25 per month, had grown more depend-
ent than ever on tips for their survival. Working conditions were as
bad as ever, "even worse than before the strike of 1912," according
to the union.[10] Hotel and restaurant work was still unsafe, unsanitary,
and, above all, uncertain. Employment agencies, having once been
restricted by the IHWU, were back in business, charging workers half
or more of their first month's income for the privilege of toiling under
such deplorable conditions.[11]

IFW leaders, sensitive to charges of "dual unionism," tried to
steer clear of the rival HRE by targeting nonunion establishments.
But the mere presence of organizers in the field—particularly in
contrast to the HRE's glaring inactivity—caught the eye of many

AFL members, some of whom promptly defected to the more aggressive IFW. Even powerful Local 1, the HRE's most successful group of waiters, suffered heavy losses. In February and March 1917, during the first two months of the IFW's mass organizing drive, Local 1 reported 433 "withdrawals." To put this figure in perspective, the February-March exodus represented fully one-fourth of Local 1's entire membership and was more than twenty times greater than the total number of withdrawals for the preceding six months.[12] Without knowing more about who withdrew and why, it is impossible to say what proportion left to join the IFW. But the coincidence of the IFW's organizing campaign and Local 1's sudden loss in membership certainly points to a well-traveled road from business to industrial syndicalism.

The strategically located cooks and other kitchen helpers formed the IFW's nucleus, around whom gravitated other hotel workers and, increasingly, waiters. By the summer of 1918, with more than four thousand members, the IFW was able to maintain a weekly newspaper, the *Hotel Worker,* featuring articles written in English, Italian, French, German, and Greek.[13] Its format included strident denunciations of capitalism and exploitation alongside brief exposés of conditions and wage rates in different houses. More and more workers poured in, reportedly by "the hundreds" on good recruiting days, until the IFW was in firm control of the city's largest hotels.[14]

Union elections were held in the fall of 1918. Coming out on top was Otto Wagner, whose background typified the new generation of IFW leaders. Wagner, a Socialist party member in his native Germany, had emigrated to America at the age of twenty-four. After securing work in a large Manhattan hotel, first as a lowly busboy and then as a waiter, he drifted into union activism. But lacking both U.S. citizenship and a skilled trade, he found the HRE's doors closed to him. Having "lost faith in political action," Wagner, like so many other disillusioned immigrants, turned to direct action on the job, professing his allegiance to "syndicalism." At his side was Cesare Lesino, a highly respected chef and well-traveled militant. The Paris-trained Lesino, veteran of both the HRE and the IWW, led armies of admiring kitchen workers and bakers into the new union, increasing its ranks to nearly fifteen thousand eager yet untested recruits.[15]

The IFW at War

The IFW, like the rest of the nation, was on a war footing. Although the armistice ending World War I had been signed months earlier, the civilian labor force remained mobilized, with pressures building to get more able-bodied men into basic industry to alleviate continuing shortages of essential war materials. Under this state of readiness, labor recruiters were encouraged to raid nonessential industries, including New York's already thinned-out hotel and restaurant trade. As a vigorous nightlife returned to the city after the war, experienced culinary workers were in short supply, and increasingly so.[16] With the demand for labor running high, restive hotel and restaurant workers called for immediate action to create a "uniform rate of pay" of $15 per week for all culinary workers, waiters and cooks alike.

The IFW's leaders were torn. Considering only the relations of economic force, the time to strike was now. "When labor is plentiful," Wagner wrote in the *Hotel Worker,* "economic determinism constantly forces wages down, one man underbidding the other. War conditions, however, changed this competition [in favor of the union]."[17] Yet, despite favorable labor market conditions, the IFW's fighting ability had been compromised by recent government raids on its New York City headquarters, a depleted treasury, and the generally antilabor climate created by wartime patriotism. Wagner, balancing his syndicalist sensibilities with political realism, declared a selective strike, calling out hotel workers at the Waldorf-Astoria, McAlpin, and Claridge, nearly fifteen hundred of whom responded on October 26, 1918.[18]

The war-related scarcity of labor forced hotel employers to confront the union on a more level playing field than in the past. Without access to a large pool of strikebreakers, they shifted their defenses from the economic to the political front, turning to the federal government for support. Appealing to the U.S. Employment Service, the hotel operators characterized their striking employees as "essential" to their business and thus in violation of continuing wartime regulations outlawing any interruption of essential services. When government officials were unable to force the strikers back to work, the employers threatened them with military conscription. Still they refused to back down. "There is no possibility of our losing the strike," a confident Paul Bourget assured his fellow waiters.[19]

With nowhere else to turn, the employers began to hire women as strikebreakers. Their opportunism was not lost on the union. "A week ago," Bourget noted, "the hotel managers declared the men waiters and cooks to be essential to the success of their business." But with the recent failure of government intervention, these same "essential" workers had suddenly become superfluous. Opportunistic or not, the employment of women strikebreakers was openly applauded by a spokesman for the federal Employment Service. "I have no interest in the hotels nor in the strike," he explained, "except in so far as the strike may release men and render them available for war service. My only interest is to get men to do Uncle Sam's work."[20] Sounding a similarly patriotic note, the commercial press condemned the walkout as "ill-timed" and its participants as "nearly fifty per cent enemy alien" and urged the public "to accept improvised service" provided by less experienced waitresses.[21]

The use of women strikebreakers exposed the Achilles' heel of culinary unionism. Although women made up a sizable minority of the labor force, they had been largely confined to the traditional "female ghettos" of the hotel laundry and the housekeeping unit or restricted to part-time waitressing in cafeterias and smaller diners. So long as women were excluded from full-time employment in the kitchens and dining rooms of first-class hotels and large restaurants— the main targets of industrial organization—they could be safely ignored by unions, as indeed they had been before World War I. But as soon as "the men fell to fighting each other," as the female floor manager at a leading hotel described the recent strike, "the kitchens began to be short on men and long on women. They came into nearly every department the chef controls."[22]

Feminization opened the door not only to the kitchens but also, to a lesser extent, to the unions. Before the wartime surge in membership, organized labor was effectively off-limits to women culinary workers. A 1914 government survey of twenty locals operating in New York's hotel and restaurant trade turned up one female member. A follow-up study conducted in 1920, one year after both the HRE and the IFW sent women organizers into the field, placed the figure at more than one thousand. While an impressive gain, the house of labor remained very much a patriarchy.[23]

The slowly changing face of labor was evident from the strikers' ranks. Included among the original group of fifteen hundred strikers were more than fifty women, whose numbers grew substantially during the walkout. Still, they were the exception, as many more of their sisters crossed picket lines in search of better-paying waitressing jobs in the first-class hotels and restaurants. Lured also by "Dan Cupid," hundreds of young "sentimental girls," as Wagner described them, were recruited to strikebreaking in search of "true love." The city's most eligible bachelors, promised a typical newspaper story, regularly "lose their hearts" to waitresses, making such courtships "usually rapid and romantic, too."[24] Best of all, strikebreaking was risk-free, or nearly so. Precisely because they were women, and therefore capable of playing on stereotypes of femininity and innocence, neither the public nor the police were willing to tolerate the usual degree of intimidation and physical confrontation on the picket line. With the union ordering its pickets "to make themselves as inconspicuous as possible," the "strikebreakers in skirts" encountered little resistance.[25]

IFW leaders remained outwardly confident, waiting for the women to, in Bourget's words, "drop from overwork." Bourget added, "[The employers] can't exist without the men who have learned the waiter's and cook's trade in years of experience"—apparently forgetting who cooked and served him his own meals at home! When the women showed themselves to be both tireless and able learners, IFW leaders turned in desperation to the law, hoping to accomplish through the courts what they had been unable to win through direct action alone. Pointing to various state laws prohibiting women from serving alcohol, Bourget forecast huge financial losses, running into "thousands of dollars," for any establishment where male strikers were unavailable to tend bar and serve drinks. But the law—as any good syndicalist knows—is only as good as its enforcement, and neither the employers nor the police were in a vigilant mood. The big election night parties in early November, at which liquor flowed freely, came off without a hitch.[26]

Unable to throw effective picket lines into the path of female strikebreakers, the IFW returned to the courtroom, arguing that the struck hotels were violating protective legislation that prohibited waitresses from working after 10:00 P.M. or for more than nine consecutive hours. But the state industrial commissioner ruled that the law did not apply to first-class hotels. Frustrated once again by the courts, IFW leaders returned to their syndicalist roots, calling out hotel workers at the Knickerbocker, St. Regis, Vanderbilt, and Plaza. With the number of strikers nearing three thousand, chances of a settlement seemed increasingly remote. The walkout dragged on through the middle of November, when angry hotel operators suddenly declared their opposition to collective bargaining and cut off all contact with the union.[27] IFW leaders responded by authorizing the first mass picketing around the struck hotels. At a closed-door meeting later that week, union representatives from 100 hotels and 150 restaurants empowered their leaders to call a general strike. Just when, Wagner was not saying. "It would be ridiculous for us to divulge the point of attack on the Hotel Men's Association as it would be for an army to notify the enemy where it expected to make a drive," he told a group of anxious reporters. "All we can say now is that the entire membership is ready to respond."[28]

Opposition to the hotel owners was also voiced from a less likely source, the restaurateurs, whose business was thriving as a result of the walkout.[29] Not wanting to provoke a costly strike of their own, particularly with the busy Thanksgiving holiday a few days off, they offered to meet with the union. On Wednesday night the Society of Restaurateurs, the main trade association, caved in to the union and promised to provide substantial wage increases, subject to formal approval by its member firms. With Thanksgiving only hours away, both sides adjourned, leaving the task of formal ratification until after the holiday rush. At a union meeting the following morning, scheduled originally to launch the general strike, news of the agreement "was greeted by a roar of applause" from the rank and file.[30]

IFW leaders, urged on by the crowd, went ahead with their plans to march on the hotel district, only now their actions were billed as a victory celebration rather than the beginning of an industrywide walkout. The four thousand exuberant marchers included strikers and, for the first time, their wives and children. "My daddy is a cook," read one sign displayed by a young girl, "but I do not get any of his good cooking." Other signs, particularly those carried by family members, brought out the personal side of the walkout. "I know my papa," one child's sign read, "only since he joined the union"—a poignant comment on the long hours that prevailed before unionization. Another sign, held by a striker's wife, justified a wage increase to afford "necessities for our children." And leading the procession was a four-year-old boy, the son of a striking cook. Dressed in a miniature army uniform, "complete from visored cap to leather leggings," he presented a most patriotic image in stark contrast to the charges of "enemy alien" directed at the strikers.[31]

Thanksgiving came and went—and with it the restaurateurs' commitment to ratifying the agreement, which disappeared a few days later when they locked out unionized cooks and waiters at three leading Manhattan restaurants as a show of solidarity with the hotel operators. The union has been "double-crossed," an angry Wagner told the press. "Now we know that the willingness of the employers to talk over the terms of settlement of our demands for wage increases was a trick to prevent a strike on Thanksgiving day, when the union had the restaurant men at its mercy."[32] By ignoring the importance of timing, IFW leaders had been beaten at their own game. Wagner declared "a fight to the finish" and responded to the employer lockouts by authorizing strikes at all three establishments, the first of several walkouts that brought ten large restaurants to terms with the union by week's end. The ringleaders of this group were then expelled from the Society of Restaurateurs, which was coming under increasing pressure from the more intransigent and better-organized Hotel Men's Association.[33]

Splits within the ranks of organized labor also began to appear. While progressive Local 1 of the HRE quietly supported the IFW's efforts, its parent organization was openly hostile. HRE international president Sullivan took it upon himself to keep the federal government fully informed about the IFW's subversive ways, even fingering individual activists. He regularly condemned the IFW for opening its doors to noncitizens and, in several letters to the War Department, urged federal agents to investigate immigrant unionists, who had "no sympathy whatsoever for America or her institutions."[34] Sullivan put his fervent Americanism into practice, apparently having "a hand" in the government's decision to raid IFW headquarters before the walkout. But even at his patriotic worst Sullivan played a less destructive role than his boss, the venerable Sam Gompers, whose actions during the strike angered many culinary workers. Early in the walkout, when a delegation from the IFW approached Gompers about possibly affiliating with the AFL, he brusquely turned them away with little or no explanation.[35] Then, as the strike dragged on into December, Gompers twice walked through picket lines at the Hotel Astor, first to attend a dinner hosted by the Academy of Political Science, which was being boycotted by most other union supporters, and a few days later to dine with upper-class members of the Council on Foreign Relations. In his defense Gompers claimed that he appeared at both functions only after the meals had been prepared and served by strikebreakers. But Wagner and his followers were not persuaded, and promptly filed antilabor charges with the AFL central office against its own international president.[36]

Seven long weeks of fighting had left both the union and the employers weary but still standing. Looking for a knockout punch, IFW leaders raised anew the specter of an industrywide walkout. "A general strike on New Year's day," Wagner announced to the press, "would prevent the proprietors from receiving an income of several million dollars." If this figure was not credible, the threat of a walkout on December 31 certainly was, particularly for those employers who had been hit by the same tactic in 1912. Memories of the costly 1912 strike were again stirred up when workers at the Hotel Belmont, where it all began six years ago, walked out in the middle of December.[37]

The Belmont's manager, anticipating a walkout, had women strikebreakers waiting in the wings. It was the straw that finally broke the IFW's sexist back. Instead of regarding the strikebreakers as incorrigible class enemies, union leaders hired women organizers in an effort to win over their wayward sisters. This strategic reorientation was accompanied by a discursive shift on the part of union leaders who for the first time spoke of women strikebreakers in terms traditionally reserved for male unionists. No longer portrayed as frail young girls blinded by authority, they were now seen as militant industrial rebels. "The women will not be the docile slaves the employers expect," Wagner predicted. "No one who has a spark of revolt can tolerate the evil conditions that prevail in the largest hotels. The women, too, will rebel against wages of $40 a month and long hours." The hotel operators were not taking any chances. When workers at the Hotel Martinique walked out a few days later, management replaced them with African Americans rather than women.[38]

Wagner remained optimistic, placing his syndicalist faith in a successful general strike. An army of strikebreakers, he insisted, would not be enough to rescue the millions in lost revenue resulting from a citywide walkout on New Year's Eve. On the morning of December 31 the union put its case before the public one last time. "The employers have rejected every offer for negotiations, and so we are out to fight to a finish," Wagner told reporters.[39] That evening, as the dinner hour approached, five thousand culinary workers spilled out into the streets in a spontaneous celebration of their collective strength, the coming year, and, above all, the fact that they, like most other New Yorkers, were finally able to enjoy the New Year's holiday without working. This festive mood carried over for the next several days, as offers of support and financial assistance poured in. But the contributions soon dried up. And the public, once so sympathetic, grew impatient with the continuing strike. Dispirited and disorganized, workers began to drift back to the job in late January, bringing the bitter three-month battle to an inglorious end.[40]

Back to the Point of Production

The collapse of the general strike exposed the IFW as little more than a house of cards resting on a shifting and unstable rank-and-file foundation. Recognizing the need to rebuild from the ground up, union leaders suspended their weekly agitational newspaper in early February 1919. When the *Hotel Worker* reappeared six weeks later, its revolutionary rhetoric had been toned down considerably, in recognition, Wagner conceded, that "it did not represent the aims, the policy and the interests of the organization and the membership." None of this meant abandoning, even softening, the struggle against capitalism. On the contrary, Wagner admonished his new readers to remain ever vigilant against their "most ancient, most unscrupulous and most powerful enemy, Capitalism." But targeting the system was not enough—or rather it was too much for the average culinary worker to grasp. Featuring expanded coverage of working conditions, grievances, and organizing, the "newborn" *Hotel Worker* was conceived "to serve the interests of the workers in our industry in particular." Seeking a more authentic workers' voice, Wagner urged the rank and file, "Contribute to the paper. If you are not able to write the language very well, write any old way except the bosses' way."[41]

The rebuilding process extended the IFW's reach to new jurisdictions. In April more than one thousand lunch counter workers were brought into the union. Endowed with a "comfortable treasury," these newest recruits took to heart the lessons of the recent strike and elected an executive board consisting of five "wideawake men and two women even more wideawake."[42] To strengthen the union's presence on the job, shop committees were organized in all establishments with five or more workers. This radical decentralization shifted the action from IFW headquarters to the job, where local shop committees assumed full responsibility for recruiting, collecting dues, and ruling on grievances. In moving toward tighter workplace organization at the point of production, IFW leaders were self-consciously modeling their practice of "modern unionism" after the British shop steward system.[43]

Through its expanding network of shop committees, the IFW exercised increasing power on the job. Comparing the union's reign to a "waiters' soviet," Michael Hegarty, an experienced headwaiter at a local Manhattan restaurant, took legal action to break what the *New York Herald* described as the IFW's iron "grip" on the industry. Naming Wagner and three others as defendants, Hegarty filed a damage suit for $10,000, alleging that his recent dismissal was a result of union pressure. Unionized waiters, he claimed, refused to work with him after learning that he had reported alleged instances of tip padding. The restaurant's owner initially backed Hegarty but knuckled under when the union threatened strike action if he was not immediately discharged. Hegarty's dismissal, regardless of its merits, was a vivid demonstration of the IFW's growing potency on the job.[44]

The IFW's decentralized "modern unionism" began to converge with HRE Local 1's increasingly militant shop floor orientation. Spurred on by recent IFW success in organizing lunch counter women, Local 1 launched an ambitious drive aimed at the city's nine thousand waitresses, who were promised not just equal pay with men—itself a rather bold demand—but also an end to the traditional sexual division of labor that had waiters serving customers while waitresses did all that in addition to bussing dishes, polishing silver, and setting tables.[45] At stake here were issues of gender equity and, in keeping with the spirit of the new unionism, control over the labor process. Both objectives came together in a groundswell of support from nearly two thousand waitresses who attended a Local 1 recruiting meeting in June. It was a measure not only of the times but also of the fluidity of social identities that many of these same women, now prospective unionists, had entered their jobs as strikebreakers less than a year earlier.[46]

Despite Local 1's recent inroads, the more dynamic IFW continued to grow, reaching out to kitchen workers and lunch counter helpers employed in many of the smaller restaurants and diners. Faced with increasingly successful IFW raids into territory traditionally held by the HRE, Sullivan dispatched international organizer A. F. Martel to New York to investigate the situation firsthand. "The only solution," Martel reported, "is to take in the kitchen help" as members of waiters' Local 1 or Local 719, representing cooks. "To explain here the reasons why none of the two locals have attempted it," Martel mused, "you may as well try and solve the problem of perpetual motion"—or, perhaps more fittingly, the problem of inertia that had gripped local HRE leaders. "We can and must win," Martel concluded. Winning, in his view, would not come from trying to out-organize the more aggressive IFW but from declaring all-out war on its left-wing leaders. "All the labor forces of this city must be concentrated against them, and they must be made to understand that they are not only fighting our locals, but organized labor as a whole."[47]

War broke out less than a month later, but it was a far cry from what Martel had in mind. On the evening of August 23, 1919, with no advance warning, 6,000 waiters, led by 900 members from HRE Local 1, walked out just as the busy dinner hour was approaching, affecting several hundred medium- and low-priced restaurants throughout the city. Their demands, presented by Local 1's president, William Lehman, boiled down to a modest wage increase of $5 per week—the same increase won a few months earlier by their fellow waiters in the IFW. But this was no ordinary job action, particularly for an affiliate of the AFL. Not only did the walkout come "like a bolt from a clear sky," but it was called in flagrant violation of a signed agreement that was still in force. IFW leaders, characterizing Local 1's actions as "a radical departure from the timeworn and hidebound rules and tactics of the A. F. of L. unions," ordered their members out as a display of solidarity.[48]

Capitalizing on strategic timing, direct action, mass mobilization, and a willful disregard of contracts—much the same syndicalist repertoire guiding the IFW—Lehman and his followers held the upper hand. The ranks of strikebreakers, normally so plentiful, were depleted by the unusually small number of women applicants, suggesting that Local 1's recent effort to organize the city's waitresses was already paying off. Within a few hours most proprietors had capitulated, leaving fewer than two thousand workers still out. Later that evening, when representatives of the restaurant owners arrived at

HRE headquarters to draw up a settlement, angry pickets greeted them "with jeers and cries of 'Capitalists.' "[49]

Local 1 and the IFW were becoming indistinguishable not only in practice but in institutional form as well. Both unions were now focused exclusively at the point of production, where they built highly disciplined organizations capable of mobilizing the rank and file through unrestricted direct action. Even the critical distinction between craft and industrial structure had lost much of its force, as the city's HRE locals, led once again by rebellious Local 1, formed an industrywide body to better coordinate their common efforts.[50] But perhaps the most telling sign of convergence was Local 1's growing responsiveness to immigrants. Bucking his own national organization, Lehman was one of the few delegates at the 1919 HRE convention to come to the defense of foreign workers, speaking out against proposals that would ban noncitizens from the union and force all locals to conduct business meetings in the English language. The appointment of Local 1's first immigrant organizers a few months later solidified Lehman's commitment to the kind of multiethnic unionism championed by Wagner and the IFW.[51]

Of course, not all differences between the IFW and the HRE were so easily smoothed over. At the commanding heights of both organizations, ideologues retained their distinctive visions of unionism: Wagner continued to press his case against the capitalist system as a whole, whereas Lehman confined his attack to individual capitalists. But such ideological concerns, however important to highly placed activists in each camp, mattered far less to the majority of culinary workers at the bottom. "The rank and file has no industrial philosophy," Wagner admitted in a confidential interview conducted shortly after the 1918 general strike. "All it cares for is wages and conditions, and anyone getting those will get their adherence."[52]

What Wagner forgot to add was that his union, in following the organizational logic of industrial syndicalism, was especially well positioned to secure improved wages and conditions for the city's unskilled immigrant workers who continued to pour into the IFW, bringing its membership to fifteen thousand by the fall of 1919. With much of this growth attributable to mutually supportive job actions by cooks and waitpersons, representatives from the union's kitchen and dining departments began to explore ways to better coordinate their joint efforts. In October the IFW's first-ever combined business meeting of the dining and kitchen departments was held before a "packed" house. Pronouncing the death of "all crafts," the New York City branch formally reconstituted itself as an "industrial organization" under the direction of a newly elected executive board drawn from both departments.[53]

Consolidation of the IFW's kitchen and dining departments was part of a growing national movement that gave rise to similarly "amalgamated" unions in industries as diverse as textiles, steel, and mining.[54] In each case the driving force was a heavily immigrant, largely unskilled labor force that had been neglected by the AFL. Embracing more inclusive forms of industrial organization that relied principally on direct action, the "amalgamationists" saw their unions as vehicles not only for advancing their immediate interests but also, in the language of revolutionary syndicalism, as shells of the new society. "Labor must take over industry," insisted the *Hotel Worker*, "operate it through its unions and see to it that exploitation is done away with." In struggling to raise the standard of living, the workers' "main object is to wrest more and more control over the industry and share in the management of their work." Contracts or agreements that in any way delimited and regulated the class struggle were expressly outlawed.[55]

Amalgamation fever spread rapidly among the city's culinary workers. No one was immune, not even the journeymen bakers, a highly privileged group of craft workers who were represented by an independent union. Organized into seven hundred fifty closed shops throughout the metropolitan area, the unionized bakers, numbering about five thousand, were a force to be reckoned with. Combining high levels of skill with aggressive shop floor control, they essentially ran the industry, dictating wages and conditions through written agreements with individual employers while retaining the right to strike at any time. As the embodiment of a hybrid syndicalism that combined businesslike methods with industrial combativeness, their attraction to the IFW was mutual. Following several months of delicate negotiations, the journeymen bakers joined hands with the IFW in May 1920, giving birth to a new organization: the International Workers in the Amalgamated Food Industries.[56]

Toward One Big (Amalgamated) Union

The Amalgamated, as the new union was known, followed in the footsteps of its predecessor. Its constitution opened with the familiar "principle of the Class Struggle" and closed by outlawing all time agreements with employers. In between, the rights and obligations of membership were spelled out in considerable detail. Placing the Amalgamated on an even more solid organizational foundation, the new constitution mandated improved procedures for collecting initiation fees and monthly dues, paying per capita local taxes, suspending delinquent members, and raising strike funds.[57]

The upstart Amalgamated immediately locked horns with HRE Local 1, as both unions, vying for allegiance from unorganized waiters, waitresses, and lunch counter workers, fought hard to distinguish themselves in battle. By the summer of 1921 scores of restaurants, hotels, and cafeterias were overrun by industrial warfare, fending off recurrent waves of wildcat strikes. Such guerrilla tactics only added to an already confusing situation, pitting strikers against nonstrikers and both groups against their unions. Accusations flew in all directions, with leaders of Local 1 and the Amalgamated drawn into an escalating war of words over who was the worst "sellout," "scab" and "union-buster." If any of it was to be believed, neither organization was above the worst sort of opportunism: the Amalgamated reportedly put its members to work at wage levels beneath those previously established by Local 1, while Local 1 freely supplied "real union labor" to any establishment that had been hit by Amalgamated job actions.[58]

The competition for new members failed to produce a clear winner, with both unions recording modest gains, partly at the other's expense. When everyone was accounted for, the Amalgamated, having suffered huge losses over the past year from nonpayment of dues, was back up to a solid core of about 5,000 paid-up members. More exact figures are available for the HRE. Reorganized Local 5, representing hotel waiters, was up to nearly 600 members by the fall of 1921, and Local 719 finally began making headway with the cooks, more than doubling in size to about 250 members. The big winner was Local 1, which grudgingly admitted 300 new recruits, raising its total membership to nearly 1,700.[59]

In the face of the Amalgamated's impressive gains, Local 1's controlled growth came under sharp attack from its parent organization. Reviewing the situation in New York, Hugo Ernst, president of the progressive San Francisco HRE, stated matter-of-factly, "They have a job trust which they call Waiters' Union Local No. 1." Ernst, who had been traveling the country reporting on various locals, presented his findings in the July 1923 issue of the *Mixer and Server*. Local 1, he wrote, "has absolute control" that extends well beyond the customary concerns of wages and conditions. Under terms of their agreement, for example, any member having worked for as little as one week could not be discharged without approval from the local executive board, which alone determined the merits of the case; employers could be tried and, if found guilty, fined by the union for insulting their employees; for job-related injuries not covered by state compensation, disabled members were entitled to full pay during the entire period of their recuperation; and, adding insult to injury, employers were required to pay the union $5 for the dubious "privilege of signing the agreement." Such bold accomplishments were a source of embarrassment for radicals like Ernst who took strong exception to the exclusionary membership practices that made it all possible. Local 1 did not have more members, he concluded, because "they would endanger the complete control of the jobs."[60]

Local 1 defended itself through a letter to the editor that appeared in the September issue of the *Mixer and Server*. Harry Morris, a member of Local 1, challenged Ernst's remarks as "a libel" against his union. "In the first place," he insisted, "our membership is not closed; we are taking in new members all the time." Ernst was correct in reporting that jobs are filled by the union rather than by individual proprietors. But "if that condition is what impelled Brother Ernst to name Local 1 as a 'job trust,'" Morris said, "then I believe that if all our sister locals were the same kind of job trusts, our brothers and sisters throughout our international union would be considerably better off." Call it what you will—job trust or union—the fact is, Morris argued, Local 1 had secured wages and conditions that "are as good if not better than the best anywhere in the country."[61]

Morris's defense was in some ways beside the point. No one was questioning Local 1's collective bargaining achievements. The question was, at what cost? While Local 1's ability to extract concessions from employers solidified support from its existing members, it did so by excluding large numbers of new recruits, turning them into potential strikebreakers. Worse still, Local 1's strength had the unintended effect of weakening employer opposition to the Amalgamated, which, despite its openly left-wing leadership, lacked the economic muscle of the more ideologically conservative HRE. So, ironically, it was the stunning success of the AFL in this particular case that provided generally favorable conditions for the Amalgamated's continued growth.

And grow it did, fueled by a major recruiting drive in the spring of 1923. Waiving the usual modest initiation fee along with any reinstatement charges, the Amalgamated opened its doors to "thousands of old members" willing to pay as little as $2 for two months' advance dues. "Why it looks like 1918 again to see so many old faces," remarked one longtime member. Active shop committees were reconstituted in most of the large unorganized hotels and restaurants. Within one month more than fifteen hundred members were added to the rolls.[62] By the spring of 1924 the union was strong enough to take on the powerful Salvin-Thompson Corporation, which owned and operated ten of the city's finest first-class restaurants. In early April the manager of Long Island's exclusive Pavilion Royal, the flagship of the Salvin-Thompson chain, suddenly announced that its six-year relationship with the Amalgamated was over and that all current staff had to resign immediately from the union as a condition of continued employment. More than five hundred men, representing the unionized workforce of all ten houses, promptly quit work, leaving New York's "flashiest restaurants . . . completely deserted." A few nonunion waiters were secured through the private Manhattan Waiters' Association, but to no avail. "[The] scabs," reported the *Free Voice,* the Amalgamated's monthly newspaper, "are absolutely inefficient, as the service demanded at these places is of such high distinction that only men with years of special training can come up to the requirements."[63]

The only remaining source of experienced waiters was the rival HRE. As recently as two years before, Local 1 had readily furnished "real union" labor to replace Amalgamated strikers. But this time solidarity prevailed over narrow organizational interests, and Local 1, pledging its full support for the walkout, refused all requests to provide strikebreakers.[64] Unable to staff its restaurants, Salvin-Thompson turned to the courts for relief, seeking to enjoin the union from picketing outside its establishments. When the injunction was issued a few days later, cloaked in what the *Free Voice* described as "a mass of legal phraseology and word twisting," the striking waiters were "added to the long, long list of victims" of "capitalist class justice."[65]

From inside a corrupt legal system whose "sympathies naturally went to the capitalist side," the union found an unexpected ally in the U.S. district attorney, who promptly closed the entire Salvin-Thompson chain, pending an investigation into reported liquor law violations. Minimizing the court's role, union leaders attributed their "signal victory over these stubborn bosses" to the strikers' militancy and solidarity. The *Free Voice* saw this as a lesson to owners everywhere: "It is best for their pocketbooks to conduct their business in peace and harmony with the union."[66]

In privileging economic direct action in the struggle against capital, the Amalgamated's unreconstructed syndicalism did not sit well with a small but increasingly vocal "left-wing" faction grouped around the newly formed Workers (Communist) party.[67] The first signs of a rift appeared late in 1925 when Ludwig Lore, a party member and leader of the bakers, refused to endorse a Communist-sponsored resolution calling for the creation of a Labor party. Only a few months earlier Lore had been praised by the Communist *Daily Worker* for championing a Trade Union Educational League initiative urging consolidation of the city's multiple bakery unions and locals. But his outspoken opposition to political struggle was too much for the party elite, who summarily expelled Lore as a "detestable opportunist, right winger," and leader of the Amalgamated's "most reactionary forces." In the end, however, Lore's syndicalism was vindicated when delegates attending the union's convention in December voted down the same Labor party resolution.[68]

The Amalgamated was still defending itself from the Communist left when its old nemesis on the right, the HRE, invaded its jurisdiction with the formation of Local 16, aimed at hotel waiters. This latest HRE assault had an unusually familiar quality, led as it was by three recent defectors from the Amalgamated's hotel branch. Conceived as a mass-based alternative to Local 1's high dues and restricted membership, Local 16 braced itself for the expected flood of new recruits. But the waiting masses kept their distance. Battling both the Amalgamated's hostility and Local 1's studied indifference, Local 16 sputtered along after stabilizing at about two hundred fifty members.[69]

With its rivals on the left and right now in check, the Amalgamated returned to the business of fighting employers. Union leaders launched a major drive in the spring of 1926, concentrating on the hundreds of unorganized cafeterias, coffee shops, and automats that were popping up all over the city. Small in scale as well as profitability, this fast-growing segment of the catering industry was also the most exploitive, characterized by little security, low pay, and high stress. The conditions were, as the *Free Voice* put it, "enough to make an angel revolt."[70]

And increasingly that is what the labor force consisted of—"angels," or young women, often teenagers, who had the necessary stamina to keep up with the rapid customer turnover found in less expensive eateries. "A waitress' job is so inhumanely strenuous," noted one observer, "that none but the huskiest of girls can stand the pace for more than a short time." Chronic fatigue and nervous breakdowns were not uncommon. Eating meals on the run while dashing back and forth between overheated kitchen and drafty dining room was hardly conducive to good health. Six months on the job, a New York City waitress remarked, "and you have to go to a hospital."[71]

Earning barely more than a dollar a day in wages in 1927, "fast food" waitresses were totally dependent on tipping to survive. Getting food to the table soon enough to please even the most impatient diners was a must. What one waitress described as "the ever-present need of 'making it snappy' " turned them into "coffee fiends" just to keep going. In the face of surly and abusive customers, the waitress was expected to bite her tongue, smile, and apologize. She was always on stage, performing in ways that pleased and flattered her mostly male clientele. The obvious parallels with the world's oldest profession were not lost on middle-class reformers who condemned waitressing as "semi-prostitution."[72]

Such degrading conditions made waitresses, in the words of one organizer, "readily susceptible to a genuine unionization drive." But there was little room for them in the New York HRE, where women, although representing almost 30 percent of the city's wait staff, accounted for fewer than one hundred of Local 1's nearly two thousand members.[73] Their underrepresentation had many sources. Partly it was due to orthodox Jewish religious practices that excluded women from the core of Local 1's constituency employed in male-staffed kosher restaurants and delicatessens. More generally, traditional employer preferences for waiters—a carryover from Old World customs that associated masculine servility with dining sophistication—kept women on the fringes of the trade, confined to the lowest-paying and hardest-to-organize small cafés, coffee shops, and lunchrooms.[74]

Some waitresses also shunned unions, whether fearing employer retribution or out of a false sense of "professionalism." The few who did join the HRE often preferred the company of their sisters, organizing themselves into separate waitress locals that flourished mostly in the Midwest and on the West Coast. These prefigurative feminist forms of organization gave waitresses a stronger and more unified voice in setting relevant union policies. When a resolution to narrow the gender gap in earnings was introduced at the 1927 national HRE convention, male delegates were all over the map, some in support, some against, and some in between. But not the women, who uniformly opposed the resolution, arguing that if their low-waged status was eliminated, they would gradually be eased out of the industry by comparably priced male labor.[75]

Such pragmatism, however, was still not enough to guarantee women employment in the presence of a strong union shop, as Local 1 had demonstrated during contract negotiations a few years earlier. In the spring of 1922, with the union threatening a general strike in response to a pending wage cut, New York's restaurateurs offered a compromise that, in opening the doors to female labor, promised to protect union jurisdictional rights along with profits. As proposed, employers would be allowed to hire unionized waitresses—whose weekly wages at the time were $5 less than waiters—if their businesses were operating at a deficit. Terming the proposal "reasonable and just," a federal mediator, in his words, "pleaded with the union" to accept the offer. But after three hours of debate, Local 1's predominantly male membership, siding with the current sexual division of labor, voted down the employers' proposal. The wage cut was rescinded and the traditional brotherhood of waiters was restored—at the expense of their unionized sisters.[76]

While the scrappy waiters' union won the opening round, the fight was far from over. The harsh economic realities that led New York's smaller restaurants to ask Local 1 for concessions only got worse, particularly in the hotel industry where a massive postwar building boom created a deepening slump. In 1920 the national hotel occupancy rate—calculated as a ratio of the number of available rooms to the total number of guests—stood at a robust 85 percent. By 1928 it had fallen to 67 percent, or 8 percent below what industry analysts saw as the "break even" point for running a marginally profitable operation.[77] Faced with growing competition and shrinking profits, many of the larger employers lashed out at organized labor, abrogating contracts and demanding still more concessions while bearing down harder than ever on their employees.

This one-sided class war took a heavy toll on culinary unionism. With both the HRE and the Amalgamated on the defensive, new organizing ground to a halt. Commenting on the HRE's stagnating campaign in New York, a normally upbeat field organizer admitted that "mass meetings do not take well in this city—individual work is what is necessary here; it is slow but sure." Growing unemployment, particularly among cooks, further undermined the union's already sagging membership.[78] The overextended Amalgamated sustained even greater losses. Its once-thriving hotel workers branch was in "deplorable condition," declared Martin Obermeirer, former union secretary. He conceded that failure to organize new workers had weakened the union and that its "members [had] given up hope to build up a strong organization."[79]

Rebuilding the Amalgamated

A slender ray of hope appeared from behind the shadows of union disorganization, as conditions inside many hotels and restaurants continued to deteriorate. In early spring of 1929, Obermeirer, now head organizer for the Amalgamated's recently consolidated Hotel and Restaurant and Cafeteria Workers Branch, launched a mass recruiting campaign aimed at cafeteria workers, more than one thousand of whom signed union cards in barely two weeks. "We are told that slavery has been abolished," commented "JS," a recent union recruit, "but right here in New York City workers are slaving 12, 14 and 15 hours under the most miserable conditions." After completing a busy three-hour mealtime shift at a local cafeteria, JS was paid sixty cents, from which the owner deducted five cents, "because," JS said, "he claimed I ate five cents more of food than I was supposed to eat." It could be worse, as JS discovered when he secured work as a busboy, earning all of $18 for a seven-day week. Again money was deducted from his gross earnings, this time a hefty $5 fee for the employment agency, leaving him with $13 for seventy-five hours of work—just over seventeen cents per hour.[80]

Other cafeteria workers recounted similar stories of exploitation and abuse. A self-described "cafeteria slave," an experienced waiter and family man, told of his most recent job in a lunchroom, where he was paid 35 cents for "two hours of hard work." "And they say the slave days are over," he added. While the pay was undeniably bad, the hours were worse still, typically twelve-hour shifts, six and a half days per week. "The work is very hard," explained another waiter. "When I go home at night to my dirty room full of bedbugs, I am so tired I don't even want to see a movie."[81]

Working nonstop around the clock left little time for routine maintenance or even cleanup, particularly in the kitchen and other areas that were out of the customers' sight. "The cracks in the floor are filled with stinking dirt, pieces of rotten food, soaked with urine," observed another waiter, in a description reminiscent of conditions exposed by the IWW during the 1912 strike. "It is unfit for hogs, let alone human beings." Customers would "never come back [if they could] see how their food was prepared," commented another waiter. "I have seen the cook, with sweat running off of his body, especially in the summer, and running right into the food he is cooking." A veteran of the cafeteria trade observed, "Everything left over is used another day. If meats are left over, they are chopped up, [given] a French name, [and served again]." Added another waiter, "It is nauseating to go into the filthy place. When a strike is called, we will go out 100 per cent."[82]

That is just what they did when Obermeirer called out the cafeteria workers employed in Manhattan's garment district, a stronghold of left-wing unionism. On the morning of April 4, 1929, five hundred food workers left their jobs, demanding an eight-hour day and a six-day week, hiring through the union rather than private employment agencies, and equal pay for equal work, including weekly minimums of $22 for busboys and dishwashers and $35 for cooks and the wait staff. As the lunch hour approached, crowds of strikers and their supporters, drawn mainly from the ranks of the Communist-led Needle Trades Workers' Industrial Union, assembled in front of many of the most popular restaurants, effectively shutting them down. Within a few days nearly two thousand workers were out, tying up 95 of the area's 125 restaurants.[83]

The employers, having recently organized into the United Restaurant Owners Association, worked closely with city police in orchestrating the arrest of almost two hundred picketers during the first week. With the strikers' ranks growing daily, the owners grew desperate. Many hard-pressed smaller businesses hired "private detectives" to carry out armed assaults on union leaders, sending several activists to the hospital. The larger chains pooled their resources in search of formal legal remedies, eventually securing a blanket injunction against mass picketing. Union leaders disingenuously threw up their hands, claiming they were powerless to stop the workers from picketing as part of a "spontaneous protest . . . against the injunction." In open defiance of the courts, hundreds of strikers continued mobilizing, facing down police, and marching off to jail.[84]

Young women represented a "very high" percentage of the nearly seven hundred strikers arrested by the end of April. Militants like eighteen-year-old Sylvia Weiner, arrested five times, Rose Kaplan, considered "one of the most persistent violators" of the injunction, and dozens of lesser-known women strikers were "coming to the forefront," wrote one observer, "staunchly marching on the picket lines, engaging in encounters with scabs, the bosses, thugs, and the police." Innocent "angels" no more, many young waitresses exchanged their open-shop halos for union cards as the only defense against escalating attacks on the picket lines and through the courts.[85]

The tide began to turn against the strikers in May after the walkout spilled outside the garment district to the exclusive restaurants along Fifth Avenue where middle-class customers had little compunction about crossing picket lines. With Obermeirer and fellow union leader Samuel Kramberg facing contempt charges for violating a recent Supreme Court injunction against "oppressive picketing," angry strikers resorted to more disruptive forms of direct action, releasing smoke bombs inside dining halls, overturning tables, and throwing dishes on the floor as frightened patrons rushed the exits. "The situation has become one of absolute anarchy," declared the owners' legal counsel. "We have never seen anything like it in this city."[86]

Public support for the walkout ebbed as the HRE entered the fray, battling the Amalgamated for representation rights. Cafeteria workers' Local 302, having done almost nothing to organize new workers during its four years of existence, seized on the energy generated by the walkout to launch an ambitious recruiting drive—from the top down, by signing up owners whose employees, under terms of the contract, automatically became members of the HRE. With "union shop" stickers proliferating in the front windows of restaurants and cafeterias throughout the city, street fighting erupted between Amalgamated pickets and "strikebreaking" members of Local 302. An understandably confused public, including many union-conscious garment workers, withdrew their active support as the walkout degenerated into a violent jurisdictional battle. By the middle of June, the original body of three thousand strikers—having absorbed fifteen hundred arrests, numerous jail sentences, thousands of dollars in fines, and countless blows from police batons and HRE fists alike—finally threw in the towel.[87]

Perhaps the most significant outcome of the two-month struggle was the unprecedented collaboration that emerged between the HRE and restaurateurs, stemming from their mutual fear of growing Communist influence among the city's culinary workers. To the untrained eye, the Amalgamated appeared as just another "Communist front group," an illusion assiduously cultivated by the party through the *Daily Worker*'s extensive and uniformly favorable coverage of the walkout. Obermeirer, as head of the strike committee, made little secret of his allegiance to the party, or of his indebtedness to his many "comrades" within the Amalgamated.

But what most disturbed HRE officers was the specter of communism within their own ranks. When Robert Long, leader of cooks' Local 719, refused to serve up his members as strikebreakers during the walkout, he and his followers were expelled from the HRE's citywide food workers' council. "Comrade Long" later found a home in the Amalgamated, taking most of Local 719's two hundred members with him.[88] Local 302's strikebreaking activities also ran afoul of its own executive board, a majority of whom were allegedly Communist party members and on that basis alone expelled. Even elitist Local 1 was a target of determined Bolshevik "borers from within." Alarmed by accounts of Communist "infiltration" into several New York area locals, delegates attending the HRE's 1929 national convention adopted a resolution calling for the immediate expulsion of any union member associated with the Communist party.[89]

But the Communists were bigger than any resolution, particularly as the shadow of economic depression spread across the land. By the end of 1929, the party had sufficient strength within the Amalgamated to force a protracted floor fight at the union's biannual convention over the question of affiliating with the Trade Union Unity League (TUUL), formed in August as the dual unionist successor of the Communist-led Trade Union Educational League. Introduced by Obermeirer's cafeteria workers, the proposal to join the red union federation failed to win majority support from the delegates and was referred to the membership. In a contested referendum, in which returns from several delinquent left-wing locals in Philadelphia were invalidated, the rank and file sustained the earlier vote of convention delegates.[90]

The Communists, although still seething over what they regarded as a stolen election, were not so sectarian as to abandon the Amalgamated. Early in 1930 the TUUL rallied around the Amalgamated when one of its cafeterias, the Moon, closed down and reopened a few days later, as the Monroe, under contract to the HRE, complete with a Local 302 "union shop" label prominently displayed in the front window. On opening day several customers, claiming to have been "fooled by the scab sign," engaged in a "great demonstration" once they saw pickets gathering outside. Police were called to the scene, and a small riot broke out.[91] Skirmishes continued in and around the Monroe over the next few weeks, capped by a major demonstration on February 20, when, during the height of the lunch hour, eighteen-year-old Anna Spieker jumped onto a table and yelled, "Everybody out. This place is on strike." In the commotion that followed, reported the *New York Times,* "tables were upset and glass tops smashed, crockery was hurled to the floor and patrons rushed to the street without paying their checks." The only serious injury was to the Monroe, which was forced to close for repairs.[92]

The Amalgamated scarcely had time to acknowledge the "left-wing unions" for their solidarity in battling Local 302 when the Communists abruptly broke ranks. In April the TUUL called a meeting of New York's "progressive" culinary unionists, out of which was formed the Food Workers Industrial Union (FWIU). Obermeirer was one of the first to line up behind the FWIU, taking most of the Amalgamated's eight hundred cafeteria workers with him. Amalgamated officials called an emergency reorganization meeting for all "loyal members" of the hotel and cafeteria branch. While many "old-timers" eventually returned to the fold, the increasingly young and restless culinary workers looked to militant leaders like Obermeirer and other FWIU firebrands who promised a sharp break with the failures of the past.[93]

Communists, Crooks, and
the Triumph of the AFL

The early years of the Great Depression came close to killing off the hotel and restaurant trade, as widespread economic uncertainty put a damper on dining out, recreational travel, and most other leisure pursuits on which the industry depended. With the economic pinch of the late 1920s tightening into a suffocating profit squeeze, employers wrung everything they could out of labor. "Wage cuts are the first order of business in every hotel and restaurant," observed an Amalgamated organizer in the fall of 1930. Slashing wages, often 20 percent or more, reduced the culinary workers' standard of living "to its minimum." Many waiters, however, fared even worse after their employers stopping paying wages altogether, making them entirely dependent on tips. The prewar split watch returned along with fourteen-hour shifts and the seven-day workweek. With many headwaiters becoming "bolder and more tyrannical," workers faced discharge "for no reason whatsoever."[94]

The Amalgamated did its best to navigate the treacherous waters of the Great Depression. But as more of its experienced leaders jumped ship for the FWIU, the union was barely afloat by 1931. "One of the reasons why the bosses are so bold," admitted the *Free Voice,* "is because they think the union is out of existence." And for good reason. With only a handful of houses under contract and a citywide membership of less than three thousand, the Amalgamated "didn't amount to anything," recalled Jay Rubin, a founder of the FWIU. "There was no organization at that point. There were just individuals, people who grew up in the hotel industry, and naturally they were part of the Amalgamated."[95]

The seemingly moribund HRE struggled simply to stay alive. Its only "organizing" amounted to little more than theft, led by Local 302's strategy of raiding the membership of other unions, particularly the pugnacious FWIU. In one cafeteria after another, boasted an organizer for Local 302, employers "signed up with our people before opening"—and, as the Communists pointed out, without first bothering to consult the workers.[96] Viewing with envy Local 302's accomplishments, hotel waiters' Local 16 came back from the dead by making similar sweetheart deals with employers. By 1932 Local 16 had secured verbal agreements with many of the exclusive Broadway res-

taurants and nightclubs. Its success was "puzzling," noted two observers, as "Local 16 was small, with only a handful of members, and
with no strength to force anyone to do anything." In fact, both Local
302 and Local 16 had considerable clout—not by virtue of organizing
new workers but rather from their connections to racketeers who
were deeply involved in both locals.[97]

The FWIU, target of more than one hundred antipicketing injunctions in 1931 alone, showed the most signs of life, conducting
countless job actions to force union recognition. Through the pages
of the *Food Worker*, the union's monthly newspaper, the rank and
file shared grievances and organizing tactics while learning more than
most wanted to know about the horrors of capitalism. A typical product of the party's "third period" sectarianism, the *Food Worker* at
times devoted more space to derailing rival unions than attacking
employers. Based largely among Obermeirer's militant cafeteria
workers, with some support from grocery clerks and bakers, the
FWIU developed a small but stable following of about fifteen hundred by the spring of 1933.[98]

Passage of the National Industrial Recovery Act (NRA), with its
section 7a giving workers greater freedom to unionize, failed to spark
an immediate upsurge of organizing among New York's culinary
workers. But the ensuing public debate over a federal code for regulating industrial relations in the hotel and restaurant industries galvanized unions into action. In August, when the proposed restaurant
code was announced, employers, barely able to contain their glee,
anticipated "extreme controversies" over its acceptance. Essentially
proposing to turn back the clock to the nonunion era, the code endorsed the split watch, a fifty-four-hour week, and a minimum wage
of twenty-eight cents per hour. Unionists across the board were out-
raged. Members of the HRE "were up in arms," declared international president Edward Flore. Addressing a mass meeting of New
York's food council, Flore promised to call a "general strike" to protest those provisions of the code that treated workers "like slaves."
Amalgamated and FWIU officials reacted with even greater anger and
bitterness.[99]

With the code hearings under way, New York's veteran culinary
workers as well as many newcomers poured into the unions, bringing
with them a new spirit of hope and militancy. The aging but tireless
Amalgamated, after reporting in April that the union had been

"broken," announced in October that hundreds of members were joining each day. Cautioning their newest recruits not to rely on the latest
"swindle from the boss" in the form of the NRA, the *Free Voice* urged
its readers, "Show your manhood or womanhood this time. You must
take a stand on the side of the other workers who are organizing."[100]

One of those workers was Andre Fournigault, a cold meat chef at
the exclusive Waldorf-Astoria. In mid-January 1934, Oscar, the hotel's
celebrated maitre d', assembled his staff to discuss their possible
union affiliations in light of the NRA. Seeking to promote membership in the Federation of Hotel Guilds—a toothless professional association that functioned as a company union—Oscar was reportedly
speechless on learning that most of his employees already belonged
to the Amalgamated. A few days later Fournigault, who had "successfully tickled elite palates" for years, was dismissed without explanation. The Amalgamated, in which Fournigault was a cooks' delegate
and outspoken militant, accused the Waldorf of discriminating against
its members and threatened immediate action.[101]

At 7:00 P.M. the next evening the Waldorf's entire kitchen and wait
staff of six hundred took matters into their own hands, walking out
en masse to force Fournigault's reinstatement. Hotel managers, although "virtually helpless in the face of the union's swift action," tried
to maintain a bold front as hundreds of disappointed diners left in a
huff. "The Sert Room Orchestra played on as when the *Lusitania*
sank," wrote correspondent Herbert Solow. "And the Waldorf, regarded by bosses and men as the industry's flagship, went down." A
cursing Oscar pleaded with the strikers to return, but only a handful
did so. The rest mobbed union headquarters, urging their leaders to
turn up the heat.[102]

HRE Local 16, the recent target of a citywide probe into criminal
racketeering, joined hands with the hotel employers in red-baiting
the Amalgamated and seeking injunctive relief against picketing. "I
will not call out a single man or woman in sympathy," pledged a
spokesman for Local 16. "We are not cooperating with the Amalgamated in any way." Nor were the Communists, despite their public
declarations for united action. When FWIU Local 119, representing
hotel workers, failed in its bid to take over the walkout, union leaders
ordered their members to bore from within—or, in the newly revised
Popular Front vocabulary, to "merge" with the Amalgamated's rank
and file.[103]

The prospect of merging with the Communists was particularly repellent to the leaders of the walkout, most of whom were associated with New York City's vibrant "left opposition" to Stalinism. Benjamin Gitlow, part of the recently expelled Jay Lovestone faction within the party, did not mince words. "I am a Communist," he told a gathering of strikers. "I warn you, don't affiliate with any Communist organization." "This is an industrial organization," Gitlow insisted, invoking a familiar syndicalist message, "and that is a political organization."[104] Similar warnings were sounded by James Cannon, leader of the Trotskyist Communist League of America and a frequent speaker at rallies. Trotskyist influences also extended to the two union officials directly involved in the walkout, B. J. Fields, organizer for the cooks and a union secretary, and fellow Greek, Aristodimos Kaldis, with a large following among waiters.[105]

Communist sniping at the strike's anti-Stalinist leadership escalated along with the growing walkout. As the original job action against the Waldorf expanded into a general strike of almost thirty thousand, Amalgamated officials came under sharper attack from the party faithful, who accused them of "hobnobbing with the N.R.A., stirring up the most vicious 'red scare,' deliberately calling for disunity, thereby injuring and endangering the strike." The Amalgamated's idea of class conflict, charged the *Daily Worker*, was to file a "cringing, belly-crawling protest to President Roosevelt [while] attempting to quiet down and hold back the militant spirit of the strikers." All efforts at resolving the walkout were dismissed by the Communists as "sellouts" and "betrayals."[106]

Communist-led strikers, many with spouses and young children at their sides, began battling police in nightly street demonstrations outside some of Manhattan's most fashionable eating places. After nearly two weeks of increasingly violent confrontations, federal mediators forged a tentative agreement whereby the hotel operators offered to take back all strikers and dismiss their replacements if the union pulled its pickets. The pickets were removed in mid-February, but the strikebreakers remained.[107] Mayor Fiorello La Guardia, incensed by the employers' duplicity and subsequent refusal to meet with union representatives, unleashed the sanitation department, which began carrying out highly publicized health inspections of the city's first-class luxury hotels. The walkout ended days later, on the same terms originally proposed by federal mediators.[108]

True to form, the employers failed to comply with the agreement. Despite assurances to rehire all strikers, "hundreds of workers have been refused their jobs," reported the *Daily Worker*. More than two weeks after seeking reinstatement, only 3 out of 300 strikers had been taken back at the Hotel New Yorker, 25 out of 150 at the Park Central, and 60 out of 600 at the Waldorf-Astoria. In the face of widespread blacklisting, FWIU activists organized a rank-and-file movement within the Amalgamated to oust the union's paid officials, "whose policies," it was charged, "lost the hotel strike." At a routine membership meeting in late March, Fields, Caldis, and their supporters were voted out and replaced by the union's executive board as the temporary governing body, with backing from a rank-and-file "committee of 30" charged with enforcing their authority.[109]

With FWIU cadres now firmly in control of the Amalgamated, plans were laid for merging the two organizations. Meeting in April, a joint committee endorsed the goal of "One Big Union" for the food industry. Plans for consolidating the two organizations were put on hold as the merger proposal was taken up by each local of the Amalgamated, including several in which minimal Communist influence allowed submerged syndicalist reservations to surface concerning the "political leadership" of the FWIU. With the Amalgamated's bakers still undecided through the fall, the union's hotel and restaurant workers were already acting as one, taking their direction from the rejuvenated FWIU.[110]

The Communists, now fully in the swing of the Popular Front, began making overtures to the HRE, the same group of "social fascists" they had condemned only months earlier. After exchanging correspondence, the two sides met for the first time in the spring of 1935 to explore the possibility of a formal merger. Heading the HRE delegation was Emmanual Koveleski, an outspoken critic of both the Amalgamated and the FWIU. At his side were the newly installed international vice president, William Lehman, formerly head of powerful waiters' Local 1, and Miguel Garriga, an experienced officer recently assigned to organize the city's cooks. Across the table, representing the FWIU, sat party stalwarts Jay Rubin, the union's national secretary, Sam Kramberg of the cafeteria workers, and Martin Obermeirer and William Albertson from hotel workers' Local 119.[111]

From this seemingly incongruous body emerged the framework for the FWIU's application to join the HRE. With international president Flore's blessing, the food workers' delegation was invited to present their case before the HRE's national executive board. On the day of the hearing Paul Coulcher and Harry Koenig from waiters' Local 16, along with Max Pincus from cafeteria workers' Local 302, appeared out of nowhere to condemn the proposed merger. The board, promising to take their dissenting views under advisement, began to deliberate in private.[112]

It was clear to the board, as it was to most observers, that Coulcher, Koenig, and Pincus were motivated less by their concern for the working class than by their own pocketbooks. All three men were known associates of "Dutch" Schultz, the notorious gangster, who had invaded the culinary industry in 1932, looking for a new source of income to compensate for the expected loss of bootleg revenues with the pending repeal of Prohibition. As part of his master plan to "organize" the city's restaurants and cafeterias, Dutch sent his henchmen into Locals 16 and 302 where they forcibly "supervised" union elections by silencing the opposition with "pistols, rubber hose, and other weapons."[113]

Underworld figures, working closely with officers from Locals 16 and 302, began "organizing" from the top down, forcing employers into the Metropolitan Restaurant and Cafeteria Association, whose members paid more than $2 million per year in initiation fees, dues, and routine shakedowns. But it was money well spent. In exchange the owners received "protection" in the form of the HRE's union label, which kept at bay the more militant Amalgamated and FWIU. Protection money also kept dissident HRE members in line. When Local 302 veteran Abe Borson tried to conduct business the old-fashioned way, by organizing workers, he was taken for a "ride" to a quiet suburb, told to "get on [his] knees and pray," shot, and left for dead. As revelations of criminal activity in New York reached Flore, the union's executive board—forced to choose between allying with the FWIU's Communists or Dutch Schultz's criminals—came down on the left and endorsed the proposed merger.[114]

The Communists' fight to join labor's mainstream was now in the hands of the rank and file. Emboldened by the board's favorable recommendation, FWIU Locals 110, representing cafeteria workers, and 119, representing restaurant waiters and waitresses, renewed earlier offers to merge with their HRE counterparts, Locals 302 and 16. By the fall of 1935 the demand from the rank and file was, as Rubin and

Obermeirer recalled, "too great to be denied," and an agreement for merger was signed between the two cafeteria locals.[115]

Local 16, still firmly under the thumb of Coulcher and Koenig, held out—but not for much longer. An extensive investigation by the Office of the District Attorney into labor racketeering was nearing its conclusion, with several officers of Locals 302 and 16 facing indictments. Koenig, a prime suspect in the investigation, was shot, gangland style, a few months later while attending the HRE's national convention. Lying on his deathbed, Koenig refused, under vigorous questioning, to identify his assailants, saying only "So long" as he lost consciousness. Pincus, formerly of Local 302, committed suicide after he, Coulcher, and several lesser union officers were charged with criminal racketeering. Finally freed from the grip of organized crime, the membership of Local 16 welcomed FWIU Local 119 with open arms in the fall of 1936.[116]

Local 119's "self-liquidation," carried out in the name of a higher unity, brought to a close a quarter century of independent left-wing unionism. "We bow out with a feeling of great joy," declared the *Food Worker* in its final issue. And understandably so, for while the FWIU was gone, most of its objectives had been realized. The culinary workers had been transformed from a disorganized mass into a highly disciplined proletarian army that employers were now bound to respect. Having unified themselves as members of a single union, they began their march toward the promised land of industrial organization, arriving three years later with the formation of a citywide foods council. Leading the way were former officers in the Amalgamated and the FWIU, including open Communists like Obermeirer, Rubin, Albertson, and Kramberg, all of whom were elected to important offices in the new organization.[117] Just as the Wobblies had urged, the culinary workers built their "new society within the shell of the old"—forming One Big Union, organized along industrial lines, and led by radicals—all from inside the AFL.

Conclusion

More than two decades after their abandonment by the IWW, New York's culinary workers finally arrived at the door of the AFL. Their journey was neither smooth nor predictable, guided only by the sketchiest of road maps left behind by the Wobblies. Following the familiar landmarks of industrial syndicalism, the rank and file relied on labor solidarity, mass mobilization, and unrestricted direct action to find their way across what was still a largely uncharted organizational landscape.

New York's culinary workers began their journey in 1916, stopping first at the International Federation of Workers in the Hotel and Restaurant Industry, an industrial organization modeled after the IWW and led by former Wobblies and their allies. Union leader Otto Wagner, a self-described syndicalist, built a substantial following among the city's less skilled culinary workers. Although the rank and file, by Wagner's own admission, did not share his revolutionary convictions, they were drawn to the IFW's organizational logic of industrial syndicalism, which they deployed with increasing effectiveness against employers and rival business syndicalists alike.

The city's craft unionists were divided in their response to the IFW. Waiters, members of powerful Local 1, came closest to embracing its combative "modern unionism." Over the objections of national HRE leaders, local waiters regularly supported IFW job actions, from which they drew important lessons of their own about timing, direct action, and solidarity. In the end, however, Local 1's reliance on conventional job control, rather than mass mobilization, steered its predominantly male membership toward the logic of small numbers, restrictionism, and contracts that formed the basis of its otherwise organizationally potent business syndicalism.

While Local 1's carefully guarded admissions offered a sharp contrast to the IFW's high-profile mass recruiting, both unions focused their energies on building up workers' power at the point of production. It was not enough, however, to simply lead the rank and file into combat, as the Wobblies had done years earlier. In the aftermath of the IFW's unsuccessful citywide strike in 1918, Wagner and other leaders patiently rebuilt the union from the ground up, creating a dense network of workplace committees that reached down to the shop floor as a means of mobilizing the rank and file. Its doors now open wider than ever, the reorganized IFW was soon overrun by a larger and more diverse membership that, particularly with the addition of women from traditionally unorganized sectors, substantially changed the face of industrial unionism in New York.

Seeking still more expansive quarters to accommodate the mass of fresh recruits, the culinary workers moved next to the Amalgamated

Food Workers Union. This new house of labor was built on the same foundation of organizational integrity and industrial syndicalism that had supported the IFW. Under increasing attack from rival unionists on its right and left, the Amalgamated doggedly pursued its own independent course, avoiding the exclusionary business syndicalism of the HRE, on the one side, and the politicized agenda of the nascent Communist movement, on the other. Finally, after more than a decade of continuing interunion raids and escalating employer attacks, the city's culinary workers abandoned the Amalgamated for the Communist-led Food Workers Industrial Union.

The ideologically driven FWIU was the Communists' answer to the Amalgamated's unabashed syndicalism. But beneath its politicized exterior, the FWIU rested on much the same organizational foundation as its predecessors. The FWIU's appeal, as its Communist leaders later admitted, depended less on the union's refined politics than on its base proletarianism, less on following the correct political line than on maintaining militant picket lines. Only a small fraction of its members, fewer than 10 percent, ever joined the Communist party; and most of those who did, according to union founder and president Jay Rubin, were simply "militant people" who, like food workers generally, were drawn to the FWIU's combative syndicalism.[118] Having been formed only a few years earlier as the sworn enemy of the HRE, the mercurial left-wing union proved to be in the end its greatest benefactor. With the FWIU's self-liquidation in 1935—a product of the historical conjuncture of the Great Depression, the growing presence of organized crime within the industry, the rise of "progressive" forces within the rival AFL union, and the Communists' own sudden interest in coalition building—the feisty red union quietly passed out of existence, leaving the HRE as the exclusive house of labor for New York's culinary workers.

The mass of less skilled culinary workers thus made their way from the IWW to the AFL in search of a stabler institutional expression of industrial syndicalism. Throughout the many twists and turns that defined their trajectory, they were guided by the practices of labor solidarity, mass mobilization, and unrestricted direct action. With each new obstacle placed in their path—whether by hostile employers, an unsympathetic legal system, a fickle public, or rival unionists— the rank and file responded by pursuing ever-tighter, more disciplined organizational expressions of industrial syndicalism. Even after joining the HRE in 1936 and signing their first time contracts, the culinary workers continued for many years to wield their familiar weapons of labor solidarity, mass mobilization, and direct action at the point of production.

The HRE's success, then, was not a consequence of the growing conservatism, pragmatism, economism, or any other "ism" supposedly characteristic of American workers. Support for the HRE was never premised on a widespread conversion to the ideological views of its top leadership, any more than the failure of its industrial rivals was predicated on a rejection of their political radicalism. The trajectory of culinary unionism in New York followed the time-worn organizational logic of industrial syndicalism, not ephemeral political programs of the right or left.

Chapter Six

Syndicalism, Pure and Simple

The men and women who labored in obscurity on the docks of Philadelphia and in the kitchens and dining rooms of New York City had more in common than their anonymity as historical actors. Having been drawn into open conflict with their employers, both groups turned in 1913 to the revolutionary IWW for direction and support. While the culinary workers used the Wobblies as little more than a way station on the road to a stabler form of industrialism, the longshoremen remained within their grasp for more than a decade. In time, however, both jurisdictions fell under the sway of the more conservative AFL.

Much the same story of organizational succession has been told for countless other American cities and industries. Its plot, familiar to even casual observers of the labor movement, revolves around the working class coming into its own. Leaving behind its youthful indiscretions, symbolized by a childish flirtation with the earlier "uplift unionism" of the Knights of Labor and the empty revolutionary promises of the left-wing Socialists and Wobblies, the rank and file finally grows up, removes the utopian scales from its eyes, and accepts the AFL as the organization that best "fits" the conservatism that comes with advancing age.[1]

The trajectory of organized labor has thus been conventionally understood as the product of a long-germinating conservatism, deeply rooted in the psychology of a mature working class that by the turn of the century had grown to love capitalism while denying its own existence. Flourishing in the hothouse atmosphere of American liberalism, this "pro-capitalist, anticlass" consciousness soon established itself, eventually taming or uprooting the few remaining weeds of industrial radicalism. The subsequent blossoming of the AFL, as generations of scholars have argued since Perlman, was merely the institutional expression of this "homegrown" proletarian conservatism.[2]

The thesis of proletarian conservatism, although at times approaching the status of "academic dogma" among students of twentieth-century American labor, has seldom rested on anything more substantial than an "article of faith."[3] In point of fact, what we know today about ordinary working people of the past is based far less on the few surviving relics of their private thoughts than on their observable deeds, thereby falling once again into the familiar trap of inferring individual mental states from group behavior—in effect, trying to blindly read consciousness from collective action. If, given the scarcity of reliable historical data on worker mentalities, the decision to focus empirically on their practical activity makes sense, the almost inevitable leap to consciousness does not.[4]

And yet the distant—some might say, impenetrable—world of consciousness has remained the principal focal point for theorizing about American workers and their organizations for more than half a century.[5] Whether conceptualized as an appropriately guarded "job consciousness" by the old labor history, a tragically failed "false consciousness" by Western Marxism, or a popularly based "class consciousness" by the new social history, the common starting point is one that privileges ideas over action, as if "it is somehow necessary for men and women to encompass society intellectually before they can attempt to change it." "This premise," Gordon Marshall points out, "is not confirmed by the history of class action on either a revolutionary or on a more modest scale."[6]

Indeed, in retracing the actual steps of the longshoremen and culinary workers, actions speak much louder than words, particularly for the "inarticulate mass" of ordinary dockworkers, waitresses, and cooks who never had an opportunity to say what they thought of the capitalist system and their place within it. In any case, whether they loved or hated capitalism is arguably less telling than what they did to survive under it as dependent wage earners, just as whether they were "class" or "job" conscious is less revealing than what they actually did as workers to organize themselves in opposition to employers and the state. Still, actions do not speak for themselves. To make sense of what the rank and file did, their behavior must be understood contextually, as a product of historical "options under pressure" that at particular points in time defined the changing universe of possibilities they faced.[7]

The opening decades of this century offered millions of unorganized American workers the clearest of ideological choices: a revolutionary IWW bent on overthrowing capitalism or a reformist AFL committed to rising within it. But on the docks of Philadelphia and in the hotels and restaurants of New York City, where the two organizations battled head-to-head, their competing views of capitalism were seldom communicated directly to the rank and file. Revolution and reform may have been important concerns within the headquarters of both unions, inside the hidden war rooms of the FBI, the Justice Department, and the employer associations, and in the far-off editorial offices of magazine and newspaper publishers but not on the job, the picket line, or the floor of local union meetings where organizational loyalties were forged. However much the rank and file knew of the ideological contrast between the IWW and the AFL, it never appeared to weigh very heavily in their choice of unions.

Whereas the formal ideologies guiding the IWW and the AFL were distinct yet inconsequential, their immediate union objectives were neither. Despite the vast ideological chasm at the top of both organizations, at the bottom their local affiliates often came together on many of the same demands. On the Philadelphia waterfront the IWW, operating through Local 8 of its Marine Transport Workers' Industrial Union, took the early lead in improving wages, hours, and conditions for the port's longshoremen. But the rival AFL union, Local 1116 of the ILA, was never far behind, finally pulling even with the Wobblies in 1925 when its leaders embraced as their own the same wage and hour demands originally put forward by Local 8. Except for the ILA's goal of securing a contract, the left-wing Wobblies and the right-wing AFL ended up supporting most of the same immediate objectives.

It was even more difficult to distinguish trade union programs in New York's hotel and restaurant industry, where powerful waiters' Local 1 of the HRE sometimes followed and sometimes led the IWW and its leftist successors in demanding concessions from employers. Lacking the waiters' traditions of job control, other HRE locals generally lagged behind their industrial counterparts, but only temporarily. Once they had built up sufficient organizational muscle, the craft unions willingly took on their pugnacious rivals, matching them blow for blow, demand for demand, until their trade union programs had become all but indistinguishable. Well before the HRE's triumph in 1936, immediate objectives had ceased to figure as a distinguishing characteristic of the city's culinary unions.

The contest for union loyalty, then, was not decided by appealing exclusively to either the mind or the belly: the competing views of capitalism endorsed by IWW and AFL leaders mattered hardly at all to the rank and file while the growing convergence in immediate objectives erased those programmatic differences that seemingly mattered most. In choosing between the AFL and its industrial rivals, the longshoremen and culinary workers were guided neither by a Gramscian "war of ideological position" nor a Perlmanian "revolt of the stomach" but rather by the experience of workplace struggle that drew them to the union whose logic of collective action best "fitted" their own class capacities rooted in the organization of the labor process.[8]

The IWW's industrial syndicalism offered by far the better fit for the masses of less skilled workers who loaded ships, prepared food, and waited tables. Lacking the strategic advantages of craft workers, their capacity to disrupt production fluctuated with the undulating rhythms of work as vessels and customers came and went. Whether the particular product of their labor was a 300-pound slab of raw beef deposited in the hold of a ship or a 12-ounce cooked steak delivered on fine china, the longshoremen and the culinary workers relied on a kind of "situational" power that could only be realized by retaining the right to strike when conditions were most favorable.

The unrestricted right to strike, however, was meaningless without the organizational capacity to cripple, if not halt, production. Highly localized job actions, even when propitiously timed, were not enough. Pulling dockworkers off a single pier or calling waiters out at one hotel might be temporarily disruptive, perhaps even costly to profit-conscious shippers and restaurateurs. But such isolated actions seldom threatened the economic viability of larger employers, given both the relative ease of replacing unskilled labor and the possibility of directing empty ships and hungry customers to neighboring piers and restaurants. For the economically vulnerable longshoremen and culinary workers, the best defense was to mount a strong offense in the form of inclusive unions that were capable of mobilizing and sustaining industrywide collective action. Labor solidarity was not simply an empty slogan on the docks and in the hotels and restaurants but a necessary condition of success.

Industrial syndicalism thus complemented the organizational capacities of the longshoremen and culinary workers whose support for the IWW and its left-wing successors rested on a logic of collective action defined by membership inclusivity, mass mobilization, and reliance on worker self-activity in place of contracts. On both the Philadelphia waterfront and in New York's larger hotels and restaurants where previous unionization efforts had been blocked by capitalist intransigence and labor force segmentation, the practice of industrial syndicalism removed both obstructions: taming hostile employers through the unrestricted exercise of direct action on the job while bridging racial, ethnic, sexual, and occupational divisions among workers through organizational logics that privileged expansive forms of solidarity rooted in class.

As the embodiment of industrial syndicalism on the docks, Local 8 retained the allegiance of Philadelphia's thirty-five hundred regularly employed longshoremen for more than a decade. Its demise in 1926 was occasioned not by some inexorable shift in worker consciousness toward "conservatism" but by the changing balance of class forces on the waterfront and within the larger society, as capital, the state, rival unionists, black separatists, and even their own national IWW leaders lined up against the port's embattled longshoremen. Local 8's "failure," if it can be called that, was clearly one of power, not organizational practices.

Similarly, the IWW's "failure" to create a durable base of support inside New York's kitchens and dining rooms had more to do with the particular shortcomings of Wobbly leadership during the disastrous 1913 citywide strike than with any failing of industrial syndicalism. Indeed, the organizational logic of labor solidarity, mass mobilization, and direct action outlived the IWW by more than two decades, remaining the dominant repertoire of collective action guiding three separate food workers' unions, each one driven toward greater inclusiveness and tighter organizational discipline in response to stiffening opposition from employers and rival unionists. The demise of industrial unionism in New York in 1936—as in Philadelphia a decade earlier—did not come as a result of any profound change in worker consciousness. All that changed was the political line of their Communist leaders whose Popular Front enthusiasm for unity at any cost killed off an otherwise vital tradition of independent, left-led culinary unionism.

The AFL affiliates that triumphed in Philadelphia and in New York City each bore a striking resemblance to the industrial union it had vanquished. On the waterfront the ILA incorporated not only most of Local 8's former Wobbly officers but also many of its organizational practices, including its innovative policy of biracial leadership along with its commitment to portwide solidarity. In the hotels and restaurants, where "institutional isomorphism" had been the rule for some time, the HRE completed its metamorphosis into a quasi-industrial union in 1935 with the appointment of prominent Communists to direct its organizing efforts and the subsequent creation of a citywide "food council" to more effectively coordinate joint action across occupational boundaries.[9] Except for entering into time contracts with employers, the victorious AFL unions came to embrace many of the same practices that defined the rival organizations they had recently defeated.

The AFL's self-transformation was the price of its victory. In earlier head-to-head competition, its business syndicalism of small numbers, big dues, and wordy contracts had proven no match for the industrial syndicalism of the Wobblies and their successors. Unable to beat its industrial challengers, the AFL ended up all but joining them, taking on many of their organizational practices. While the continuing presence of a viable union opposition on the docks and in the hotels and restaurants discouraged local AFL leaders from backsliding into pure business syndicalism, the absence of a critical mass of skilled workers simultaneously removed any incentive to do so.[10]

Yet the AFL's ability to remake itself in the image of its industrial competition would not have been possible without a common grounding in the syndicalism that shaped the struggles of Philadelphia's longshoremen and New York's culinary workers, ultimately leading them from the IWW to the AFL. This was not syndicalism in theory but in action, a syndicalism pure and simple, bereft of formal ideology, whether left or right. It was not about abolishing the state, building workers' soviets, or plotting social revolution. Its methods did not rely solely on general strikes, industrial violence, or sabotage, just as its followers were not all reckless anarchists, wild-eyed bomb throwers, or industrial saboteurs.

Workplace syndicalism was none of these things. Rather it was embodied in the struggle of ordinary working men and women to extract some greater measure of comfort and security from a capitalist system that regularly withheld both. Their means of doing so—by vigorously contesting individual capitalists through direct action at the point of production—was the essence of American syndicalism. Its significance, as a contemporary student of syndicalism observed in 1913, did not lay in either its long-term vision or its immediate demands "but in the spirit of independence and militancy which it has kept alive, and energetically fostered, in the hearts of the labouring classes."[11]

American Syndicalism Reconsidered

The syndicalism that led American workers into battle earlier in this century was premised on rejecting the electoral arena as the main field of combat and the state as the principal target of attack. In that the revolutionary IWW and the reformist AFL were in firm agreement. Largely avoiding the political terrain, both organizations concentrated their forces at the point of production where they engaged employers in a bitter and often-violent war of direct action for control of their job territory. However differently they drew the boundaries of that territory, and however much they disagreed on how best to capture it, the craft unions and their industrial rivals fought under the same broad syndicalist banner that privileged production over politics as the primary site of working-class struggle.

The resulting marginalization of politics, which reached its height during the formative years of the AFL and the IWW, has remained a distinguishing feature of American unionism ever since. While never able to entirely absent itself from the political process, organized labor has exercised far less influence on government policy and electoral outcomes in the United States than in practically any other industrialized democracy.[12] Even at its most politically influential moments— the 1930s when the New Deal coalition was first formed and at the apex of liberalism some thirty years later before the coalition began to unravel—the relationship between American labor and the Democratic party was never more than a "partial equivalence," if that, to the Socialist and Social Democratic labor party alliances found throughout Western Europe.[13]

As one of the cornerstones of "American exceptionalism," labor's relatively limited role in U.S. political life has been the subject of considerable research and theorizing. Like the larger body of literature of which it is a part, explanations for working-class apoliticism run wide and deep, pointing to such diverse factors as the depoliticization of labor struggles resulting from the (limited) extension of the franchise before industrialization; the late-nineteenth-century separation of work and community that isolated economic from political struggles; the federal government's hostility, weakness, or unresponsiveness to workers, which rendered the state politically irrelevant; the lack of a viable and enduring labor party; the general success of repression and co-optation in containing insurgent political movements; and the pervasive influence of liberal, antistatist values. What all of these otherwise disparate, at times contradictory, explanations share is an underlying presumption that a lack of political engagement demonstrates not only American labor's "exceptionalism" but its failings as well.[14]

Using institutionalized politics as the principal measure of success, American labor has, not surprisingly, come up short, with its syndicalist orientation generally characterized as a primitive, even reactionary, mode of struggle that was poorly suited to raising worker consciousness much less razing the capitalist system.[15] Where the old labor historians followed Perlman in dismissing "job syndicalism" as a "pure reaction to conditions" without revolutionary ambitions, their Marxist counterparts likewise belittled struggles at the point of production as, in Lenin's celebrated formulation, a "mere economism" that inhibited the growth of some as yet unrealized "class consciousness." In either case American syndicalism—like the workers' movement it inspired—did not add up to anything more than a political zero.[16]

Judged on its own terms, however, syndicalism was less of a political failure than a political refusal. Its politics, when invoked, were neither left nor right but indeterminate. Thus Polly Baker, who, as a die-hard Wobbly, led Philadelphia's longshoremen into battle against the shipowners in the early 1920s, was driven by the same syndicalism a decade later into opposition against the political agenda of the Communist-influenced International Longshoremen's and Warehousemen's Union (ILWU), the ILA's dogged Congress of Industrial Organizations (CIO) challenger. While remaining open to the ILWU's modified industrial syndicalism of labor solidarity, mass mobilization, and contractual direct action, Baker denounced its ideological functionaries as a meddling and destructive "intelligentsia."[17] Significantly, the ILWU's leaders responded, not by defending their radical politics or even acknowledging them, but by impugning Baker's own syndicalist credentials, calling him a "well-known rat" and "labor faker" for "selling out" the longshoremen. The charge was not without foundation.[18] Baker, having ascended the ILA bureaucracy to become one of its international vice presidents, had risen far from his humble Wobbly origins in the rank and file. But, even at his red-baiting worst, vice president Baker never lost touch with the workplace syndicalism that continued to hold the longshoremen to the ILA, insulating them from repeated raids conducted during the late 1930s by the left-wing ILWU.[19]

The relationship between syndicalism and political leftism evolved very differently in New York's culinary industry, where Baker's counterpart, Martin Obermeirer, ended up allying with the Communist party. True to his syndicalist roots, Obermeirer spoke more often and more favorably of the party's industrial radicalism, hardly ever mentioning its political radicalism. By deftly translating the exotic ideological discourse of communism into the more recognizable practice of industrial syndicalism, Obermeirer and his comrades built a substantial and durable following in the city's hotels and restaurants, creating in the process one of the few Communist strongholds within the AFL.[20]

The clashing ideological views of Baker and Obermeirer, like those of Bill Haywood and Sam Gompers a generation before them, were of far less consequence to the rank and file than their shared syndicalism. In either organizational form—industrial or business syndicalism—the workplace struggles of American labor have been characterized by what most observers regard as "a unique degree of intensity" seldom found among the more politicized labor movements of Western Europe.[21] Compensating for their lack of political strength, workers in the United States have found it necessary to overdevelop their economic muscles, waging battles against employers that have generally been among the hardest-fought, most protracted, and bloodiest anywhere in the industrialized world.[22]

If one of the most combative and strike-prone working classes of the twentieth century is still perceived as "conservative," it is because its syndicalism has been seen as little more than an unmitigated political failure. Whether examined through the lens of Perlman's job consciousness or Lenin's economism, the industrial battles fought by American workers have appeared narrow and one-sided, more notable for the radical politics that are usually missing than for the uncompromising militancy that is often present. While students of exceptionalism have generated countless explanations for the late-nineteenth-century Socialist path that was never taken, the more intriguing question—given the labor movement's subsequent trajectory—is how its indigenous syndicalism sustained a peculiarly "American style" of class struggle that, at its most effective, "undermined the sway of capital over the quotidian lives" of ordinary working men and women.[23]

This is not to suggest that every act of worker defiance carried within it the seeds of wider revolt against the system. Some did, but most, clearly, did not. Nor is it to lapse into a "sentimentalism of the left" that, as Lawrence McDonnell argues, magnifies "the coherence and success of worker resistance to capitalism" by diminishing the "human costs and political thralldom of what has survived."[24] To be sure, the battles that were won must be weighed against those that were lost, not fought, or never even imagined. The resulting balance is the only meaningful measure of success or failure. That a particularly virulent strain of capitalism survived in the United States, however, is not to deny the antisystemic possibilities embodied in syndicalism's practical resistance to the economic reign of capital at the point of production.[25]

None of this is offered as a defense of labor's apoliticism. American unions were no doubt handicapped in many ways by their marginalization from the political battles that raged outside the sphere of production. If the state, as some historians contend, appeared distant and remote to most workers, it seldom treated them as such. Contrary to the liberal mythology of laissez-faire, the U.S. state was from its inception deeply involved in making, interpreting, and enforcing a wide range of laws and administrative procedures that decisively influenced the industrial terrain on which labor and capital engaged one another.[26] It may be, as Jean Monds has argued, a "workerist illusion" to think that struggles at the point of production were ever sufficient to bring down early-twentieth-century capitalism. If so, it is equally illusory to think that without such struggles the working class, or its self-appointed "vanguard," could have ever hoped to seize and retain power.[27]

"The dilemma of the American left," McDonnell writes, "has ever been, how to get from 'here' to 'there'?"—that is, from exercising workers' economic power at the point of production to wielding class-based political power in the wider society.[28] Certainly an important question. But it is neither the only nor, arguably, the most meaningful way to understand a national labor movement whose character is defined more by the "here" of militant workers' struggles than by an idealized and distant radical politics located out "there," always just beyond reach. Understanding what is "here" as syndicalism—rather than an expression of political failure or conservatism—casts a very different light on the "mere economism" that, in most accounts, leads America's "anticlass, pro-capitalist" workers to embrace an especially feeble "job-conscious unionism."

American syndicalism, it is true, has sometimes sunk to the depths of mere economism, even lower. Militant craftsmen allied with the AFL have pursued union policies that, in systematically excluding racial minorities, women, recent immigrants, and the unskilled, ended up dividing, disorganizing, and ultimately disempowering the working class as a whole. At other times these same "elitist" skilled workers have been excluded by groups like the IWW that wrote them off as a "reactionary labor aristocracy" not worth organizing. Craft and industrial workers, members of the AFL and the IWW alike, have on occasion found it possible to advance their interests only by "compromising" with employers, violating their own organizational principles, and abandoning other wage earners. But such practices, it bears repeating, have existed alongside the dominant syndicalist repertoire of aggressive job control and militant direct action guiding American labor.[29]

The broad syndicalist wave that crested in the years around World War I has never entirely receded. Its rising floodwaters engulfed the United States during the mass working-class insurgency of the 1930s when basic industry was unionized, often employing many of the same organizational practices pioneered by industrial syndicalists a generation earlier.[30] Even what most observers regard as the CIO's most distinctive contribution to the strategic arsenal of American workers— the sit-down strike—was actually a Wobbly creation. More than three decades before the dramatic factory occupation at Flint, Michigan, in 1937, some three thousand workers at a General Electric plant in upstate New York, members of an IWW local, sat down on the job in "regular syndicalist fashion," occupying the plant for sixty-five hours to protest the dismissal of three fellow unionists. The 1906 GE strike, like so many other IWW efforts, was lost, but its lessons about militant direct action at the point of production lived on.[31]

In much the same way that the IWW's industrial syndicalism fitted the organizational capacities of an unskilled, newly formed labor force around World War I, the CIO's reliance on industrywide organization, rank-and-file self-activity, and direct action enabled mass production workers to conquer basic industry a generation later. Although the new industrial unions, unlike their predecessors, signed time agreements with employers, their strength continued to reside in the same logic of collective action that privileged large numbers, solidarity, and mass disruption at the point of production—without which, as the Wobblies used to say, "a piece of paper saying 'recognition' isn't worth anything."[32]

The youthful and ambitious CIO, ever alert to new organizing possibilities, nearly doubled in size during its first few years, growing from about 800,000 dues-paying members in 1936 to roughly 1.4 million by 1940. But during those same years the aging and supposedly somnolent AFL grew at almost the same rate, from 2.6 to 4.2 million members—a real increase greater than the entire paid-up membership of the CIO in 1940.[33] Membership comparisons alone, however, do not tell the full story of relative organizational strength, as the CIO's smaller forces were strategically concentrated in the core of the manufacturing economy among mass production workers in auto, steel, electrical, rubber, and textiles, or in such vital extractive industries as mining, petroleum, and natural gas. The AFL's larger army, in contrast, was more widely dispersed across the economic periphery, from highly skilled construction workers to machine operators to truck drivers.

In combat with employers, the AFL and the CIO also deployed their troops differently, reflecting their contrasting logics of collective action and resulting strategies of industrial warfare. The method of guerrilla war pursued by the business syndicalist AFL produced a higher number of skirmishes between 1937 and 1940: 5,300 recorded strikes as compared to 4,400 for the rival CIO. Yet, the CIO, heir to the Wobblies' industrial syndicalism, mobilized far more combatants—2.5 million strikers versus 1.5 million for the AFL—in waging a broadly based war of position against some of the nation's most powerful corporations.[34]

Like veterans of different military campaigns, the AFL's grizzled old warriors and the CIO's Young Turks had little in common, except for the one thing that may have mattered most: their underlying syndicalism. Neither organization, although clearly benefiting from New Deal social legislation that was more favorable to labor, ever viewed politics as much more than a second front in the war against capital.[35] The CIO eventually waded deeper into the chilly political waters of postwar America, but it did so mostly out of self-defense, often as a means of protecting its fragile working-class base on the shop floor from the growing stream of antiunion bills flooding Congress. In taking the fateful plunge into politics, the goal of industrial unionists— much like their more slowly politicizing craft union counterparts at the time—was primarily to keep their organization afloat in increasingly rough seas, not to launch a vessel for independent political action. Borrowing a page from the officially nonpartisan AFL, CIO strategists focused their electoral energies after 1946 on mobilizing a broad cross-section of sympathetic voters to "reward their friends and punish their enemies." While neither organization ever came close to vying for political power within the larger society, both in their own way produced some of the most effective workplace opposition ever mounted against the "industrial despotism" of modern capitalism.[36]

The "spirit of independence and militancy" that syndicalism "energetically fostered in the hearts of the labouring classes" earlier in this century has been dampened but never crushed. It has survived, albeit in weakened form, the extension of contract unionism during the 1930s, the wartime bureaucratization of industrial relations, the postwar expulsion of the Communist-backed left wing of the CIO, and the subsequent consolidation of the labor-capital accord. With the forces of industrial authority closing in on all sides, organized workers have not so much retreated as simply pulled back, regrouping at the point of production where they have managed with varying success to preserve a shrinking social space from which to collectively resist each new managerial assault.[37]

If the "logic" of class collaboration embedded in contract unionism has appeared irrefutable to most academic observers, it has generally persuaded the rank and file only insofar as it has advanced their interests.[38] Otherwise unionists have shown little compunction about defying its central tenet—the no-strike clause—by participating in unauthorized "wildcat" strikes and other proscribed actions.[39] In the face of often-severe sanctions for willful contract violations, workers have found other ways to circumvent rather than break the agreement. A strategy that the Wobblies used to call "striking on the job" continues to inspire the various "in-plant" and "inside" campaigns that have been devised over the years to restrict production: soldiering, working to rule, and countless other contractually "protected" forms of direct action. Such "defensibly disobedient" job actions, David Wellman shows, are capable of subverting even the strongest of contracts.[40]

At most the modern institution of collective bargaining has influenced the scope of industrial conflict. Nothing could eliminate it, not even the much-celebrated postwar "accord" between big labor and big capital. Despite sweeping claims in the 1950s about the "containment" and "institutionalization" of class conflict in the United States, industrial relations in the country's heartland were anything but cordial.[41] Between the late 1940s and the mid-1960s, when the accord was presumably the law of the land, the auto and steel industries were each hit by no fewer than four major work stoppages, in addition to significant "labor revolts" from the bottom carried out by electrical workers, longshoremen, coal miners, machinists, teamsters, and others.[42] The unraveling accord was in shreds a few years later as strike activity reached record levels. By 1970 work stoppages accounted for fully 37 percent of all "man days idle" in the United States, up dramatically from 15 percent just four years earlier. "The productivity of the worker is low," observed a special government task force in 1973, pointing to "absenteeism, turnover rates, wildcat strikes, sabotage, poor-quality products, and a reluctance by workers to commit themselves to their work tasks."[43]

The industrial discipline that seemed so elusive during the relatively prosperous 1970s has returned with a vengeance in today's downsized, globally competitive economy. Deindustrialization and accelerated capital mobility have redrawn traditional battle lines, pulling labor and its supporters away from the trenches of the shop floor to the court of public opinion where the new multinational corporations appear increasingly vulnerable. Sophisticated "corporate campaigns" directed at shareholders, mass protests and boycotts aimed at consumers, and highly publicized legal challenges to corporate decision making have placed organized labor on a more solid footing as it heads into the next century.[44]

The labor movement that will be taking American workers into the new millennium is different in many respects from the one that led them through the twentieth century. Unions now reach into many more areas of the economy, and their membership is that much more representative of the paid labor force and the wider society.[45] The ideological utopias that animated many of its founders have yielded to more modest but no less humane goals of economic fairness and social justice. Warring organizational chauvinists have been replaced by a new generation of idealistic men and women who sit atop a single, unified labor movement that—for all the talk in recent years of union decline—is some twenty times larger and vastly more powerful than it was at the dawn of the twentieth century.

Only the most hardened of cynics could fail to see the promising signs on the horizon. The same labor movement that has been "reviled, held in contempt, or ignored entirely for a generation," as two longtime observers recently noted, "is making sounds like a giant waking from a long slumber." Employers, however, are not trembling in their boots just yet. In the industrial relations arena, where unions are still more like David than Goliath, the smart money is, at present, with the reigning corporate Titans.[46]

But the odds are slowly changing, as unions pour more and more energy and resources into restoring the labor movement as a "mighty force" in American society.[47] Labor and community coalitions are forming on a scale never before seen in this country. At the same time many unions are breaking out of their self-imposed isolation by forging alliances with feminists, civil rights groups, environmentalists, and other new social movements that were formerly seen as part of the problem.[48] On the legal front organized labor and its allies have declared an all-out war on the large body of law that they see increasingly directed at—rather than simply about—them. And unions have even begun to exercise their political muscle in ways not seen since World War II, contributing record sums in recent elections and playing a decisive role in several close state races and ballot measures.[49]

It may all come to naught, however, unless organized labor is somehow able to revitalize itself at the base. Doing so will not be easy. Industrial restructuring continues to erode the historic foundations of American unionism, steadily chipping away at our nation's basic manufacturing industries and in the process transforming their surrounding blue-collar communities into modern-day ghost towns. Yet even here, in the new "industrial wastelands" that have come to dominate the landscape in many regions, the fight is far from over, as production workers and their unions are learning to exploit recent corporate strategies that have left multinational capital more vulnerable than ever to work stoppages at key points within the "global assembly line." In the new world of lean production dominated by "just in time" inventories and growing economic interdependence, a well-timed walkout by six thousand auto workers in central Michigan can easily cripple the largest manufacturing corporation in the country, reminding its seemingly omnipotent CEOs, in words scrawled on a picket sign, "GM may be the heartbeat but the workers are the backbone."[50]

Even as labor's own pulse grows fainter in Detroit's downsizing auto plants and Pittsburgh's rusting steel mills, it is increasingly audible in places like Las Vegas with its booming service sector economy. Led by the hotel workers' union, the desert oasis of gambling has become, according to John Sweeney, president of the AFL-CIO, "the hottest union city in America," largely through the efforts of determined rank and filers like Lynne Myrden, a silver-haired greatgrandmother, restaurant hostess, and "labor firebrand" who "recalls with pride the five times she has been arrested in union sit-ins" since 1984. And she is not alone. Many of her co-workers have reportedly "plunged into union activity with an abandon rarely seen since labor's heyday in the 1930s," sitting-in, walking picket lines, and building solidarity.[51]

It is too early to tell whether Las Vegas has found "the path to a resurgence of growth in the labor movement," as the AFL-CIO's director of organizing believes. What is clear is that success elsewhere will require a similar "tenacity in strikes," relying on the "solidarity" and "unusual militancy" of workers like Lynne Myrden to rebuild the union movement from the ground up, one workplace at a time.[52] It remains a most timely lesson—first learned by an earlier generation of culinary workers at the opposite end of the country—that the true measure of American labor is the strength of its syndicalism, pure and simple.

Notes

Chapter One. Explaining Union Allegiance

1. Carnegie is quoted in Stephen Brier, supervising ed., *Who Built America? Working People and the Nation's Economy, Politics, Culture, and Society,* vol. 2: *From the Gilded Age to the Present* (New York: Pantheon, 1992), 160.

2. Union membership figures for the United States are from Leo Wolman, *The Growth of American Trade Unions, 1880–1923* (New York: National Bureau of Economic Research, 1924), 33. German and French union membership figures are from William A. McConagha, *Development of the Labor Movement in Great Britain, France, and Germany* (Chapel Hill: University of North Carolina Press, 1942), 75, 179. George Sayers and Robert Price, *Profiles of Union Growth* (Oxford: Basil Blackwell, 1980), 37, 87, 133.

3. Wolman, *Growth of American Trade Unions,* 62.

4. The founding meeting of the IWW is covered in most of the standard organizational histories, including Paul Brissenden, "The I.W.W.: A Study of American Syndicalism" (Ph.D. dissertation, Columbia University, 1919), chap. 2, esp. 71; Philip S. Foner, *History of the Labor Movement in the United States,* vol. 4: *The Industrial Workers of the World, 1905–1917* (New York: International Publishers, 1965), chap. 1; and Melvyn Dubofsky, *We Shall Be All: A History of the Industrial Workers of the World,* 2d ed. (Urbana: University of Illinois Press, 1988), 81–87.

5. Of the roughly 2 million union members in the United States in 1905, nearly 1.6 million were affiliated with the AFL. See Wolman, *Growth of American Trade Unions,* 122.

6. On the relationship between the IWW and the AFL, see Foner, *History of the Labor Movement;* Dubofsky, *We Shall Be All;* Brissenden, "I.W.W."; and Joseph Robert Conlin, *Bread and Roses Too: Studies of the Wobblies* (Westport, Conn.: Greenwood Press, 1969).

7. The quote on an "industrial crime" is from Dubofsky, *We Shall Be All*, 94.

8. Gompers is quoted in Harold C. Livesay, *Samuel Gompers and Organized Labor in America* (Boston: Little, Brown, 1978), 107. On the precursors of the AFL's business unionism, see Philip Taft, "On the Origins of Business Unionism," *Industrial and Labor Relations Review* 17, no. 1 (October 1963): 2–39. Gompers's relationship to Marxism evolved over time and was far more complex than is suggested by his eventual repudiation of the Socialist party. By his own account, Gompers believed that organizing workers at the point of production was more consistent with Marx's own thinking than were the efforts of Socialists and others who saw unions simply as vehicles for organizing the political struggle against capitalism. However critical he became of Socialist politicians in later years, the young Gompers endorsed their "ultimate ends, including the abolition of the wage system." See William Dick, *Labor and Socialism in America: The Gompers Era* (Port Washington, N.Y.: Kennikat Press, 1972), 31. For dissenting views on Gompers's self-styled Marxism, see Bernard Mandel, *Samuel Gompers: A Biography* (Yellow Springs, Ohio: Antioch Press, 1963); and Stuart Bruce Kaufman, *Samuel Gompers and the Origins of the American Federation of Labor, 1848–1896* (Westport, Conn.: Greenwood Press, 1978). For a recent, admittedly provocative, reassessment of Gompers's affinities with Marxism, see Michael Merrill, "The Other Great Evasion: Samuel Gompers, the AFL, and Workers Power in the United States," paper presented at the annual meeting of the Social Science History Association, 1993. Still another view of Gompers sees him as embracing a "populist" rhetoric that resonated with the sensibilities of American workers while avoiding the political liabilities of an "alien" Marxism. See Michael Kazin, *The Populist Persuasion: An American History* (New York: Basic Books, 1995), 55.

9. The quote on the futility of voting is from Dubofsky, *We Shall Be All*, 83. The reference to "slowshulism" is from Conlin, *Bread and Roses*, 122.

10. Trotsky is quoted in Gabriel Kolko, "The Decline of American Radicalism in the Twentieth Century," *Studies on the Left* 6, no. 5 (September-October 1966): 15. Haywood's comment is from his testimony before Congress in "Final Report and Testimony," Submitted to Congress by the Commission on Industrial Relations, vol. 11 (Washington, D.C.: GPO, 1916), 64th Cong., 1st sess., Senate Doc. No. 415, p. 10583. Haywood's life is the subject of biographies by Joseph R. Conlin, *Big Bill Haywood and the Radical Union Movement* (Syracuse: Syracuse University Press, 1969); and Peter Carlson, *Roughneck: The Life and Times of Big Bill Haywood* (New York: W. W. Norton, 1983).

11. Debs is quoted in Dubofsky, *We Shall Be All*, 96. Given the IWW's generally porous organizational boundaries, poor record-keeping, and high turnover rates, membership figures are rough approximations at best. The estimate of two to three million members is from Melvyn Dubofsky, *Indus-*

trialism and the American Worker, 1865–1920 (Arlington Heights, Ill.: AHM Publishing, 1975), 103. Monthly averages are based on membership data furnished by IWW General Secretary Vincent St. John, as reported by Brissenden, "I.W.W.," 267, 268, 357.

12. Selig Perlman, *A Theory of the Labor Movement* (New York: Macmillan, 1928), viii–ix. On the widespread and continuing influence of Perlman's theory, see Charles A. Gulick and Melvin K. Bers, "Insight and Illusion in Perlman's *Theory of the Labor Movement,*" *Industrial and Labor Relations Review* 6, no. 4 (July 1953): 510–31; Andrew Dawson, "History and Ideology: Fifty Years of 'Job Consciousness,' " *Literature and History* 8 (Autumn 1978): 223–42; John H. M. Laslett, "The American Tradition of Labor Theory and Its Relevance to the Contemporary Working Class," in Irving Louis Horowitz, John C. Leggett, and Martin Oppenheimer, eds., *The American Working-Class: Prospects for the 1980s* (New Brunswick: Transaction Books, 1979), 3–30; James S. Roberts, "The New Labor History in America: Problems and Prospects," *Archiv für Sozial Geschichte* 23 (1983): 523–39; and Howard Kimeldorf, "Bringing Unions Back In (Or Why We Need a New Old Labor History)," *Labor History* 32, no. 1 (Winter 1991): 91–103.

13. The basic thrust of Perlman's work, I would argue, has withstood surprisingly well the many waves of attack over the years, including the massive assault launched by the "new" labor historians more than a quarter century ago. While the turn to social history has illuminated vast stretches of human experience that escaped Perlman's narrow institutional focus, it has generally failed to engage the central tenets of Perlman's theory concerning the basis of union loyalty. With this latest round of scholarship having thus far failed to produce a more synthetic statement of class formation, Perlman's work remains, as Michael Kazin argues, "by default, the only intelligent, overarching explanation of why American workers behave the way they did and do." See Michael Kazin, "Struggling with the Class Struggle: Marxism and the Search for a Synthesis of U.S. Labor History," *Labor History* 28, no. 4 (Fall 1987): 497. On the challenges of forging a "new synthesis" in labor studies that transcends the old Wisconsin School of Commons and Perlman, see the early and influential statement by David Brody, "Labor History in the 1970s: Toward a History of the American Worker," in Michael Kammen, ed., *The Past Before Us: Contemporary Historical Writing in the United States* (Ithaca: Cornell University Press, 1980), 252–69, and his more recent views in "Reconciling the Old Labor History and the New," *Pacific Historical Review* 62, no. 1 (February 1993): 1–18. Also see the collection edited by J. Carroll Moody and Alice Kessler-Harris, *Perspectives on American Labor History: The Problems of Synthesis* (Dekalb: Northern Illinois University Press, 1989); Philip Scranton, "The Workplace, Technology, and Theory in American Labor History," *International Labor and Working-Class History* 35 (Spring 1989): 3–22; and Jerry Lembcke, "Labor History's 'Synthesis Debate': Sociological Interventions," *Science and Society* 59, no.

2 (Summer 1995): 137–73, followed by a symposium in *Science and Society* 60, no. 4 (Winter 1996–97): 467–94.

14. The thesis of "collective brain damage" is, as Frank Parkin argues, the common "diagnosis" offered by twentieth-century Marxists in accounting for the "false consciousness" or "embourgeoisement" of the Western working class. See Frank Parkin, *Marxism and Class Theory: A Bourgeois Critique* (New York: Columbia University Press, 1979), 81.

15. "Given governmental repression of all radical working-class movements," Vanneman and Cannon argue, ". . . the workers' decisions to align themselves with the more successful AFL says little about their lack of class consciousness; it reflects a simple rationality in the face of given historical alternatives." See Reeve Vanneman and Lynn Weber Cannon, *The American Perception of Class* (Philadelphia: Temple University Press, 1987), 31.

16. The especially violent and militant character of working-class struggle in the United States is well documented. See, for example, Seymour Martin Lipset, *The First New Nation: The United States in Historical and Comparative Perspective* (Garden City, N.Y.: Anchor Books, 1967), 204–7; Phillip Taft and Phillip Ross, "American Labor Violence: Its Causes, Character and Comparative Perspectives," in Hugh Davis Graham and Ted Robert Gurr, eds., *Violence in America: Historical and Comparative Perspectives* (New York: Bantam, 1969), 1:221–301; H. M. Gitelman, "Perspectives on American Industrial Violence," *Business History Review* 47, no. 1 (Spring 1973): 1–23; Ronald Filippelli, ed., *Labor Conflict in the United States: An Encyclopedia* (New York: Garland, 1990); and Victoria Charlotte Hattam, *Labor Visions and State Power: The Origins of Business Unionism in the United States* (Princeton: Princeton University Press, 1993), 9–10.

17. " 'Why is there no socialism' thus becomes a problem of explaining the *disjuncture* of industrial relations and political practice in the United States." See Eric Foner, "Why Is There No Socialism in the United States?" *History Workshop* 17 (Spring 1984): 60. While this disjuncture may have been wider in the United States, it was by no means absent from early-twentieth-century Western European working-class movements. See Geoff Eley and Keith Nield, "Why Does Social History Ignore Politics?" *Social History* 5, no. 2 (May 1980): 262.

18. The militancy or industrial radicalism of the rank and file has seldom been the explicit focus of the new labor historians, whose critical sights, when trained on the workplace, have targeted the ideological and political conservatism of American workers that was a cornerstone of the old Wisconsin School of labor history. On the contrast between political and industrial radicalism, see the insightful comparative analysis of French and U.S. workers by Scott Lash, *The Militant Worker: Class and Radicalism in France and America* (Rutherford, N.J.: Fairleigh Dickinson University Press, 1984).

19. Social scientists and historians alike have generally followed Lenin in dismissing militant workplace struggles as a "mere economism," presumably

incapable of challenging capital's hegemony in production. See, for example, Laslett, "American Tradition of Labor Theory," 8; Michael Mann, *Consciousness and Action Among the Western Working Class* (London: Macmillan, 1973), 24–33; and Anthony Giddens, *The Class Structure of the Advanced Societies* (New York: Harper & Row, 1973), 205–15. For a more complex rendering of "economism," see Laurie Clements, "Reference Groups and Trade Union Consciousness," in Laurie Clements and Tom Clarke, eds., *Trade Unions Under Capitalism* (Atlantic Highlands, N.J.: Humanities Press, 1978), 320–23; David Matza and David Wellman, "The Ordeal of Consciousness," *Theory and Society* 9, no. 1 (January 1980): 1–27; Rick Fantasia, *Cultures of Solidarity: Consciousness, Action, and Contemporary American Workers* (Berkeley and Los Angeles: University of California Press, 1988), 237–39; John Kelly, *Trade Unions and Socialist Politics* (London: Verso, 1988), 101, 118; and Michael Wallace, "Aggressive Economism, Defensive Control: Contours of American Labour Militancy," *Economic and Industrial Democracy* 10, no. 1 (February 1989): 7–34.

20. There has been surprisingly little attention devoted to Local 8, until quite recently. Aside from brief references scattered throughout more general labor histories, for many years the only scholarly study devoted to Philadelphia's longshoremen was an unpublished seminar paper written in 1975 by Janet Asteroff, then a graduate student in history at the University of Wisconsin. See Janet Asteroff, "The Intrusion of Ideology: Wobbly Marine Workers of Philadelphia, 1913–1926," Box 10, Folders 7, 8, Fred Thompson Papers, Reuther Archives. Two very fine recent works by young historians have filled this gap: Lisa McGirr, "Black and White Longshoremen in the IWW: A History of the Philadelphia Marine Transport Workers Industrial Union Local 8," *Labor History* 37, no. 3 (Spring 1995): 377–402; and Peter Cole, "Shaping Up and Shipping Out: The Philadelphia Waterfront During and After the IWW Years, 1913–1940" (Ph.D. dissertation, Georgetown University, 1997). Cole's study is by far the most thorough and balanced account to date of Local 8.

21. The instability of most IWW efforts is a major theme in David Saposs, *Left-Wing Unionism: A Study of Radical Policies and Tactics* (New York: International Publishers, 1926). The Local 8 leader is Walter Nef, whose views are drawn from his correspondence with Agnes Inglis, dated July 3, 1936, Agnes Inglis Papers, Labadie Collection, Special Collections Library, University of Michigan (hereafter cited as Inglis Papers).

22. The history of New York's culinary unionism has been told as part of the larger story of the industry. See Jay Rubin and M. J. Obermeirer, *Growth of a Union: The Life and Times of Edward Flore* (New York: Comet Press, 1943); Mathew Josephson, *Union House Union Bar: The History of the Hotel and Restaurant Employees and Bartenders International Union AFL-CIO* (New York: Random House, 1956); Morris A. Horowitz, *The New York Hotel Industry: A Labor Relations Study* (Cambridge, Mass.: Harvard University

Press, 1960); and Dorothy Sue Cobble, "Sisters in the Craft: Waitresses and Their Unions in the Twentieth Century" (Ph.D. dissertation, Stanford University, 1986).

23. On the logic and application of "parallel demonstration" as a research strategy, see Theda Skocpol and Margaret Somers, "The Uses of Comparative History in Macrosocial Inquiry," *Comparative Studies in Society and History* 22, no. 2 (April 1980): 176–78.

24. Just as many students of the AFL have attributed its success, at least in part, to the conservatism of American workers, students of the IWW have tended to portray their supporters as products of a diffuse, frontier radicalism. See the influential study by Melvyn Dubofsky, "The Origins of Western Working Class Radicalism, 1890–1905," *Labor History* 7, no. 2 (Spring 1966): 131–54. Yet, despite all of the research that has been carried out on the IWW over the past three decades, the mental worlds of the Wobbly rank and file are still, as William Preston concluded years ago, "a vast uncharted historical wasteland. . . . [N]o historian knows how much tacit support for Wobblies existed . . . or to what extent the militant activists represented, then or now, a much larger but historically inert mass of radical protest." See William Preston, "Shall This Be All? U.S. Historians versus William D. Haywood et al.," *Labor History* 12, no. 3 (Summer 1971): 435–53.

25. Henry Pelling, *American Labor* (Chicago: University of Chicago Press, 1960), 221; Russell Jacoby, "Political Economy and Class Unconsciousness," *Theory and Society* 5, no. 1 (January 1978): 11–18; P. K. Edwards, *Strikes in the United States, 1881–1974* (Oxford: Basil Blackwell, 1981), 251; Michael Kazin, "A People Not a Class: Rethinking the Political Language of the Modern U.S. Labor Movement," in Mike Davis and Michael Sprinker, eds., *Reshaping the U.S. Left: Popular Struggles in the 1980s* (London: Verso, 1988), 257. Neatly summarizing the consensus view, Harold Wilensky writes, "American labor is conservative. Compared to European labor, it shows a low degree of class consciousness." See Harold L. Wilensky, "Class, Class Consciousness, and American Workers," in Maurice Zeitlin, ed., *American Society, Inc.: Studies of the Social Structure and Political Economy of the United States* (Chicago: Rand McNally College Publishing, 1977), 461.

26. Gerald N. Grob, *Workers and Utopia: A Study of Ideological Conflict in the American Labor Movement, 1865–1900* (Chicago: Quadrangle Books, 1969), 189, 181; Michael Harrington, *Socialism* (New York: Bantam, 1972), 131. The reference to unionists as "upholders of the capitalist system" is from Dick, *Labor and Socialism*, 4. John Patrick Diggins, *The Rise and Fall of the American Left* (New York: W. W. Norton, 1992), 67.

27. The supposed affection of American workers for capitalism is a recurrent theme in the literature. Werner Sombart, writing in 1905, observed the "intimate . . . relation of the American laborer to capitalism" and continued, "I believe he enters into it with all his heart: I believe he loves it."

Sombart is quoted in Livesay, *Samuel Gompers,* 126. The flip side of this argument, of course, is that workers therefore do not hate capitalists. "With relatively few exceptions," asserts neo-Marxist Bertell Ollman, "[workers] don't really and deeply hate capitalists . . . because they have never been able to set off a sufficiently unencumbered target to hate." See Bertell Ollman, "Toward Class Consciousness Next Time: Marx and the Working Class," *Politics and Society* 3, no. 1 (Fall 1972): 12.

28. Vanneman and Cannon, *American Perception of Class,* chaps. 1, 2. Similarly, Andrew Dawson argues that "the absence of [labor-based] working-class political institutions in the United States has been almost uniformly ascribed to a lack of class consciousness among American workers." See Andrew Dawson, "The Parameters of Craft Consciousness: The Social Outlook of the Skilled Worker, 1890–1920," in Dirk Hoerder, ed., *American Labor and Immigrant History, 1877–1920s: Recent European Research* (Urbana: University of Illinois, 1983), 135. On the general methodological problems of gaining access to "subjective worlds that were once occupied by people who are now dead," see Paul Rock, "Some Problems of Interpretative Historiography," *British Journal of Sociology* 27, no. 3 (September 1976): 353–69; and John H. Goldthorpe, "The Uses of History in Sociology: Reflections on Some Recent Tendencies," *British Journal of Sociology* 42, no. 2 (June 1991): 211–30. The resulting difficulty of inferring ideas from behavior has redirected sociological scholarship away from elaborating ever more complex typologies of worker "consciousness" to focusing on the sources of collective action. For programmatic statements of this position, see Gordon Marshall, "Some Remarks on the Study of Working-Class Consciousness," *Politics and Society* 12, no. 3 (1983): 263–301; and Ira Katznelson, "Working-Class Formation: Constructing Cases and Comparisons," in Ira Katznelson and Aristide Zolberg, eds., *Working-Class Formation: Nineteenth-Century Patterns in Western Europe and the United States* (Princeton: Princeton University Press, 1986), 3–41. The strongest and most compelling case against studying consciousness apart from practice has been made by Fantasia, *Cultures of Solidarity,* esp. chap. 1.

29. The literature on socialism's incompatibility with American culture is extensive, stretching across the theoretical and political spectrum. See, for example, Leon Sampson, *Towards a United Front* (New York: Farrar and Rinehart, 1933); Louis Hartz, *The Liberal Tradition in America: An Interpretation of American Political Thought Since the Revolution* (San Diego: Harcourt Brace Jovanovich, 1955); Lipset, *The First New Nation,* pt. 2; Werner Sombart, *Why Is There No Socialism in the United States?* ed. C. T. Husbands, trans. Patricia M. Hocking and C. T. Husbands (White Plains, N.Y.: International Arts and Sciences Press, 1976; originally published 1906); Daniel Bell, *The End of Ideology: On the Exhaustion of Political Ideas in the Fifties* (Glencoe: Free Press, 1960), chap. 12; and Antonio Gramsci, "Americanism and Fordism," in Gramsci, *Selections from the Prison Note-*

books of Antonio Gramsci, ed. and trans. Quintin Hoare and Geoffrey Nowell Smith (New York: International Publishers, 1971), 277–318.

30. Hartz, *Liberal Tradition;* Edward Countryman, "American Liberalism and the Problem of American Socialism," in Jean Heffer and Jeanine
Rovet, eds., *Why Is There No Socialism in the United States?* (Paris: Ecole
des Hautes Etudes en Sciences Sociales, 1988), 87–100. There is also a more
"materialist" argument in which the structure of the party system is seen as
inhibiting third-party efforts, thus producing a conservative consensus. See
Richard J. Oestreicher, "Urban Working-Class Political Behavior and Theories of American Electoral Politics, 1870–1940," *Journal of American History* 74, no. 4 (March 1988): 1257–86; and Seymour Martin Lipset, "Radicalism or Reformism: The Sources of Working-Class Politics," *American
Political Science Review* 77, no. 1 (March 1983): 1–19.

31. Seymour Martin Lipset and Reinhard Bendix, *Social Mobility in Industrial Society* (Berkeley and Los Angeles: University of California Press,
1959); Stephen Thernstrom, "Socialism and Social Mobility," in John H. M.
Laslett and Seymour Martin Lipset, eds., *Failure of a Dream? Essays in the
History of American Socialism,* rev. ed. (Berkeley and Los Angeles: University of California Press, 1984), 408–26.

32. Stanley Aronowitz, *False Promises: The Shaping of American Working Class Consciousness* (New York: McGraw-Hill, 1973), chap. 3; John Bodnar, "Immigration, Kinship, and the Rise of Working-Class Realism in Industrial America," *Journal of Social History* 14, no. 1 (Fall 1980): 45–65.

33. See, for example, Bruce Laurie, *Artisans into Workers: Labor in
Nineteenth-Century America* (New York: Hill and Wang, 1989); Linda
Schneider, "The Citizen Striker: Workers' Ideology in the Homestead Strike
of 1892," *Labor History* 23, no. 1 (Winter 1982): 47–66; and Sean Wilentz,
"Against Exceptionalism: Class Consciousness and the American Labor
Movement, 1790–1920," *International Labor and Working-Class History* 26
(Fall 1984): 1–24. The old labor history, to its credit, never denied the ex-
istence of these earlier radicalizing currents, only that they represented the
mainstream of labor development.

34. Kim Voss, *The Making of American Exceptionalism: The Knights of
Labor and Class Formation in the Nineteenth Century* (Ithaca: Cornell University Press, 1993), xi.

35. The past decade has witnessed an explosion of scholarship locating
the failure of U.S. labor radicalism in the strength of institutional and social
structural forces, not in the presumed weakness of worker ideology. On the
conservatizing role of the judiciary, see Christopher Tomlins, *The State and
the Unions: Labor Relations, Law, and the Organized Labor Movement in
America, 1880–1960* (Cambridge: Cambridge University Press, 1985); Michael Wallace, Beth A. Rubin, and Brian T. Smith, "American Labor Law:
Its Impact on Working-Class Militancy, 1901–1980," *Social Science History*
12, no. 1 (Spring 1988): 1–29; William H. Forbath, *Law and the Shaping of*

the *American Labor Movement* (Cambridge, Mass.: Harvard University Press, 1991); Holly J. McCammon, " 'Government by Injunction': The U.S. Judiciary and Strike Action in the Late 19th and Early 20th Centuries," *Work and Occupations* 20, no. 2 (May 1993): 174–204; and Daniel R. Ernst, *Lawyers Against Labor: From Individual Rights to Corporate Liberalism* (Urbana: University of Illinois Press, 1995). The state's role during the decisive years around World War I has been explored by Gerald Friedman, "The State and the Making of the Working Class," *Theory and Society* 17, no. 3 (May 1988): 403–30; Hattam, *Labor Visions and State Power*; and Jeffrey Haydu, *Making American Industry Safe for Democracy: Comparative Perspectives on the State and Employee Representation in the Era of World War I* (Urbana: University of Illinois Press, 1997). On the role, more generally, of political processes in deflecting the left, see Theodore Lowi, "Why Is There No Socialism in the United States? A Federal Analysis," *International Political Science Review* 5, no. 4 (1984): 369–80; Judith Stepan-Norris and Maurice Zeitlin, " 'Who Gets the Bird?' or, How the Communists Won Power and Trust in America's Unions," *American Sociological Review* 54 (1989): 503–23; and Karen Orren, *Belated Feudalism: Labor, the Law, and Liberal Development in the United States* (Cambridge: Cambridge University Press, 1991). Ethnic and racial stratification as a counterweight to class mobilization has been taken up by Gwendolyn Mink, *Old Labor and New Immigrants in American Political Development: Union, Party, and State, 1875–1920* (Ithaca: Cornell University Press, 1986); and Eric L. Hirsch, *Urban Revolt: Ethnic Politics in the Nineteenth-Century Chicago Labor Movement* (Berkeley and Los Angeles: University of California Press, 1990). Organizational dynamics have been explored by Goran Therborn, "Why Some Classes Are More Successful than Others," *New Left Review* 138 (March-April 1983): 37–55; Jerry Lembcke, *Capitalist Development and Class Capacities: Marxist Theory and Union Organization* (New York: Greenwood Press, 1988); Gary Marks, *Unions in Politics: Britain, Germany, and the United States in the Nineteenth and Early Twentieth Centuries* (Princeton: Princeton University Press, 1989); and Carol Connel and Kim Voss, "Formal Organization and the Fate of Social Movements: Craft Association and Class Alliance in the Knights of Labor," *American Sociological Review* 55 (April 1990): 255–69. The role of employer resistance is examined by Larry Griffin, Michael Wallace, and Beth Rubin, "Capitalist Resistance to the Organization of Labor Before the New Deal: Why? How? Success?" *American Sociological Review* 51, no. 2 (April 1986): 147–67; Jeffrey Haydu, "Employers, Unions, and American Exceptionalism: A Comparative View," *International Review of Social History* 33, no. 1 (1988): 25–41; and Sanford M. Jacoby, "American Exceptionalism Revisited: The Importance of Management," in Sanford Jacoby, ed., *Masters to Managers: Historical and Comparative Perspectives on American Employers* (New York: Columbia University Press, 1991), 173–200. Repression, at the hands of both private and public actors, has been emphasized by Daniel R. Fusfeld, *The Rise and Repression of Radical Labor in the United States, 1877–1918* (Chicago: Charles H. Kerr, 1980); and Patricia Cayo Sexton, *The War on Labor and the Left: Understanding America's Unique Conservatism* (Boulder: Westview Press, 1991).

36. The theoretical tenets of the resource mobilization perspective are laid out in pathbreaking works by John D. McCarthy and Mayer N. Zald, *The Trend of Social Movements in America: Professionalization and Resource Mobilization* (Morristown, N.J.: General Learning Press, 1973); and Charles Tilly, *From Mobilization to Revolution* (New York: Random House, 1978). For a more recent overview of research and theorizing on social movements, see the fine collection edited by Doug McAdam, John D. McCarthy, and Mayer N. Zald, *Comparative Perspectives on Social Movements: Political Opportunities, Mobilizing Structures, and Cultural Framings* (New York: Cambridge University Press, 1996). On the impact and promise of the new institutionalism within labor studies, see Jonathan Zeitlin, "From Labour History to the History of Industrial Relations," *Economic History Review* 40, no. 2 (1987): 159–84; Eric Arneson, "Crusaders Against Critics: A View from the United States on the 'Rank and File' Critique and Other Catalogues of Labour History's Alleged Ills," *International Review of Social History* 35, no. 1 (1990): 106–27; and Ira Katznelson, "The 'Bourgeois' Dimension: A Provocation About Institutions, Politics, and the Future of Labor History," *International Labor and Working-Class History* 46 (Fall 1994): 7–32.

37. Amy Bridges, "Becoming American: The Working Classes in the United States before the Civil War," in Katznelson and Zolberg, *Working-Class Formation,* 620–21.

38. Hirsch, *Urban Revolt,* 210. On the relationship more generally between urban space and political radicalism, see Ira Katznelson, *City Trenches: Urban Politics and the Patterning of Class in the United States* (New York: Pantheon, 1981); Judith Stepan-Norris, "The Integration of Workplace and Community Relations at the Ford Rouge Plant, 1930s–1940s," *Political Power and Social Theory* 11 (1997): 3–44; and Roger V. Gould, *Insurgent Identities: Class, Community, and Protest in Paris from 1848 to the Commune* (Chicago: University of Chicago Press, 1995).

39. On the Knights of Labor, see Voss, *The Making of American Exceptionalism;* and Leon Fink, *Workingmen's Democracy: The Knights of Labor and American Politics* (Urbana: University of Illinois Press, 1983). For a more general analysis of the role of repression in containing American labor radicalism, see Fusfeld, *Rise and Repression;* and Sexton, *War on Labor.*

40. "American trade unionists at the end of the nineteenth century were not revolutionaries. . . . [B]y the 1890s a majority of trade unionists in the United States rejected anarchism, socialism, and syndicalism." See Martin Shefter, "Trade Unions and Political Machines: The Organization and Disorganization of the American Working Class in the Late Nineteenth Cen-

tury," in Katznelson and Zolberg, *Working-Class Formation,* 198. The traditional and still dominant view of the AFL as a bastion of craft conservatism has been questioned by Christopher L. Tomlins, "AFL Unions in the 1930s: Their Performance in Historical Perspective," *Journal of American History* 65, no. 4 (March 1979): 1021–42; Michael Kazin, *Barons of Labor: The San Francisco Building Trades and Union Power in the Progressive Era* (Urbana: University of Illinois Press, 1987); David Montgomery, "Thinking about American Workers in the 1920s," *International Labor and Working-Class History* 32 (Fall 1987): 4–24; and Dorothy Sue Cobble, *Dishing It Out: Waitresses and Their Unions in the Twentieth Century* (Urbana: University of Illinois Press, 1991).

41. Robert Hoxie, *Trade Unionism in the United States* (New York: D. Appleton, 1920), 155. Challenging those who dismiss the Wobblies as merely "a colorful footnote in the American labor story," Staughton Lynd has recently declared that "the Wobblies were right." He then goes on to praise their "horizontal process" of organizing workers across industries and even countries, as the best strategy for countering the growing power of today's multinational corporations. See Staughton Lynd, *Living Inside Our Hope: A Steadfast Radical's Thoughts on Rebuilding the Movement* (Ithaca: Cornell University Press, 1997), 198.

42. Hoxie, *Trade Unionism,* 154, 160, 159; Perlman, *Theory,* 288n, 227. Louis Levine, however, argued that syndicalism was "born of conditions of life in America." See Louis Levine, "The Development of Syndicalism in America," *Political Science Quarterly* 28, no. 3 (September 1913): 452. The only labor movement that actually called itself syndicalist—the Syndicalist League of North America, led by William Z. Foster—never sank deep roots in American soil, reaching a peak membership of "perhaps 2,000" in no more than a dozen branches. See James R. Barrett's introduction to Earl C. Ford and William Z. Foster, *Syndicalism* (Chicago: Charles H. Kerr, 1990; originally published as a pamphlet in 1912), viii.

43. John Graham Brooks was one of the first to attach the syndicalist label to the IWW, in his *American Syndicalism: The I.W.W.* (New York: Macmillan, 1913). On the international dimensions of syndicalism, see Larry Peterson, "The One Big Union in International Perspective: Revolutionary Industrial Unionism, 1900–1925," in James F. Cronin and Carmen Sirianni, eds., *Work, Community, and Power: The Experience of Labor in Europe and America, 1900–1925* (Philadelphia: Temple University Press, 1983), 49–87; Wayne Thorpe, *"The Workers Themselves": Revolutionary Syndicalism and International Labour, 1913–1923* (Dordrecht: Kluwer, 1989); and Marcel van der Linden and Wayne Thorpe, eds., *Revolutionary Syndicalism: An International Perspective* (Aldershot, U.K.: Scolar Press, 1990). Perhaps the only common features of syndicalism are its antistatist orientation and its reliance on worker self-activity at the point of production. In its familiar left-wing incarnation, syndicalism has served as an ideological weapon for

opposing capitalism, though there have been right-wing and, more commonly, nonideological expressions as well. Institutionally, it has championed craft organization in some countries and industrial organization in others. See John Spargo, *Syndicalism, Industrial Unionism and Socialism* (New York: B. W. Huebsch, 1913); and Conlin, *Bread and Roses,* chap. 1. Capturing the formlessness of syndicalism, Wobbly supporter Bessy Beatty, writing in 1914, described it "as nebulous as mood rings, . . . as varying as the face of a moody woman." Beatty is quoted in Salvatore Salerno, *Red November, Black November: Culture and Community in the Industrial Workers of the World* (Albany: State University of New York Press, 1989), 46.

44. The quote on the Wobblies challenging production is from Mike Davis, "The Stop Watch and the Wooden Shoe: Scientific Management and the Industrial Workers of the World," in James Green, ed., *Workers' Struggles, Past and Present: A "Radical America" Reader* (Philadelphia: Temple University Press, 1983), 98. The reference to "radical labor leadership" is from Harold Freeman, *Toward Socialism in America* (Cambridge: Schenkman Publishing, 1980), 145. The reference to a "class-conscious movement" is from Roberta Ash, *Social Movements in America* (Chicago: Markham, 1972), 10, 213.

45. The quote on Wobblies making converts is from James R. Green, "The Brotherhood of Timber Workers, 1910–1913: A Radical Response to Industrial Capitalism in the Southern U.S.A.," *Past and Present* 60 (August 1973): 179. Debs is quoted in Michael Goldfield, *The Decline of Organized Labor in the United States* (Chicago: University of Chicago Press, 1987), 48. The characterizations of Gompers are from Aronowitz, *False Promises,* 153; Frank Annunziato, "Commodity Unionism," *Rethinking Marxism* 3, no. 2 (Summer 1990): 23; and Maurice Isserman, " 'God Bless Our American Institutions': The Labor History of John R. Commons," *Labor History* 17, no. 3 (Summer 1976): 326.

46. Will Hershberg, "American Marxist Political Theory," in Donald Drew Egbert and Stow Persons, eds., *Socialism and American Life* (Princeton: Princeton University Press, 1952), 1:491.

47. Lipset, *The First New Nation,* 171, 180–81.

48. Kazin, *Populist Persuasion,* chap. 3.

49. Despite Lipset's emphasis on cultural factors in explaining the character of American labor as embodied in the AFL, he also recognizes the role of syndicalism, which he sees as part of the antistatism of national political culture. See Seymour Martin Lipset, *American Exceptionalism: A Double-Edged Sword* (New York: W. W. Norton, 1996), 37.

50. Melvyn Dubofsky, "The Rise and Fall of Revolutionary Syndicalism in the United States," in van der Linden and Thorpe, *Revolutionary Syndicalism,* 210.

51. David Montgomery, "The 'New Unionism' and the Transformation of Workers' Consciousness in America, 1909–1922," *Journal of Social His-*

tory 7, no. 4 (Summer 1974): 509. Montgomery's thesis came under sharp attack by sympathetic critics. See James R. Green, "Comments on the Montgomery Paper," *Journal of Social History* 7, no. 4 (Summer 1974): 530–35; Jean Monds, "Workers' Control and the Historians: A New Economism," *New Left Review* 97 (May-June 1976): 81–104; Lawrence T. McDonnell, " 'You Are Too Sentimental': Problems and Suggestions for a New Labor History," *Journal of Social History* 17 (Summer 1984): 629–54; and Daniel Clawson, *Bureaucracy and the Labor Process: The Transformation of U.S. Industry, 1860–1920* (New York: Monthly Review Press, 1980), 160–66. For a more sweeping syndicalist-influenced interpretation of American labor history, see the classic study by Jeremy Brecher, *Strike!* (Greenwich, Conn.: Fawcett, 1972).

52. In treating syndicalism as a practice of resistance, Montgomery followed the lead of Andre Tridon, who in 1913 described syndicalism as "a practice not a theory." See Andre Tridon, *The New Unionism* (New York: B. W. Huebsch, 1913), 17.

53. The term "business syndicalism" is used here to apply to a particular organizational logic of mobilization and not, as in Michael Kazin's use of the term, the fusion of militant tactics with economically stable bargaining relations. See Kazin, *Barons of Labor*, 150.

54. For an analysis of the "macro historical structural forces" leading the AFL to embrace an exclusionary "logic of particularism," see Antoine Joseph, "The Solidarity of Skilled Workers: Creating a Logic of Particularism," *Journal of Historical Sociology* 6, no. 3 (September 1993): 288–310.

55. On Gramsci's views regarding industrial legality and trade unionism in general, see Richard Hyman, "Workers' Control and Revolutionary Theory," in Ralph Miliband and John Saville, eds., *The Socialist Register* (London: Merlin Press, 1974), 257–65.

56. Luca Perrone, "Positional Power, Strikes and Wages," *American Sociological Review* 49, no. 3 (June 1984): 412–26. On the historical relationship between strategic location within production and growth of unionization, see Benson Soffer, "A Theory of Trade Union Development: The Role of the 'Autonomous' Workman," *Labor History* 1, no. 2 (Spring 1960): 141–63.

57. The concept "organizational weapon" is borrowed from the discussion of Leninist party organization in Philip Selzick, *The Organizational Weapon* (New York: McGraw-Hill, 1952). On the role of "craft radicals" in the United States and Britain, see Jeffrey Haydu, *Between Craft and Class: Skilled Workers and Factory Politics in the United States and Britain, 1890–1922* (Berkeley and Los Angeles: University of California Press, 1988).

58. On the role of unions in stratifying labor by race and gender, see the influential analysis by Edna Bonacich, "A Theory of Ethnic Antagonism: The Split Labor Market," *American Sociological Review* 37, no. 5 (October 1972): 547–59; and Ruth Milkman, "Organizing the Sexual Division of

Labor: Historical Perspectives on 'Women's Work' and the American Labor Movement," *Socialist Review* 10, no. 1 (January-February 1980): 95–150.

59. For an illuminating discussion of the ways in which the struggles of American workers have gone "beyond the confines of 'wage and job consciousness' or 'bread and butter' unionism," see David Montgomery, "The Past and Future of Workers' Control," in Green, *Workers' Struggles*, 389–405.

60. The critique of theoretical economism has been aimed at Marxian accounts of class that focus exclusively on production relations. See, for example, Louis Althusser, *Essays in Self-Criticism* (London: New Left Books, 1976), 85–88; Charles Bettleheim, *Class Struggles in the U.S.S.R. First Period: 1919–1923* (New York: Monthly Review Press, 1976), preface; and William H. Sewell, Jr., "Classes and Their Historical Formation: Critical Reflections on E. P. Thompson's Theory of Working-Class Formation," in Harvey J. Kaye and Keith McClelland, eds., *E. P. Thompson: Critical Perspectives* (Cambridge: Polity, 1990), 50–77. For a compelling empirical defense of focusing at the point of production as the principal site of class formation and consciousness, see the influential body of work by Michael Burawoy, *Manufacturing Consent: Changes in the Labor Process under Monopoly Capitalism* (Chicago: University of Chicago Press, 1979), esp. chap. 9; and *The Politics of Production: Factory Regimes under Capitalism and Socialism* (London: Verso, 1985).

61. For recent arguments favoring the "turn to history" in sociology, see Andrew Abbott, "From Causes to Events: Notes on Narrative Positivism," *Sociological Research and Methods* 20, no. 4 (May 1992): 428–55; Ronald Aminzade, "Historical Sociology and Time," *Sociological Methods and Research* 20, no. 4 (May 1992): 456–80; Larry Griffin, "Narrative, Event-Structure Analysis, and Causal Interpretation in Historical Sociology," *American Journal of Sociology* 98, no. 5 (March 1993): 1094–1133; William H. Sewell, Jr., "Three Temporalities: Toward an Eventful Sociology," in Terrence J. McDonald, ed., *The Historic Turn in the Social Sciences* (Ann Arbor: University of Michigan Press, 1997), 245–80; and Margaret R. Somers, "We're No Angels: Realism, Rational Choice, and Relationality in Social Science," *American Journal of Sociology* 104, no. 3 (November 1998): 722–84.

Chapter Two. Industrial Syndicalism on the Philadelphia Waterfront

1. Besides Local 8, the IWW built durable pockets of unionism in only a handful of other locations, most notably among machine workers in Cleveland where a Wobbly local survived from 1934 to 1950. See Roy T. Wortman, *From Syndicalism to Trade Unions: The I.W.W. in Ohio, 1905–1950* (New York: Garland, 1985), 8.

2. Correspondence from W. T. Nef to Agnes Inglis, dated July 3, 1936, Inglis Papers.

3. Sterling D. Sperro and Abram L. Harris, *The Black Worker: The Negro and the Labor Movement* (New York: Atheneum, 1974; originally published 1931), 335. Herbert Northrup, *Organized Labor and the Negro* (New York: Harper & Brothers, 1944), 144. McGirr, "Black and White Longshoremen," 379, 388. The thesis that Local 8 was simply an evolved "business union" has been challenged in a recently completed dissertation by the historian Peter Cole, who describes the dockworkers as "radical," largely on the basis of their policies of racial equality and union militancy—the same features that lead most other observers to see Local 8 as a typical business union with, at most, progressive racial policies. See Cole, "Shaping Up," 444. What both Cole and his critics miss, I would argue, is an understanding of the ways in which conventional renderings of "radical" and "business" union-ism—as proxies for the IWW and the AFL—share a common syndicalist foundation that has at the same time managed to support two very different logics of collective action.

4. The only case of collective action on the Philadelphia waterfront before 1898 was the temporary organization of coal heavers in 1835, three hundred of whom went on strike that year for higher wages and a ten-hour day. See Cole, "Shaping Up," 41. Maud Russell, *Men Along the Shore* (New York: Brussel & Brussel, 1966), 10, 50; Charles B. Barnes, *The Longshoremen* (New York: Russell Sage Foundation, 1915), 112; and Cole, "Shaping Up," 48–49.

5. Russell, *Men Along the Shore*, 50–52, 248; Myland Rudoph Brown, "The I.W.W. and the Negro Worker" (Ed.D. dissertation, Ball State University, 1968), 61.

6. The Knights' presence is mentioned in Jonathan Garlock, *Guide to the Local Assemblies of the Knights of Labor* (Westport, Conn.: Greenwood Press, 1982), 454. The best survey of union strength in the North Atlantic at this time is Barnes, *Longshoremen.*

7. George F. Sproule, comp. and arr., *The Port of Philadelphia: Its Facilities and Advantages* (Harrisburg, Penn.: Board of Commissioners of Navigation for the River Delaware and Its Navigable Tributaries, 1914), 41, 49 ff.

8. On the ethnic makeup of Boston's unionized waterfront workers, see Barnes, *Longshoremen,* 181–84.

9. The ethnic character of New York's labor force is discussed in Barnes, *Longshoremen,* 5.

10. On the ethnic makeup of Philadelphia's longshoremen, see Sperro and Harris, *Black Worker,* 333; and Joe Biginski, tape-recorded interview with Howard Kimeldorf, Philadelphia, May 3, 1989.

11. The role of ethnic and racial tensions is covered in Philip S. Foner, "The IWW and the Black Worker," *Journal of Negro History* 55, no. 1

(January 1970): 51. Cole argues that the prevalence of black workers on the Philadelphia waterfront was the product of an unspecified "racism" that relegated African Americans to jobs like longshoring that were physically demanding, insecure, and low paying. See Cole, "Shaping Up," 62, 116. But such unattractive working conditions also existed on the Boston and New York docks where, in the presence of a strong craft union, blacks were excluded, whereas in unorganized Philadelphia, without union exclusion, they came to dominate. Ironically, it was the shipowners in Philadelphia and elsewhere who often worked to create a more racially and ethnically diverse labor force—not out of a commitment to social equality, needless to say, but as a means of preventing worker solidarity.

12. The IWW "invasion" that spring targeted the city's textile workers, not the longshoremen who had shown little interest in earlier Wobbly agitational efforts on the waterfront. See *Philadelphia Public Ledger* (hereafter cited as *PPL*), June 10, 1913, 1.

13. National Adjustment Commission, Hearing Before the National Adjustment Commission, *In the Matter of the Demands of the Longshoremen of the North Atlantic Coast Ports as to Wages, etc.*, September 30, 1918–October 3, 1918, New York City. Typewritten copy, Houghton Library, Harvard University, 101, 91.

14. Testimony of John A. Dunn, Box 117, Folder 7, p. 11981; Charles Carter, Box 117, Folder 7, p. 12021; John J. Walsh, Box 114, Folder 5, p. 9331; all found in *U.S. v. William D. Haywood et al.*, Trial Transcript, IWW Papers.

15. Walsh testimony, Box 114, Folder 5, p. 9331, IWW Papers.

16. Walsh testimony, Box 114, Folder 5, p. 9333, IWW Papers.

17. For a general discussion of the casual nature of longshore work, see Charles P. Larrowe, *Shape-Up and Hiring Hall: A Comparison of Hiring Methods and Labor Relations on the New York and Seattle Waterfronts* (Berkeley and Los Angeles: University of California Press, 1955); and Vernon H. Jensen, *Hiring of Dock Workers and Employment Practices in the Ports of New York, Liverpool, London, Rotterdam, and Marseilles* (Cambridge, Mass.: Harvard University Press, 1969). For a more richly textured account of hiring practices on the waterfront, see Bruce Nelson, *Workers on the Waterfront: Seamen, Longshoremen, and Unionism in the 1930s* (Urbana: University of Illinois Press, 1988).

18. *Solidarity*, October 4, 1913, 1.

19. *Solidarity*, May 24, 1913, 2.

20. The quote on spreading demands is from *Solidarity*, October 4, 1913, 1; *PPL*, May 18, 1913, n.p., found in Newspaper Clipping File, Urban Archives, Temple University, Philadelphia, Pennsylvania (hereafter cited as Clipping File).

21. *Solidarity*, October 4, 1913, 1.

22. *Philadelphia Evening Bulletin* (hereafter cited as *PEB*), May 20, 1913, n.p., Clipping File.

23. On the enforcement of labor discipline at sea, see Nelson, *Workers on the Waterfront,* chap. 1. On the employer's vulnerability to job action by longshoremen, see Howard Kimeldorf, *Reds or Rackets? The Making of Radical and Conservative Unions on the Waterfront* (Berkeley and Los Angeles: University of California Press, 1988).

24. The direct-actionist orientation of waterfront workers is covered in Nelson, *Workers on the Waterfront;* and Kimeldorf, *Reds or Rackets?*

25. *Solidarity,* May 24, 1913, 4. On the role of ethnic solidarity in the Lawrence textile strike, see Dubofsky, *We Shall Be All,* chap. 10.

26. Racially segregated white and black locals were the rule in most southern ports organized by the ILA, and the practice was often adopted in many northern ports as well. See Lester Rubin, *The Negro in the Longshore Industry,* Report No. 29, The Racial Policies of American Industry (Philadelphia: Industrial Research Unit, Wharton School, University of Pennsylvania Press, 1974); Eric Arneson, "It Ain't Like They Do in New Orleans: Race Relations, Labor Markets, and Waterfront Labor Movements in the American South," in Marcel van der Linden and Jan Lucassen, eds., *Racism and the Labour Market: Historical Studies* (New York: Peter Lang, 1995), 57–100; and Eric Arnesen, "Biracial Waterfront Unionism in the Age of Segregation," in Calvin Winslow, ed., *Waterfront Workers: New Perspectives on Race and Class* (Urbana: University of Illinois Press, 1998), 19–61.

27. "Colored Workers of America: Why You Should Join the I.W.W," Folder: Colored Workers of America, Box 158, IWW Papers.

28. The quote on the IWW protecting "the colored man" is from Philip S. Foner, *Organized Labor and the Black Worker, 1619–1973* (New York: Praeger, 1974), 113. The Protestant minister is quoted in *PPL,* June 23, 1913, 2.

29. Richard R. Wright, Jr., "The Negro in Pennsylvania: A Study in Economic History" (Ph.D. dissertation, University of Pennsylvania, 1912), 94, 98.

30. Stewart Bird, Dan Georgakas, and Deborah Shaffer, eds., *Solidarity Forever: An Oral History of the IWW* (Chicago: Lake View Press, 1985), 184–85.

31. Correspondence from F. W. Taylor to Mr. Eugene O'Neill, dated May 24, 1913, Fred Walter Taylor Papers, Folder: "River Front Strike 1913," Historical Society of Pennsylvania, Philadelphia (hereafter cited as Taylor Papers). It is worth noting that this is not the same Frederick W. Taylor, also from Philadelphia, whose name is associated with scientific management.

32. Correspondence from F. W. Taylor to Messrs. Furness, Withy, & Co., dated May 26, 1913, Taylor Papers.

33. Correspondence from F. W. Taylor to Messrs. Furness, Withy, & Co., Ltd., dated June 3, 1913, Taylor Papers.

34. *PEB,* May 22, 1913, n.p., Clipping File.

35. *PPL,* May 24, 1913, n.p., Taylor Papers.

36. *PEB,* May 22, 1913, n.p., Clipping File.

37. Correspondence from F. W. Taylor to Messrs. Furness, Withy, & Co., Ltd., dated June 3, 1913, Taylor Papers.

38. Correspondence from F. W. Taylor to Messrs. Furness, Withy, & Co., Ltd., dated June 3, 1913, Taylor Papers.

39. *Solidarity,* October 4, 1913, 1.

40. Correspondence from F. W. Taylor to Messrs. Furness, Withy, & Co., Ltd., dated June 11, 1913, Taylor Papers. "Stevedores Strike—Philadelphia," minutes from meeting held June 10, 1913, Taylor Papers.

41. Taylor's warning about "maintaining the IWW" is from correspondence from F. W. Taylor to Messrs. Furness, Withy, & Co., Ltd., dated June 11, 1913, Taylor Papers. The employer quote about "a huge joke" is reported in *Solidarity,* May 30, 1914, 1.

42. *PPL,* June 10, 1913, 1; and June 18, 1913, 2.

43. *Solidarity,* October 4, 1913, 1, 4.

44. Stenographic Report—8th Annual Convention of the IWW, September 1913, Folder 2–1, Box 2, IWW Papers, pp. 7, 28; *Solidarity,* October 4, 1913, 4. Members of branch 2 were employed on piers that were controlled by the International Mercantile Marine Company, the stevedoring firm that most vigorously—and at times successfully—resisted Local 8. See Cole, "Shaping Up," 132.

45. *Solidarity,* May 30, 1914, 1; *Solidarity,* October 4, 1913, 4; Brown, "The I.W.W. and the Negro Worker," 67.

46. Correspondence from Phillip Hembosy (?) to Mr. Frank Morrison, dated September 25, 1913, Microfilm Reel 39, *American Federation of Labor Records: The Samuel Gompers Era,* microfilm (Sanford, N.C.: Microfilming Corporation of America, 1979) (hereafter cited as Gompers Papers).

47. On the ILA's organizational efforts on the Gulf Coast and their general openness to black workers, see Rubin, *Negro in the Longshore Industry;* Arneson, "It Ain't Like They Do in New Orleans"; and Cole, "Shaping Up," 386.

48. Correspondence from Phillip Hembosy (?) to Mr. Frank Morrison, dated September 25, 1913, Microfilm Reel 39, Gompers Papers.

49. "Stenographic Report—8th Annual Convention, Industrial Workers of the World, 1913," Box 2, Folder 1, p. 28, IWW Papers.

50. Correspondence from F. W. Taylor to Messrs. Furness, Withy, & Co., Ltd., dated June 11, 1913, Taylor Papers; Correspondence from F. W. Taylor to Mr. P. A. S. Franklin, dated June 26, 1913, Taylor Papers.

51. "Philadelphia—memo from old notes taken years ago," typewritten memo by Fred Thompson, n.d., Fred Thompson Collection, Box 10, Folder

10–9, Walter P. Reuther Library, Archives of Labor History and Urban Affairs, Wayne State University (hereafter cited as Thompson Papers).

52. The ILA's restrictive hiring practices are covered in John R. Commons, "Types of American Labor Unions: The 'Longshoremen of the Great Lakes,'" *Quarterly Journal of Economics* 20 (November 1905): 59–85; Russell, *Men Along the Shore;* and Barnes, *Longshoremen.*

53. Before 1920, and occasionally thereafter, the pages of *Solidarity* are filled with nothing but praise for Local 8.

54. *Philadelphia Inquirer* (hereafter cited as *PI*), July 23, 1913, 6; *PPL,* July 22, 1913, 17; *Solidarity,* August 22, 1914, 1.

55. Correspondence from F. W. Taylor to Mr. Eugene O'Neill, dated May 24, 1913, Taylor Papers.

56. The "universal wage" did not apply to cargo handlers employed in the traditionally nonunion coastwise trade, most of whom remained outside of Local 8 until 1920. In many larger ports, including Philadelphia, coastwise shipping was relegated to part-time, casual workers, whereas "deepwater," or international, shipping formed the core constituency of unionization. For a survey of income equalization efforts in other ports, see Rubin, *Negro in the Longshore Industry.*

57. On rotating leaders, see Foner, *Organized Labor and the Black Worker,* 113. *Messenger* (October 1921): 263.

58. For more on Fletcher's personal life, see William Seraile, "Ben Fletcher, I.W.W. Organizer," *Pennsylvania History* 46, no. 3 (July 1979): 213–32; Sam Dolgoff, *Fragments: A Memoir* (Cambridge: Refract Publications, 1986), 139–41; Jeff Stein, "Ben Fletcher: Portrait of a Black Syndicalist," *Libertarian Labor Review* 3 (1987): 30–33; and Howard Kimeldorf, "Ben Fletcher," *American National Biography,* forthcoming.

59. In addition to Flynn and Quinlan, Fletcher's early years in Philadelphia may have put him in contact with many leading radicals of his day, among them John Reed and Joe Hill; see unsigned correspondence (from Fred Thompson?) to Sam and Esther, dated January 6, 1967, Box 12, Folder 26, Thompson Papers.

60. On Fletcher's early contact with the IWW, see correspondence from John B. Campbell to the Director of Military Intelligence, cover letter dated October 27, 1919, Records of the War Department General Staff, Military Intelligence Division, Correspondence, 1917–41, Record Group 165, Box 2776, File No. 10110–1460–2, National Archives, Washington, D.C. (hereafter cited as Military Intelligence Papers); Fletcher's position as corresponding secretary is from *Solidarity,* August 10, 1912, 3.

61. Jack Lever transcript of interview with Herbert Hill, Solebury, Pennsylvania, May 29, 1968, Blacks in the Labor Movement Oral History Project, Walter P. Reuther Library, Archives of Labor and Urban Affairs, Wayne State University, Detroit, Michigan (hereafter cited as Lever interview); *Messenger* (August 1919): 28–29. The comments by James Fair are from

Bird, Georgakas, and Shaffer, *Solidarity Forever,* 184. For a fuller discussion of Fletcher's life, see Seraile, "Ben Fletcher"; and Irwin Marcus, "Benjamin Fletcher: Black Labor Leader," *Negro History Bulletin* 35 (October 1972): 138–40.

62. Speed's views on Lewis and himself are from IWW 8th Convention, 28. On the backgrounds of Walsh, Nef, and Doree, see Cole, "Shaping Up," 149–50, 177–80.

63. *Solidarity,* August 1, 1914, 1; August 23, 1914, 1, 4; and November 28, 1914, 1. On the harbor boatmen, see *Voice of the People* (New Orleans), October 16, 1913, 1.

64. *Solidarity,* May 30, 1914, 1, 2.

65. *Solidarity,* May 30, 1914, 2.

66. *Solidarity,* August 1, 1914, 1.

67. *PPL,* January 28, 1915, 8; *PPL,* February 9, 1915, 2; *Solidarity,* February 13, 1915, 1.

68. *Solidarity,* February 13, 1915, 1. "The Philadelphia Controversy: Being a Complete and Detailed Statement of All That Has Occurred" (hereafter cited as "Philadelphia Controversy"), Folder 79–20, Box 79, p. 1, IWW Papers.

69. The quote on "union men" is from "Philadelphia Controversy," 1. *Solidarity,* April 15, 1916, 1.

70. *Solidarity,* April 15, 1916, 1; and May 6, 1916, 1. The lumber handlers' defection is reported in *Solidarity,* September 9, 1916, 1. Walsh is quoted in *Solidarity,* May 27, 1916, 1.

71. *Solidarity,* July 15, 1916, 1; *PPL,* July 7, 1916, 1.

72. *PPL,* July 6, 1916, 1; *Philadelphia Tribune,* July 8, 1916, 1.

73. The eyewitness is John Walsh, quoted in *Solidarity,* July 15, 1916, 1.

74. "Philadelphia Controversy," 1.

75. *Solidarity,* May 27, 1916, 1. On the persistence of "whiteness" as a racial identity for Euro-American workers, see the provocative studies by David R. Roediger, *The Wages of Whiteness: Race and the Making of the American Working Class* (London: Verso, 1991); and Bruce Nelson, "The 'Lords of the Docks' Reconsidered: Race Relations among West Coast Longshoremen, 1933–61," in Winslow, ed., *Waterfront Workers,* 155–92.

76. The ethnicity of the sugar workers is from U.S. Senate, 61st Cong., 2d sess., Doc. No. 633, *Reports of the U.S. Immigration Commission, 1907–1910, Immigrants in Industries, Part 16: Sugar Refining* (Washington, D.C.: GPO, 1911), 15:611. Doree is quoted in *International Socialist Review* (April 1917): 616.

77. *PPL,* February 22, 1917, 1, 9.

78. *International Socialist Review* (April 1917): 617.

79. *PPL,* February 22, 1917, 1; February 23, 1917, 1, 5; and March 21, 1917, 6.

80. *Solidarity,* May 30, 1914, 2.

Chapter Three. Wobblies under Siege

1. International Longshoremen's Association, *Proceedings of the Twenty-second Convention of the International Longshoremen's Association,* 1914, 45, 46; and *Proceedings of the Twenty-third Convention of the International Longshoremen's Association,* 1915, 48.

2. "Investigation of the Marine Transport Workers and the Alleged Threatened Combination Between Them and the Bolsheviki and Sinn Feiners," Confidential Report from the Office of Naval Intelligence, dated December 23, 1918, 33, Microfilm Reel 8, *U.S. Military Intelligence Reports: Surveillance of Radicals in the United States, 1917–1941* (Frederick, Md.: University Publications of America, 1984).

3. "Philadelphia Controversy," cover page.

4. *Solidarity,* April 14, 1917, 3, 4.

5. On the wartime growth of federal regulatory agencies, see Haydu, *Making American Industry Safe for Democracy.*

6. *Solidarity,* June 9, 1917, 4.

7. Untitled, Box 99, Folder 12, IWW Papers. The Philadelphia defendants were indicted along with 162 of their fellow Wobblies from around the country. On the wartime persecution of the IWW, see William Preston, Jr., *Aliens and Dissenters: Federal Suppression of Radicals, 1903–1933* (Cambridge, Mass.: Harvard University Press, 1963); Dubofsky, *We Shall Be All,* chaps. 16, 17.

8. Seraile, "Ben Fletcher," 220–21. Local 8 actually had a better wartime production record than the supposedly "patriotic" ILA whose members in other large Atlantic ports were responsible for "numerous explosions, fires and accidents" during the war. See Cole, "Shaping Up," 214–15.

9. The attorney is quoted in Seraile, "Ben Fletcher," 226.

10. Bird, Georgakas, and Shaffer, *Solidarity Forever,* 184.

11. "Radicalism and Race Riots," field report by Castle M. Brown, dated October 28, 1919, Military Intelligence Papers.

12. Correspondence from J. H. Rechal to Frank Morrison, dated January 12, 1918, Microfilm Reel 39, Gompers Papers.

13. Correspondence from Francis Fisher Kane to the Attorney General, dated February 7, 1918, Frame 257, Microfilm Reel 5, *Department of Justice Investigative Case Files,* microfilm (Bethesda, Md.: University Publications of America, 1989) (hereafter cited as IWW Film).

14. Correspondence from J. H. Rechal to Mr. Frank Morrison, dated January 12, 1918, Microfilm Reel 39, Gompers Papers. Correspondence from unknown source to Teamsters union, dated January 14, 1918, Microfilm Reel 39, Gompers Papers.

15. Correspondence from Patrick Quinlan to Frank Morrison, dated April 3, 1918, Microfilm Reel 39, Gompers Papers.

16. Report from agent J. F. McDevitt, dated May 13, 1918, Case File

No. 366145, Microfilm Reel 806, Federal Bureau of Investigation, Record Group 65, National Archives, Washington, D.C. (hereafter cited as FBI Papers).

17. U.S. Shipping Board, Marine and Dock Industrial Relations Division, *Marine and Dock Labor: Work, Wages, and Industrial Relations During the Period of the War* (Washington, D.C.: GPO, 1919), 137.

18. Report unsigned, dated October 29, 1918, Case File No. 366145, Microfilm Reel 806, FBI Papers.

19. U.S. Department of Labor, Office of the Secretary, Division of Negro Economics, George E. Haynes, Ph.D., director, *Negro Migration in 1916–17* (Washington, D.C.: GPO, 1919; reprint, New York: Negro Universities Press, 1969), 123–25.

20. The number of weekly initiates is from an unsigned report, dated July 14, 1917, Microfilm Reel 555, Case File No. 160053, FBI Papers. Estimates on the proportion of black members are from Seraile, "Ben Fletcher," 217; and John Walsh testimony, Box 112, Folder 5, p. 9356, *U.S. v. William D. Haywood et al.*, trial transcript, IWW Papers.

21. Biracialism and, as a result, weak unions were common along the Gulf Coast, except for New Orleans. See Daniel Rosenberg, *New Orleans Dockworkers: Race, Labor, and Unionism, 1892–1923* (Albany: State University of New York Press, 1988); and Eric Arneson, *Waterfront Workers of New Orleans: Race, Class, and Politics, 1863–1923* (New York: Oxford University Press, 1991).

22. Report of special agent J.K., dated May 7, 1919, Records of the U.S. Shipping Board, Record Group 32, Investigated Cases Files of the Home Office, Case File No. 1494, National Archives, Washington, D.C. (hereafter cited as Shipping Board Papers).

23. "Philadelphia Controversy," 2; *Solidarity*, December 4, 1920, 3.

24. The Wobblies' defeat in New York is covered in Kimeldorf, *Reds or Rackets?* 46–49.

25. On the MTW's faltering East Coast campaign, see *One Big Union Monthly* (May 1920): 54; Sperro and Harris, *Black Worker*, 193, 196; and Brown, "The I.W.W. and the Negro Worker," 65.

26. *One Big Union Monthly* (July 1920): 1. On the economic situation facing coastwise shipping, see *New York Times*, June 6, 1920, sec. 7, 14 (hereafter cited as *NYT*).

27. *PPL*, May 28, 1920, 6.

28. *Solidarity*, June 12, 1920, 3; *PPL*, June 1, 1920, 3.

29. The Wobblies' denial of ever signing an agreement is from *One Big Union Monthly* (July 1920): 6. Local 8's leaders, when questioned by their fellow Wobbly maritime workers, denied signing an agreement not to strike during the war. See typewritten minutes of the Transport Workers Conference, Philadelphia, dated May 27, 1919, Lusk Committee Hearings, Box Loo30 1, D165/6 Folder 14, New York State Archives, Albany. The question

of the contract remains unclear, even after all these years. In 1968 Jack Lever, who helped organize Local 8, told an interviewer, "We didn't get formal bargaining. . . . [W]e simply told people to stop work until they got what they wanted." But, when asked directly whether Local 8 ever signed a contract, Lever seemingly reversed himself and said, "We were the first ones in the IWW to negotiate formal agreements with the employers." Both quotes are from Lever interview, 17. The only way to reconcile Lever's comments is to conclude that Local 8's "formal agreement" was verbal rather than written. This was the conclusion reached at the time in a government report. See U.S. Shipping Board, *Marine and Dock Labor*, 87. The offer of a monetary reward for finding a contact is from *Solidarity*, June 12, 1920, 3.

30. Local 8's actions are reported in *One Big Union Monthly* (July 1920): 9. On the shipowners' request to the government, see *PPL*, June 1, 1920, 3.

31. Report of agent J. K. McDevitt, dated June 17, 1920, Case File No. 366145, Microfilm Reel 806, FBI Papers.

32. *PPL*, June 2, 1920, 3.

33. *Solidarity*, June 19, 1920, 6.

34. *PI*, June 5, 1920, 4; *PPL*, June 10, 1920, 12.

35. *PPL*, June 8, 1920, 15; and June 10, 1920, 12.

36. *Solidarity*, June 19, 1920, 1.

37. Report from agent J. K. McDevitt, dated June 17, 1920, Case File No. 1494, Shipping Board Papers.

38. *PPL*, July 2, 1920, 1; and July 7, 1920, 4.

39. "Philadelphia Controversy," 4–5.

40. *Solidarity*, August 21, 1920, 4; report of agent McDevitt, Case File No. 366145, Microfilm Reel 806, dated August 19, 1920, 4, FBI Papers.

41. "Philadelphia Controversy," 7, 22.

42. Doree's threat is reported in "Philadelphia Controversy," 5. Details of the union meeting are from "Philadelphia Controversy," 5, 6.

43. The expulsion order was reprinted in *Solidarity*, August 14, 1920, 2; *Fellow Worker*, August 12, 1920, 1, 2.

44. For Gompers's own views on the "Bolshevik dictatorship," see Samuel Gompers, *Seventy Years of Life and Labor: An Autobiography*, ed. and introd. Nick Salvatore (Ithaca: Cornell University Press, 1984; originally published 1924), 204–5; and Samuel Gompers, *Labor and the Employers* (New York: E. P. Dutton, 1920), 35, 37.

45. The intercepted letter, signed by "Tom," was written to James Phillips, an IWW prisoner at Leavenworth; see report of agent J. F. McDevitt, dated September 20, 1920, Case File No. 366145, Microfilm Reel 806, FBI Papers.

46. "Philadelphia Controversy," 15.

47. John S. Gambs, *The Decline of the I.W.W.* (New York: Columbia

University Press, 1966), 78–79; Big Bill Haywood, *The Autobiography of William D. Haywood* (New York: International Publishers, 1929), 360.

    48. *One Big Union Monthly* (September 1920): 6.
    49. "Philadelphia Controversy," 21, 22.
    50. "Philadelphia Controversy," 25, 23.
    51. Report of agent J. F. McDevitt, dated August 30, 1920, p. 2, Case File No. 366145, Microfilm Reel 806, FBI Papers; "Philadelphia Controversy," 11.
    52. The Wobbly loyalist is "Tom," whose letter is reproduced in a report by agent J. F. McDevitt, dated September 20, 1920, p. 3, Case File No. 366145, Microfilm Reel 806, FBI Papers.
    53. The unsigned leaflet and Local 8's response are from "Strike Bulletin No. 10," dated August 31, 1920, reprinted in "Philadelphia Controversy," 16, 17.
    54. *Solidarity*, December 18, 1920, 3.
    55. *Solidarity*, December 4, 1920, 3.
    56. *Solidarity*, December 4, 1920, 3.
    57. *Solidarity*, December 4, 1920, 3.
    58. *Solidarity*, December 4, 1920, 3.
    59. *Solidarity*, December 18, 1920, 3.
    60. *Solidarity*, December 4, 1920, 3.
    61. *Solidarity*, January 1, 1921, 3.
    62. *Solidarity*, April 2, 1921, 2.
    63. *Solidarity*, January 1, 1921, 3, 4.
    64. *Solidarity*, March 19, 1921, 2.
    65. "Statement of Prov. G.O.C. of the M.T.W.I.U. 510 I.W.W.," dated August 1921 (?), typed copy in Industrial Workers of the World Records, Accession No. 5210, Box 5, Folder 7, Kheel Center for Labor-Management Documentation and Archives, M. P. Catherwood Library, Cornell University.
    66. *Minutes of the Thirteenth Convention of the Industrial Workers of the World,* May 9–27, 1921, p. 9, IWW Papers.
    67. By the end of 1922, Local 1116 officials requested an organizer who could "work among both races," suggesting that whites were still outside the union. International Longshoremen's Association, *Proceedings of the Twenty-seventh Convention of the International Longshoremen's Association,* 1923, 136. Four years later Local 1116 remained "strictly a colored group," according to James Moocke who was on the waterfront at that time. James Moocke, tape-recorded interview, "Delaware River Oral History Project," Independence Seaport Museum, Philadelphia (hereafter Moocke interview). Similarly, Joe Kane, a retired longshoreman and union officer whose father was a member of Local 8, recalls the ILA as "all black" prior to 1926. Joe Kane, tape-recorded interview with Howard Kimeldorf, May 2, 1989, Philadelphia.

68. On the ILA's escalating attack on Local 8, see report of agent H. S. White, dated August 22, 1921, Case File No. 202600–1084, Microfilm Reel 936, FBI Papers. The quote on "colored longshoremen" is from a report by agent S. Busha, dated July 15, 1921, Case File No. 202600–1084, Microfilm Reel 936, FBI Papers.

69. Report of agent H. S. White, dated August 22, 1921, Case File No. 202600–1084, Microfilm Reel 936, FBI Papers.

70. International Longshoremen's Association, *Proceedings of the Twenty-sixth Convention of the International Longshoremen's Association,* 1921, 230.

71. International ILA president T. V. O'Connor admitted to Gompers that the IWW had "almost complete control of the waterfront" in Philadelphia. See Correspondence from T. V. O'Connor to Samuel Gompers, dated February 10, 1921, Microfilm Reel 39, Gompers Papers. The Wobblies claimed that many ILA supporters were "new to Philadelphia," as quoted in Cole, "Shaping Up," 423. This conclusion is also borne out by the fact that Local 8 did not report any drop in membership at this time.

72. Report of unidentified agent, dated April 15, 1922, received through a Freedom of Information Act request dated June 30, 1994, from the Federal Bureau of Investigation by Howard Kimeldorf, p. 14.

73. *PPL,* August 20, 1920, 3; *Negro World,* March 7, 1925, 2.

74. *Negro World,* September 25, 1922, 2.

75. Judith Stein, *The World of Marcus Garvey: Race and Class in Modern Society* (Baton Rouge: Louisiana State University Press, 1986), 92–93, 104.

76. *PPL,* May 7, 1920, 5.

77. *Messenger* (July 1921): 215.

78. *Messenger* (August 1921): 234.

79. *Messenger* (July 1921): 215.

80. Fair is quoted in Bird, Georgakas, and Shaffer, *Solidarity Forever,* 182. *Messenger* (October 1921): 262, 263.

81. The views of Ben Fletcher, the IWW's most prominent African American, are indicative. Based on his knowledge of Local 8, "the Negro," he wrote in 1929, "is passing through the period of race consciousness, for the most part." Invoking the developmental schemes of classical Marxism, Fletcher argued that such sentiments were merely a phase, destined to be swept aside by the "economic pressures of capitalism," which "[cut] off all escape for all the Negroes except a few, through race consciousness." With greater exposure to "wage slavery," Fletcher believed, the black proletariat would evolve to higher forms of "class consciousness." In thus separating race from class, and privileging the latter as a more authentic expression of the (black) workers' experience, Fletcher and his fellow Wobblies dealt with racial identities mostly by denying them. See correspondence from B.H.F. to Mr. Abram Harris, dated July 29, 1929, Abram Harris Collection,

Moorland-Spingarm Research Center, Howard University (hereafter cited as Harris Papers).

82. William M. Tuttle, *Race Riot: Chicago in the Red Summer of 1919* (New York: Atheneum, 1970); R. Halliburton, Jr., *The Tulsa Race War of 1921* (San Francisco: R and E Research Associates, 1975); Elliott Rudwick, ed., *The East St. Louis Race Riot of 1921*, microfilm (Frederick, Md.: University Publications of America, 1985).

83. *PPL,* April 28, 1919, 4.

84. *PPL,* July 8, 1919, 6.

85. *PPL,* January 13, 1920, 3; and July 18, 1921, 2.

86. *PPL,* May 31, 1921, 2.

87. *Solidarity,* November 5, 1921, 1.

88. *PPL,* October 14, 1922, n.p., Clipping File, Case No. 61–2353, Department of Justice Papers.

89. Baker is quoted in *PPL,* October 15, 1922, 16. The other union leader is quoted in report of agent #2, dated October 16, 1922, Case File No. 1494–4, Shipping Board Papers.

90. Report of agent #10, dated October 15, 1922, Case File No. 1494–4, Shipping Board Papers.

91. Report of agent #10, dated October 27, 1922, Case File No. 1494–4, Shipping Board Papers.

92. Report of agent #2, dated October 16, 1922, Case File No. 1494–4, Shipping Board Papers.

93. Report of agent #10, dated October 18, 1922, Case File No. 1494–4, Shipping Board Papers.

94. Unsigned report, dated October 18, 1922, Case File No. 1494–4, Shipping Board Papers.

95. Unsigned report, dated October 17, 1922, Case File No. 1494–4, Shipping Board Papers. Report of agent #2, dated October 22, 1922, Case File No. 1494–4, Shipping Board Papers.

96. *PPL,* October 14, 1922, n.p., Clipping File, Case No. 61–2353, Department of Justice Papers.

97. The use of New York strikebreakers, presumably members of the ILA, is from a report by agent J. F. McDevitt, dated October 16, 1922, p. 2, Case File No. 61–2353, Department of Justice Papers. A similar account of "nonunion men" being sent from New York to Philadelphia appears in *Industrial Worker,* November 4, 1922, 1. The vote against Baker is from an unsigned report (agent J. A. Sullivan?), dated October 24, 1922, p. 2, Case File No. 1494–4, Shipping Board Papers.

98. On growing tensions within Local 8, see the report from agent #2, dated October 19 and October 20, 1922, p. 1, Case File No. 1494–4, Shipping Board Papers; and report from agent #10, dated October 19, 1922, Case File No. 1494–4, Shipping Board Papers. Opposition to Baker is from

a report by agent #10, dated October 23, 1922, p. 2, Case File No. 1494–4, Shipping Board Papers.

99. "Strike News Bulletin No. 1," November 7, 1922, 1, Publicity Committee of the Marine Transport Workers' Industrial Union, No. 510, Industrial Workers of the World, Philadelphia Branch, Box 70, Folder 2, IWW Papers.

100. Speed's comments to the men are from an unsigned report (agent J. A. Sullivan?), dated October 24, 1922, Case File No. 1494–4, Shipping Board Papers. Speed's letter was intercepted by a Shipping Board operative and summarized in an unsigned report (agent J. A. Sullivan?), dated October 26, 1922, Case File No. 1494–4, Shipping Board Papers.

101. Report of agent #2, dated October 23, 1922, Case File No. 1494–4, Shipping Board Papers; report of agent #10, dated October 29, 1922, Case File No. 1494–4, Shipping Board Papers.

102. Unsigned report, dated October 30, 1922, Case File No. 1494–4, Shipping Board Papers.

103. General Office Bulletin 1925, Box 32, Folder 1, pp. 8–9, IWW Papers.

104. *PPL*, November 21, 1922, 24. Abraham Moses, tape-recorded interview with Greg Williams and Ed Kirlin, May 12, 1980, Independence Seaport Museum, Philadelphia (hereafter cited as Moses interview).

105. General Office Bulletin 1925, Box 32, Folder 1, pp. 8–9, IWW Papers.

106. Yeager is so described in an unsigned report, dated October 30, 1922, Case File No. 1494–4, Shipping Board Papers. The split between pro- and anti-Communist factions at this time revolved around a number of issues, including centralization, amnesty, and of course support for Soviet Russia. See Dubofsky, *We Shall Be All*, 457–68; and Gambs, *Decline of the I.W.W.*, 78–79.

107. Unsigned (Benjamin Fletcher?) typewritten memo, "The Facts," Box 79, Folder 79–23, p. 3, IWW Papers (hereafter cited as "The Facts").

108. "The Facts," 2.

109. The quote about unswerving loyalty is from the *Messenger* (June 1923): 741. On the IWW's "interference," see "The Facts," 4.

110. *Solidarity*, April 7, 1923, 6. The number of paid-up members in the official MTW local is based on dues remitted to the national office in 1923. See *Minutes of the First Convention of the Marine Transport Workers' Industrial Union 510, I.W.W.*, Box 70, Folder 3, pp. 9–10, IWW Papers.

111. A group photograph of Yeager's followers, taken early in 1924 in front of the official MTW hall, includes twenty-seven individuals, all of whom appear to be white. See *Industrial Pioneer*, no. 11 (March 1924): 37.

112. *PPL*, July 16, 1923, 2.

113. *PPL*, July 23, 1923, 2; August 6, 1923, 2; and August 7, 1923, 2. The attempted lynching is reported in *PPL*, September 9, 1923, 2.

114. On the ILA's promise of preferential treatment, see *Marine Worker*, July 31, 1924, 1. The comparison to the ILA is from *Marine Worker*, August 28, 1924, 1.

115. *Solidarity*, March 18, 1925, 1.

116. Erwin is quoted in "General Office Bulletin," 1925, Box 32, Folder 1, p. 7, IWW Papers.

117. *Solidarity*, March 18, 1925, 1, 4.

118. *Industrial Worker*, April 18, 1925, 2.

119. Developments in the Jarka strike are reported in *Industrial Worker*, April 18, 1925, 1; April 22, 1925, 1; and April 25, 1925, 1.

120. The police convoy is reported in *Industrial Worker*, April 22, 1925, 4. The quote on "scabbing" is from *Industrial Worker*, April 29, 1925, 1.

121. Correspondence from J. F. Dewey to Mr. H. L. Kerwin, dated April 16, 1925, p. 2, Records of the Federal Mediation and Conciliation Service, Dispute Case Files, Case File No. 170–2936, Record Group 280, Washington National Records Center, Suitland, Maryland (hereafter cited as Mediation Service Papers).

122. *Solidarity*, May 13, 1925, 4.

123. *Solidarity*, May 13, 1925, 4.

124. "Summary of Final Report of Commissioner of Conciliation," dated May 21, 1925, Microfilm Reel 1, Frame 0440, in James R. Grossman, ed., *Black Workers in the Era of the Great Migration, 1916–1929*, microfilm (Frederick, Md.: University Publications of America, 1985).

125. *Philadelphia Tribune*, July 18, 1925, 6.

126. "General Office Bulletin," 1925, Box 32, Folder 1, p. 9, IWW Papers.

127. Baker's 1934 comments appear in correspondence from Fred Thompson to (?), dated 1976 (May 10?), Box 10, Folder 6, Thompson Papers. Figures on cargo shipments are derived from U.S. Maritime Commission, *Report on Volume of Water-borne Foreign Commerce of the United States by Ports of Origin and Destination* (Washington, D.C.: GPO), for fiscal years ending 1923 and 1926.

128. Ryan's views are from International Longshoremen's Association, *Proceedings of the Twenty-ninth Convention of the International Longshoremen's Association*, 1927, 135–36 (hereafter cited as *ILA Proceedings of the Twenty-ninth Convention*). Moocke interview.

129. Moses interview; *ILA Proceedings of the Twenty-ninth Convention*, 135–36.

130. *ILA Proceedings of the Twenty-ninth Convention*, 135–36.

131. Erwin is quoted in General Office Bulletin 1925, Box 32, Folder 1, p. 8, IWW Papers. Fletcher's remark is in correspondence from B.H.F. to Mr. Abram Harris, dated July 29, 1929, Harris Papers. Retired longshore-

man Edward Kelly, whose mother rented rooms in their house to Wobblies during the heyday of Local 8, remembers them, like Fletcher does, as non-ideological. The Wobblies he knew "didn't have anything to do with communism. Nothing like that in their mind. There might have been a few. But most were pretty smart fellas. Pretty educated. They wanted to better themselves. They were decent militant fellas. They didn't want to be treated like a pup." Edward Kelly, telephone interview with Howard Kimeldorf, March 10, 1990, Ann Arbor.

132. *Minutes of the Fifteenth General Convention of the Industrial Workers of the World,* 1923, p. 50, IWW Papers.

Chapter Four. Serving Up Industrial Syndicalism on the Streets of New York

1. Correspondence from Jere Sullivan to Samuel Gompers, dated February 4, 1913, Microfilm Reel 38, Gompers Papers.

2. Rubin and Obermeirer, *Growth of a Union,* 119–20.

3. Rubin and Obermeirer, *Growth of a Union,* 120. However, Rubin and Obermeirer later draw back somewhat from this argument, attributing the IWW's "ultimate disintegration" to government repression, "not to the basic weakness of its philosophy."

4. U. S. Bureau of the Census, *Thirteenth Census of the United States Taken in the Year 1910,* vol. 4, Population, Occupational Statistics (Washington, D.C.: GPO, 1914), 573–74.

5. This ethnic profile is drawn from multiple contemporary accounts.

6. *International Hotel Work,* monthly organ of the International Hotel Workers' Union, March 1912, 1 (hereafter cited as *IHW*).

7. The commanding position of the cooks is a recurring theme in *IHW*.

8. The cook is quoted in *IHW*, April 1912, 2.

9. Based on multiple contemporary accounts. Similar claims of ethnic "unorganizability" have been advanced to account for the failure of unions in the U.S. South, even today. For a critique of this view, see Michael Goldfield, "The Failure of Operation Dixie: A Critical Turning Point in American Political Development?" in Gary M. Fink and Merl E. Reed, eds., *Race, Class, and Community in Southern Labor History* (Tuscaloosa: University of Alabama Press, 1994), 167–89.

10. On the relationship between women workers, collective action, and organized labor in the United States, see the valuable studies collected in Ruth Milkman, ed., *Women, Work and Protest: A Century of U.S. Women's Labor History* (Boston: Routledge and Kegan Paul, 1985); and Ava Baron, ed., *Work Engendered: Toward a New History of American Labor* (Ithaca: Cornell University Press, 1991).

11. The mustache ban is from the *Daily Worker,* August 4, 1926, 5 (hereafter cited as *DW*).

12. For an excellent discussion of gender relations in the food service industry, see the work of Dorothy Sue Cobble, "Sisters in the Craft"; and " 'Drawing the Line': The Construction of a Gendered Work Force in the Food Service Industry," in Baron, *Work Engendered*, 216–42. Szeliga is quoted in "Sisters in the Craft," 84–85.

13. The waiter is quoted in *IHW*, April 1912, 2.

14. *IHW*, March 1912, 5.

15. The 1915 survey is reported in Consumers' League, *The Work of the Consumers' League of the City of New York, 1915* (New York: n.p., 1916). The one-third estimate is from *Survey* 37, November 18, 1916, 174. For a useful overview of working conditions facing waitresses, see the participant observations by Amy E. Tanner, "Glimpses at the Mind of a Waitress," *American Journal of Sociology* 13, no. 1 (July 1907): 48–55.

16. *IHW*, March 1912, 5.

17. The union leader is Otto Wagner, General Secretary of the International Federation of Hotel Workers, interviewed in New York City on June 5, 1919, by D. J. Saposs, p. 2, Saposs Papers, Archives Division, State Historical Society of Wisconsin (hereafter cited as Wagner interview). Elimination of tipping was to remain a central goal of culinary unions, including the AFL, for many years to come. See "Opposition of Organized Labor to the Tipping System," *Monthly Labor Review* 25, no. 4 (October 1927): 717–20.

18. Garlock, *Guide to the Local Assemblies of the Knights of Labor*, 333.

19. See Rubin and Obermeirer, *Growth of a Union*, 44–46; Josephson, *Union House*, 14.

20. Josephson, *Union House*, 15.

21. Josephson, *Union House*, 17–18.

22. Josephson, *Union House*, 24, 37, 41.

23. Josephson, *Union House*, 57–58, 82–83.

24. Josephson, *Union House*, 85.

25. Vehling's background is told in *IHW*, November 15, 1911, 3. He is quoted in the same issue, p. 2.

26. *IHW*, November 15, 1911, 2–3.

27. *IHW*, December 15, 1911, 4.

28. Elster is described in Josephson, *Union House*, 95. Elster's appearance alongside Vehling is reported in *IHW*, November 15, 1911, 9.

29. President Sullivan's views of the New York campaign were reported to the delegates at the 1911 convention. See Hotel and Restaurant Employees' International Alliance and Bartenders International League of America, *Proceedings of the Sixteenth General Convention*, May 8–13, 1911, 96, 104. Elster's role is chronicled in Josephson, *Union House*, 94–97.

30. Membership figures are from Hotel and Restaurant Employees' International Alliance and Bartenders International League of America, *Pro-*

ceedings of the General Convention, various years; Josephson, *Union House,* 96.

31. The May Day parade is covered in *IHW,* July 1912, 2. The firing by Pearl is reported in *IHW,* May 1912, 3.

32. *New York Herald,* May 8, 1912, 3 (hereafter cited as *NYH*).

33. *NYH,* May 8, 1912, 3.

34. *IHW,* May 1912, 4.

35. The demands are from *IHW,* May 1912, 3. Fogg is quoted in *NYH,* May 10, 1912, 6.

36. *IHW,* May 1912, 5.

37. *IHW,* May 1912, 5.

38. *NYH,* May 14, 1912, 3.

39. The chef is quoted in *NYH,* May 14, 1912, 3. The observer is quoted in the *New York Call,* June 12, 1912, 1 (hereafter cited as *NYC*).

40. Cases of rheumatism and other diseases were well documented among culinary workers. See correspondence from Tassio L. Sasturico to Mr. Barrows, dated June 5, 1912, and deposition of Armand Minor, dated June 8, 1912, both in Rose Pastor Stokes Papers, Box 1, Folders 2, 3, Tamiment Library, New York University (hereafter cited as Stokes Papers). The veteran chef is Caesar Lesino, future leader of the International Federation of Hotel Workers, quoted in Josephson, *Union House,* 88.

41. *NYH,* May 16, 1912, 3.

42. *NYH,* May 18, 1912, 7. The granting of the pay scale is reported in *NYH,* May 16, 1912, 3.

43. Blocklinger is quoted in *NYH,* May 25, 1912, 3.

44. *NYH,* May 28, 1912, 3.

45. *NYH,* May 29, 1912, 3.

46. The events on May 30 are reported in *NYH,* May 31, 1912, 3. The growth in union membership is from *NYH,* June 3, 1912, 5.

47. *NYH,* May 31, 1912, 3; *NYC,* June 1, 1912, 2.

48. *NYC,* June 1, 1912, 2.

49. The merger is reported in a newspaper clipping dated June 1, 1912, Stokes Papers. *NYC,* June 1, 1912, 1, 2.

50. *NYC,* June 1, 1912, 2.

51. *NYC,* June 1, 1912, 2.

52. Newspaper clipping dated June 5, 1912, Stokes Papers.

53. Newspaper clippings dated June 5, 1912, and June 6, 1912, Stokes Papers.

54. *NYC,* June 6, 1912, 2.

55. Descriptions of unhealthy conditions are found in a special issue of *NYC,* June 12, 1912, 2, 3, 6.

56. Stokes's resignation was offered in an open letter to the strikers. See correspondence from Rose Pastor Stokes to Dear Comrades and Fellow

Workers, dated June 22, 1912, Stokes Papers. The end of the strike is covered in a newspaper clipping dated June 26, 1912, Stokes Papers.

57. *IHW*, July 1912, 1.

58. *Mixer and Server*, July 15, 1912, 28 (hereafter cited as *MS*).

59. *Solidarity*, June 15, 1912, 2. The mass meeting is covered in *IHW*, July 1912, 2.

60. *IHW*, August 1912, 1, 2.

61. *IHW*, November 1912, 8, 9.

62. The new IHWU constitution, undated, is included in the Stokes Papers.

63. *IHW*, February 1913, 9, 10.

64. *NYT*, January 2, 1913, 2; *Solidarity*, January 25, 1913, 1; Elizabeth Gurley Flynn, *I Speak My Own Piece: Autobiography of "The Rebel Girl"* (New York: Masses & Mainstream, 1955), 140–142.

65. *NYT*, January 11, 1913, 3. Sullivan is quoted in *MS*, February 15, 1913, 3.

66. The beating in the engine room is reported in *IHW*, February 1913, 9, 10. The demonstration in front of the Astor is covered in *NYH*, January 9, 1913, 1.

67. *NYC*, January 10, 1913, 1.

68. Ettor is quoted in Melvyn Dubofsky, *When Workers Organize: New York City in the Progressive Era* (Amherst: University of Massachusetts Press, 1968), 124.

69. *NYH*, January 13, 1913, 14.

70. Giovannitti is quoted in *NYH*, January 13, 1913, 14.

71. Flynn's recollections are drawn from a pamphlet entitled *Sabotage*, which she wrote in 1913, using the hotel strike as an example of "the conscious withdrawal of the workers' industrial efficiency." The pamphlet is reprinted in Rosalyn Fraad Baxandal, *Words of Fire: The Life and Writing of Elizabeth Gurley Flynn* (New Brunswick: Rutgers University Press, 1987). The quoted material appears on p. 130. Such forms of culinary sabotage were hardly news to the cooks and waiters who, among themselves, quietly threatened to "burn the fried potatoes, boil eggs hard which were meant to be soft and spill bowls of gravy on the shirt-fronts of well-dressed guests." See Frank Bohn, "The Strike of the New York Hotel and Restaurant Workers," *International Socialist Review* 13 (February 1913): 621.

72. *NYH*, January 13, 1913, 14.

73. *NYC*, January 17, 1913, 2.

74. *IHW*, February 1913, 9, 10; and March 1913, 4, 5.

75. Correspondence from Sullivan to Gompers, dated February 4, 1913, Gompers Papers.

76. *Solidarity*, February 21, 1914, 1, 4.

77. *IHW*, May-June 1913, 1, 2.

78. *IHW*, May-June 1913, 1, 2.

79. *IHW,* May-June 1913, 1, 2.

80. *IHW,* May-June 1913, 1, 2.

81. *IHW,* May-June 1913, 1, 2.

82. The "radical departure" quote is from Rubin and Obermeier, *Growth of a Union,* 119.

83. *Rebel Worker,* September 1, 1919, 4; *Fellow Worker,* June 15, 1920, 1.

Chapter Five. "More Business Sense and Stability than the I.W.W."

1. Correspondence from Dave (Saposs?) to Bill (Leiserson?), dated March 2, 1919, Box 24, Folder 21, Saposs Papers, Archives Division, State Historical Society of Wisconsin.

2. *MS,* February 15, 1913, 33–35; and March 15, 1913, 37–40.

3. Joyce is quoted in *MS,* June 15, 1913, 36. Sullivan's views are presented in *MS,* February 15, 1913, 1–3.

4. *NYT,* November 28, 1913, 3; *MS,* March 13, 1914, 3.

5. The unemployed protest is covered in Elizabeth Gurley Flynn, *The Rebel Girl: An Autobiography. My First Life (1906–1926)* (New York: International Publishers, 1973), 183, 184. Unemployed Wobblies also took direct action by refusing to pay for meals, telling proprietors to "charge it to Mayor Mitchel." See *NYT,* February 19, 1915, 11.

6. *Proceedings of the Tenth Annual Convention of the Industrial Workers of the World,* Box 2, Folder 2, p. 33, IWW Papers; *NYT,* March 31, 1915, 8.

7. The strike is covered in *NYT,* December 28, 1916, 11; and *MS,* January 15, 1916, 36, 37. For the agreement ending the strike, see "In the Matter of the New York Restaurant Keepers' Association and Waiters Union Local #1," Minutes of Arbitration Session on February 15, 1916, Paul Abelson Papers, Accession No. 5192, Box 51, Folder 9, Kheel Center for Labor-Management Documentation and Archives, M. P. Catherwood Library, Cornell University.

8. Demosthenes Nicas, tape-recorded interview with author, May 6, 1989, Bronx, New York. The IFW is also briefly discussed in Josephson, *Union House,* 104; and Marion Dutton Savage, *Industrial Unionism in America* (New York: Ronald Press, 1922), 287.

9. "Revolutionary Radicalism: Its History, Purpose and Tactics with an Exposition and Discussion of the Steps Being Taken and Required to Curb It," Report of the Joint Legislative Committee Investigating Seditious Activities, Filed April 24, 1920, In the Senate of the State of New York, Committee Chairman Clayton R. Lusk, New York Legislative Documents, 144th sess., 1921, vol. 17, no. 50. *Part 1: Revolutionary and Subversive Movements Abroad and at Home, Volume I* (Albany: J. B. Lyon, 1921). See chapter 3

on the IFW, with quoted material from pp. 916, 921, 930 (hereafter cited as Lusk Committee Report).

10. See the IFW's weekly publication, *Hotel Worker,* April 26, 1919, 5 (hereafter cited as *HW*).

11. Deteriorating conditions are discussed in *MS,* January 15, 1916, 36, 37. There is also a retrospective discussion of working conditions in the *Free Voice,* publication of the Amalgamated Food Workers' Union, formed in 1919. See *Free Voice,* May 15, 1924, 5 (hereafter cited as *FV*).

12. The decline in Local 1's membership is based on membership records from the period, available on microfilm, Hotel and Restaurant Employees' International Union, International Headquarters, Washington, D.C.

13. *HW,* June 15, 1918, 1; and April 26, 1919, 1, 5.

14. Conditions and wage rates are covered in a series of investigations entitled "Report of U.S. Asst. District Attorney," File 50754, Record Group 28, National Archives. See reports dated June 8, 1918; July 6, 1918; and July 27, 1918. The quote is from *HW,* June 15, 1918, 1.

15. Wagner interview. On Lesino's background, see Josephson, *Union House,* 58.

16. *NYH,* November 1, 1918, 2.

17. *HW,* May 24, 1919, 10.

18. The government raid is covered in *HW,* June 14, 1919, 5; and report of agent A. E. Stevenson, Case File No. 215300, Microfilm Reel 625, FBI Papers. The October 26 strike is discussed in *HW,* June 14, 1919, 10.

19. Bourget is quoted in *NYC,* November 1, 1918, 2.

20. Bourget is quoted in *NYC,* November 1, 1918, 2. The spokesman for the Employment Service is quoted in *NYH,* November 1, 1918, 2.

21. *NYH,* October 30, 1918, 1.

22. The floor manager is quoted in Lois Peirce Hughes, "Opportunities for Women in the Modern Hotel," *Journal of Home Economics* 13 (April 1921): 153.

23. "Table showing number of women in labor organizations in New York State in each industry in 1914 and 1920," Frame 948, Microfilm Reel 18, Records of the National Women's Trade Union League of America, Kheel Center for Labor-Management Documentation and Archives, M. P. Catherwood Library, Cornell University. On the "logic of craft unionism" as a major factor in the exclusion of women from AFL-dominated trades, see Milkman, "Organizing the Sexual Division of Labor."

24. *HW,* June 14, 1919, 5.

25. *NYC,* November 1, 1918, 2.

26. *NYC,* November 1, 1918, 2; and November 4, 1918, 1.

27. The ruling is reported in *NYC,* November 14, 1918, 1. The hotel operators' refusal to recognize the union is from *NYC,* November 19, 1918, 1.

28. *NYC,* November 22, 1918, 1; *NYH,* November 22, 1918, 1.

29. Report of agent R. W. Finch, dated November 26, 1918, Case File No. 215300, Microfilm Reel 625, FBI Papers.

30. *NYC,* November 26, 1918, 1; and November 29, 1918, 1.

31. *NYC,* November 29, 1918, 1, 4.

32. *NYC,* December 3, 1918, 1.

33. The expanding walkout is covered in *NYC,* December 4, 1918, 1, 2; *NYT,* December 4, 1918, 11; and *NYC,* December 6, 1918, 1, 2. The split within the employers' ranks is from *NYT,* December 7, 1918, 13; and *NYC,* December 9, 1918, 1, 2.

34. Correspondence from Jere Sullivan to Gen. Enoch Crowder, dated November 5, 1918, Case File No. 330597, Microfilm Reel 752, FBI Papers.

35. Sullivan's boast of having "a hand" in the raid is reported in *HW,* June 14, 1919, 5. Gompers's snub of the IFW is from report of agent R. W. Finch, dated November 22, 1918, Case File No. 215300, Microfilm Reel 625, FBI Papers.

36. *NYC,* December 10, 1918, 1; and December 12, 1918, 1.

37. Wagner is quoted in *NYC,* December 14, 1918, 2. The Belmont walkout is covered in *NYC,* December 17, 1918, 3.

38. Wagner is quoted in *NYC,* December 17, 1918, 3. The Hotel Martinque walkout is covered in *NYC,* December 23, 1918, 1.

39. *NYC,* December 26, 1918, 1; and December 31, 1918, 1.

40. *NYC,* January 1, 1919, 1; January 10, 1919, 3; January 26, 1919, 3; and February 1, 1919, 2.

41. *HW,* April 5, 1919, 1, 5.

42. *HW,* April 12, 1919, 1.

43. The reference to "modern unionism" and the comparison to the "English shop steward system" is from *HW,* May 24, 1919, 10.

44. *NYH,* June 24, 1919, n.p., newspaper clipping file, Box Lo35 6, D166/2, Folder 33.5, Lusk Committee Hearings, New York State Archives, Albany (hereafter cited as Lusk Committee Clipping File). Also see *New York Sun,* June 24, 1919, n.p., Lusk Committee Clipping File; and *NYT,* June 24, 1919, 13.

45. *New York Tribune,* May 24, 1919, n.p., Lusk Committee Clipping File; *New York Tribune,* May 25, 1919, n.p., Lusk Committee Clipping File.

46. *New York World,* May 28, 1919, n.p., Lusk Committee Clipping File.

47. *MS,* July 17, 1919, 27.

48. *HW,* September 10, 1919, 1.

49. The shortage of strikebreakers is from *HW,* September 10, 1919, 1. The quote from pickets is in *NYH,* August 24, 1919, 4. Also see *NYH,* August 25, 1919, 4; *New York Telegram,* August 23, 1919, n.p., Lusk Committee Clipping File.

50. A proposal to organize culinary workers along industrial lines, rather than by craft, was introduced a few months later by delegates from Chicago who were attending the 1920 HRE convention. The proposal was referred to the union's executive council. See *NYT*, June 11, 1920, 18.

51. Hotel and Restaurant Employees' International Alliance and Bartenders International League of America, *Proceedings of the Twentieth General Convention*, August 11–15, 1919, 204. The appointment of immigrant organizers is reported in *MS*, October 15, 1920, 17.

52. Wagner interview.

53. *HW*, October 15, 1919, 1; and November 15, 1919, 6.

54. On amalgamationist tendencies in other industries, see Savage, *Industrial Unionism;* and Steve Fraser, "The 'New Unionism' and the 'New Economic Policy,'" in Cronin and Sirianni, *Work, Community, and Power*, 173–96.

55. *HW*, December 15, 1919, 4.

56. *HW*, June 15, 1920, 1.

57. *HW*, July 15, 1920, 4, 5.

58. The HRE's position is from *MS*, July 15, 1921, 23; and August 15, 1921, 15. The Amalgamated's view is from *FV*, June 15, 1921, 8; and August 1, 1921, 1.

59. HRE membership data are calculated from Hotel and Restaurant Employees' International Alliance and Bartenders International League of America, *Proceedings of the General Convention*, various years.

60. *MS*, July 15, 1923, 33–35.

61. *MS*, September 15, 1923, 43.

62. The formation of shop committees is discussed in *FV*, March 1, 1923, 1, 3, 7. The reference to new members is from *FV*, May 15, 1923, 1.

63. *FV*, April 1, 1924, 1.

64. See "Summary of Final Report of Commission of Conciliation," dated May 19, 1924, Regarding Salvin & Thompson Corp, Hotels, Charles Bendheim and Homer J. Brown, Commissioners of Conciliation, and related correspondence to Mr. Kerwin, dated April 2, 1924, Folder: Hotel & Restaurant Workers, New York City, Dispute Case Files, Case File No. 170–2464, Mediation Service Papers.

65. *FV*, May 15, 1924, 1.

66. *FV*, May 15, 1924, 1.

67. The emergence and early activities of the Communist bloc within the food workers is chronicled in clippings from the *Daily Worker* and interviews with key functionaries, collected as part of a research project directed by Daniel Bell. See Folder: Amalgamated Food Workers Notes for the Period 1920–1940, Box 6, Daniel Bell Papers, Tamiment Library, New York University.

68. Lore's stand on the initiative is praised in *DW*, March 6, 1925, 3. The expulsion of Lore is covered in *DW*, December 17, 1925, 2; and December

19, 1925, 4. The delegates' action in backing Lore is reported in *FV*, December 15, 1925, 5.

69. *FV*, December 1, 1925, 1, 5; and April 1, 1926, 1.

70. *FV*, July 15, 1926, 1.

71. *Labor Unity*, March 15, 1927, 5.

72. The quote on "making it snappy" is from *Labor Unity*, March 15, 1927, 5. The comparison to prostitution is from Cobble, "Sisters in the Craft," 34.

73. The quote on women being "readily susceptible" is from *Labor Unity*, March 15, 1927, 5. The total size of the city's wait staff is from U.S. Bureau of the Census, *Fourteenth Census of the United States Taken in the Year 1920*, vol. 4, *Population 1920, Occupations* (Washington, D.C.: GPO, 1923), 1160–62. Local 1's membership is from Hotel and Restaurant Employees' International Alliance and the Bartenders International League of America, *Proceedings of the General Convention, 1927*.

74. On employer preferences for male waiters, see the study by the U.S. Women's Bureau, U.S. Department of Labor, *The Effects of Labor Legislation on the Employment Opportunities of Women*, Bulletin of the Women's Bureau, No. 65 (Washington, D.C.: GPO, 1928), chap. 8, esp. 194–98.

75. The 1927 convention is covered in Cobble, "Sisters in the Craft," 398.

76. "Final Report of the Threatened Strike of the Waiters' and Waitresses' Union Local No. 1, New York, N.Y., Against the New York Restaurant Keepers' Association, New York, N. Y.," submitted June 3, 1922 by E. S. Dunnigan and William Zaranko, Commission of Conciliation, Dispute Case Files, Case File No. 170–1712, Mediation Service Papers.

77. W. I. Hamilton, *Promoting New Hotels: When Does It Pay?* (New York: Harper & Brothers, 1930), 131, 134.

78. The organizer is quoted in *MS*, November 11, 1926, 25. On the growing number of unemployed cooks, see *MS*, February 15, 1927, 17.

79. *FV*, February 1, 1929, 3.

80. On the number of recruits, see *DW*, March 29, 1929, 1. "JS" is quoted in *DW*, April 11, 1929, 4.

81. *DW*, April 11, 1929, 4.

82. *DW*, April 11, 1929, 4.

83. *NYH*, April 5, 1929, 11; *Labor Unity*, April 13, 1929, 1, 2.

84. Union leaders are quoted in *NYT*, April 20, 1929, 20.

85. *DW*, April 23, 1929, 5; *NYH*, April 24, 1929, 32; *Labor Unity*, April 20, 1929, 1, 2.

86. *NYH*, April 23, 1929, 13; *NYT*, May 3, 1929, 13. The reference to "oppressive picketing" is from *NYT*, May 9, 1929, 2. The owner's counsel is quoted in *NYT*, April 21, 1929, 22.

87. *FV*, June 1, 1929, 1, 2; *Labor Unity*, June 15, 1929, 8; Manuel Alvarez, tape-recorded interview with author, May 11, 1989, New York.

88. On Local 719's defection to the Amalgamated, see _Labor Unity,_ May 22, 1929, 2; _FV,_ June 1, 1929, 2; and Josephson, _Union House,_ 171, 172.

89. Hotel and Restaurant Employees' International Alliance and Bartenders International League of America, _Proceedings of the Twenty-fifth General Convention,_ August 12–17, 1929, 2, 106–15; _Labor Unity,_ June 22, 1929, 3.

90. _FV,_ January 1, 1930, 3; _Labor Unity,_ February 15, 1930, 5.

91. _FV,_ February 1, 1930, 1; _MS,_ February 15, 1930, 15.

92. _NYT,_ February 21, 1930, 13.

93. _Labor Unity,_ April 19, 1930, 10; _FV,_ May 1, 1930, 1. The FWIU was formed on the heels of a massive outpouring of anger by food workers over the killing of Steve Katovis, a striking member of the TUUL's Food Clerks Local, who was gunned down by police in January 1930. See Herbert Benjamin, transcript of interview, Oral History Collection, Columbia University, 388–94.

94. _FV,_ November 1, 1930, 1.

95. _FV,_ November 1, 1930, 1. Jay Rubin, tape-recorded interview with author, May 7, 1989, Newton, Connecticut (hereafter cited as Rubin interview).

96. _MS,_ November 15, 1930, 12.

97. The two observers are Rubin and Obermeirer; see Rubin and Obermeirer, _Growth of a Union,_ 228. Harold Seidman, _Labor Czars: A History of Labor Racketeering_ (New York: Liveright, 1938), 202–4. Julius Margolin, tape-recorded interview, December 30, 1983, Oral History of the American Left Collection, Tamiment Library, New York University.

98. The number of injunctions is from William Z. Foster, _From Bryan to Stalin_ (London: Lawrence & Wishart, 1937), 225n. The party's sectarian attacks on both the Amalgamated and the HRE are found throughout the _Food Worker,_ official organ of the FWIU (hereafter cited as _FW_). See _FW_ (October 1931); (May-June 1932): 5; (December 1932): 5.

99. The employers' favorable reaction to the code is from _NYT,_ August 23, 1933, 3. The reactions of HRE officers are from _NYT,_ December 14, 1933, 9; and December 23, 1933, 6.

100. _FV,_ October 1, 1933, 1.

101. Herbert Solow, "The New York Hotel Strike," _Nation,_ February 28, 1934, 239; _NYT,_ January 24, 1934, 1, 3; Irving Bernstein, _Turbulent Years: A History of American Workers, 1933–1941_ (Boston: Houghton Mifflin, 1970), 122, 123.

102. Solow, "New York Hotel Strike," 239.

103. The Local 16 spokesman is quoted in _NYH,_ January 25, 1934, 3. _FW_ (February 1, 1934): 1.

104. Gitlow is quoted in _NYT,_ January 29, 1934, 2.

105. The role of Trotskyist influences is thoroughly covered in Dan Georgakas, "The Greeks in America," _Journal of the Hellenic Diaspora_ 14, nos.

1–2 (Spring-Summer 1987): 35–37. Also see the two-part discussion in *Labor Action,* March 15, 1934, 3; and April 2, 1934, 3.

106. The attack on Amalgamated officials is in *DW,* January 30, 1934, 6. The accusation of holding back the strikers is from *DW,* January 31, 1934, 2.

107. The street demonstrations are covered in *NYH,* January 31, 1934, 8; February 6, 1934, 1, 2; and February 11, 1934, 1, 22. The agreement is outlined in *NYT,* February 20, 1934, 23; and *NYH,* February 20, 1934, 11.

108. *NYT,* February 22, 1934, 1, 17; *NYH,* February 23, 1934, 1, 13.

109. The report of workers being refused their jobs is from *DW,* March 8, 1934, 2. The attack on Amalgamated officials for losing the strike is from *DW,* March 22, 1934, 3. The committee of 30 is covered in *FW* (April 1934): 1, 6.

110. The April meeting is reported in *DW,* May 3, 1934, 2. Opposition to Communist political leadership is discussed in *FV,* August 1, 1934, 3.

111. Rubin and Obermeirer, *Growth of a Union,* 237, 238.

112. Rubin and Obermeirer, *Growth of a Union,* 238.

113. Seidman, *Labor Czars,* 202–4.

114. The $2 million figure is from Seidman, *Labor Czars,* 204. Abe Borson's tragic story is told in *MS,* December 12, 1933, 29.

115. Rubin and Obermeirer, *Growth of a Union,* 240.

116. Rubin and Obermeirer, *Growth of a Union,* 245–50; *DW,* August 17, 1936, 3.

117. *FW* (February-March 1936): 1. The election results are reported in *DW,* December 4, 1936, 4.

118. Rubin interview. This is not to argue that Communist and AFL culinary leaders, in subscribing to a broadly similar syndicalist logic of mobilization during the early 1930s, were therefore locked into identical practices of unionism. On the contrary, the only systematic cross-industry comparative study of the impact of union leadership on collective bargaining found that Communist-led CIO unions, as compared to industrial unions without leftist leadership, generally secured contracts that were more "pro-worker"—a finding that is perfectly consistent with the distinction drawn here between industrial and business forms of syndicalism as the basis of union loyalty. See Judith Stepan-Norris and Maurice Zeitlin, " 'Red' Unions and 'Bourgeois' Contracts?" *American Journal of Sociology* 96 (March 1991): 1151–1200.

Chapter Six. Syndicalism, Pure and Simple

1. This rendering is drawn from Hoxie, *Trade Unionism,* 45 ff. It remains, in basic outline, the accepted view of the AFL in contemporary scholarship as well as in recent textbooks on American history. On the latter, see Dorothy Sue Cobble and Alice Kessler-Harris, "The New Labor History in American

History Textbooks," *Journal of American History* 79, no. 4 (March 1993): 1542–43.

2. Summarizing what has been for many years the standard view, Harold Livesay writes: "Under Gompers's firm guidance, the AF of L grew by appealing to the conservative, procapitalist sentiments of craft workers and their unions." See Livesay, *Samuel Gompers,* 128.

3. The quotes refer specifically to the thesis of "job consciousness," perhaps the most common version of proletarian conservatism. See the important critique of Perlman by Gulick and Bers, "Insight and Illusion," 510. Similarly, Montgomery argues that "the phrase 'wage and job consciousness' [has served] for half a century . . . as the shibboleth to separate 'the realists' from 'the romantics.' This toil-worn, dog-eared phrase, which could serve as well to *open* a discussion of working-class consciousness in America, has been used instead to *close* it." See David Montgomery, "To Study the People: The American Working Class," *Labor History* 21, no. 4 (Fall 1980): 500.

4. The lack of reliable historical data on worker consciousness has been responded to in recent years by social historians whose use of workers' diaries, private correspondence, and other personal sources offers greater access to the mental worlds of the (literate) rank and file. Still, such data do not address the larger methodological problem posed by the lack of fit between ideas and behavior, an incongruence that limits the utility of focusing on ideas as a means of understanding collective action. For a related critique that focuses more generally on the "disjuncture between collective action and individual belief," see Rick Fantasia, "Class Consciousness in Culture, Action, and Social Organization," *Annual Review of Sociology* 21 (1995): 272.

5. On the impenetrability of past mental worlds, see, for example, Rock, "Some Problems of Historiography"; and Goldthorpe "The Uses of History in Sociology." But see the replies to Goldthorpe in *British Journal of Sociology* 45, no. 1 (March 1994): 1–54.

6. Marshall, "Some Remarks on the Study of Working-Class Consciousness," 272.

7. "Options under pressure" is from Raymond Williams, as quoted by Ellen Meiksins Wood, "The Politics of Theory and the Concept of Class: E. P. Thompson and His Critics," *Studies in Political Economy,* no. 9 (Fall 1982): 69. Thinking of popular consciousness as historically intelligible "options under pressure," rather than as "false," "distorted" or "partial," restores both agency and the possibility of resistance to subordinate groups. For a similar understanding of class as a "structure of choices facing class actors," see Adam Przeworksi, "Proletariat into a Class: The Process of Class Formation from Karl Kautsky's *The Class Struggle* to Recent Controversies," *Politics and Society* 7, no. 4 (1977): 343–401.

8. Gramsci's concept of ideological hegemony has come under attack for overstating the coherence and pervasiveness of such "hegemonic" world-

views while also failing to fully appreciate the counterhegemonic practices that enable subordinate populations to distance themselves from the dominant ideology. See Nicholas Abercrombie, Stephen Hill, and Bryan S. Turner, *The Dominant Ideology Thesis* (London: Allen & Unwin, 1980); James Scott, *Weapons of the Weak: Everyday Forms of Peasant Resistance* (New Haven: Yale University Press, 1985); and Robin D. G. Kelley, *Race Rebels: Culture, Politics, and the Black Working Class* (New York: Free Press, 1994). The "rebellion of the belly" is a term originally employed by E. P. Thompson, "The Moral Economy of the English Crowd in the Eighteenth Century," *Past and Present* 50 (February 1971): 77. Whereas an earlier generation of institutional historians saw workers struggling for more bread, much current work points in the opposite direction in seeing collective action as a response to demands for dignity, framed as more "roses." For an illuminating essay on this tension, see Gerald M. Sider, "Cleansing History: Lawrence, Massachusetts, the Strike for Four Loaves of Bread and No Roses, and the Anthropology of Working-Class Consciousness," *Radical History Review* 65 (Spring 1996): 48–83.

9. On the general tendency toward institutional isomorphism or "organizational homogeneity," see Paul J. DiMaggio and Walter Powell, "The Iron Cage Revisited: Institutional Isomorphism and Collective Rationality in Organizational Fields," *American Sociological Review* 48, no. 2 (April 1983): 147–60.

10. While it is doubtless risky to generalize about "the" character of American unionism based on only two cases, much the same process of convergence between the IWW and the AFL was found by Elizabeth Reis in her study of efforts to unionize northern California's canneries shortly after World War I. While Reis follows convention in highlighting the ideological contrast between Wobblies and craft unionists, the overlap in organizational efforts at the ground level is so great that she is unable to say for sure whether the union most involved—the so-called Toilers of the World— is an extension of the AFL, to which it belongs, or simply a "front" for the IWW, as many contemporaries charged. As this is one of the few other empirical studies focusing on the interunion rivalry between the IWW and the AFL, her findings are in any case reassuring. See Elizabeth Reis, "The AFL, the IWW, and Bay Area Italian Cannery Workers," *California History* 64, no. 3 (Summer 1985): 175–91.

11. James A. Estey, *Revolutionary Syndicalism: An Exposition and a Criticism* (London: P. S. King and Son, 1913), 207.

12. On American labor's comparatively limited political role, see Michael Rogin, "Voluntarism: The Political Functions of an Anti-political Doctrine," *Industrial and Labor Relations Review* 15, no. 4 (July 1962): 521–35; Ruth L. Horowitz, *Political Ideologies of Organized Labor* (New Brunswick: Transaction Books, 1978), chap. 1; Lipset "Radicalism or Reformism"; Daniel B. Cornfield, "Union Decline and the Political Demands of Organized

Labor," *Work and Occupations* 16, no. 3 (August 1989): 292–322; Marks, *Unions in Politics;* and Hattam, *Labor Visions and State Power.* It would be misleading, however, to overstate the contrast between the U.S. and Western European workers' movements. If, for example, one looks at "independent political action," French unions, with their traditional lack of ties to any one political party and prohibitions against officers running for political office, might appear "less political than American labor." See Adolf Sturmthal, "Comments on Selig Perlman's *A Theory of the Labor Movement," Industrial and Labor Relations Review* 4, no. 4 (July 1951): 494. Likewise, the drift toward job control unionism throughout Western Europe has led to greater convergence with U.S. practices. See Adolf Sturmthal, *Tragedy of European Labor, 1918–1939* (New York: Columbia University Press, 1943). This theme is carried forward in a more recent cross-national study of automobile workers in the United States, Italy, Argentina, and India, which concluded that "workers everywhere agreed on major union functions and eschewed political unionism." See William H. Form, "Job Unionism versus Political Unionism in Four Countries," in Horowitz, Leggett, and Oppenheimer, *American Working Class,* 221.

13. For a rich and insightful discussion of the factors that produce different labor political alliances at the local level, see William H. Form, *Segmented Labor, Fractured Politics: Labor Politics in American Life* (New York: Plenum Press, 1995). The quote on "partial equivalence" is from the classic study by David J. Greenstone, *Labor in American Politics* (Chicago: University of Chicago Press, 1969), 361–62.

14. "The overarching specificity of the American [industrial relations] system, of course, derives from the absence of independent political representation for labor within national or state politics." See Mike Davis, *Prisoners of the American Dream: Politics and Economy in the History of the U.S. Working Class* (London: Verso, 1986), 113. At the local level, however, American unions, including even many AFL affiliates, were more politically active. The AFL's political activism peaked for a brief moment in the early twentieth century. See Julia Greene, " 'The Strike at the Ballot Box': The American Federation of Labor's Entrance into Election Politics, 1906–1909," *Labor History* 32, no. 2 (Spring 1991): 165–92.

15. Viewing politics in less institutionalized terms, David Wellman argues that American workers were apolitical only in the narrow sense of failing to sustain an active Socialist presence in the formal political arena. Rather, their politics were conducted on the job, through the "politicization of everyday life at work" as reflected in struggles to control their working environment. See David Wellman, *The Union Makes Us Strong: Radical Unionism on the San Francisco Waterfront* (Cambridge: Cambridge University Press, 1995). A similarly expansive concept of "infrapolitics" is employed by Robin D. G. Kelley to capture informal daily modes of resistance to capitalist hegemony, in his *Race Rebels,* chap. 1.

16. The reference to "job syndicalism" is from Perlman, *A Theory*, 288–89. The ill-defined concept of economism has been a favorite target of Marxists, beginning with Lenin's early critique of Russian social democracy. Lenin's critique of economism is presented most forcefully in his celebrated polemic "What Is to Be Done?" in Henry M. Christman, ed., *Essential Works of Lenin* (New York: Bantam Books, 1966), 53–175. For a more general survey of Lenin's views on trade unionism, see Thomas Taylor Hammond, *Lenin on Trade Unions and Revolution, 1893–1917* (New York: Columbia University Press, 1957).

17. Baker's openness to the ILWU's organizing principles is from "Report on Situation in ILA in Boston, Portland, Phila, Baltimore" from Sammy Kovnat, n.d., ILWU Organizing Files, Box 15, File: Organizing—East Coast—Longshore, misc. reports, leaflets 1937–1940, International Longshore and Warehouse Union Library, International Longshore and Warehouse Union, San Francisco. The anti-Communist reference to "intelligentsia" is from Clippings File, dated 1938, Urban Archives, Temple University.

18. Baker was routinely vilified in the pro-Communist labor press. See *DW*, November 2, 1934, 6; and *Labor Unity*, July 23, 1930, 5.

19. Repeated ILWU raids from 1937 through 1939 failed to win over the port's regularly employed deepwater longshoremen. CIO organizers did make some inroads among the unorganized banana workers but never had enough strength to build a viable local on the docks. See the East Coast ILWU agitational organ *Shape-Up*, March 1, 1938, 1; a more sober assessment is offered in a report by East Coast organizer Ralph Dawson in ILWU, *Proceedings of the Second Annual Convention of the International Longshoremen's and Warehousemen's Union*, April 3–14, 1939, 149–50.

20. Josephson, *Union House*, 320–29; Horowitz, *New York Hotel Industry*, 91–100.

21. Edwards, *Strikes*, 253.

22. See, for example, Edwards, *Strikes*, 241; Lipset, *The First New Nation*, chap. 5; "Editors' Introduction," Maurice Zeitlin and Howard Kimeldorf, eds., *Political Power and Social Theory* 4 (1984): xi–xiii.

23. Beth Rubin, "Class Struggle American Style: Unions, Strikes, and Wages," *American Sociological Review* 51, no. 5 (October 1986): 618. The quote on "the sway of capital" is from Stepan-Norris and Zeitlin, " 'Red' Unions and 'Bourgeois' Contracts?" 1193.

24. McDonnell, " 'You Are Too Sentimental,' " 641, 630.

25. Stated as a general proposition, it does not require an awareness of revolutionary objectives before subordinate populations can undertake actions that might precipitate revolutionary changes in society. See Therborn, "Why Some Classes Are More Successful"; and Kelly, *Trade Unions*. On the disjuncture between "revolutionary" action and "reformist" ideas, see Eley and Nield, "Why Does Social History Ignore Politics?" 261; and Dick Geary,

"Identifying Militancy: The Assessment of Working-Class Attitudes Towards State and Society," in Richard J. Evans, ed., *The German Working Class, 1888–1933: The Politics of Everyday Life* (London: Croom Helm, 1982), 225.

26. For an excellent overview of recent scholarship on labor law, see Christopher Tomlins, "How Who Rides Whom: Recent 'New' Histories of American Labour Law and What They May Signify," *Social History* 21, no. 1 (January 1995): 1–21.

27. Monds, "Workers' Control."

28. McDonnell, " 'You Are Too Sentimental,' " 644. Also see Monds, "Workers' Control"; Foner, "Why Is There No Socoialism"; and Wilentz, "Against Exceptionalism."

29. European syndicalism exhibited many of the same tendencies toward pragmatism and compromise, particularly in England. See James Hinton, *The First Shop Stewards' Movement* (London: Allen & Unwin, 1973); and Bob Holton, *British Syndicalism, 1900–1914: Myths and Realities* (London: Pluto Press, 1976).

30. The connections, organizationally, between the IWW and the CIO can be seen in Les DeCaux, *The Living Spirit of the Wobblies* (New York: International Publishers, 1978); and David Milton, *The Politics of U.S. Labor: From the Great Depression to the New Deal* (New York: Monthly Review Press, 1982).

31. The GE strike is covered in Foner, *History of the Labor Movement*, 88; and James Matles, *Them and Us: Struggles of a Rank and File Union* (Boston: Beacon Press, 1974), 71. The story of the more famous GM sitdown strike in 1937 is told exceptionally well by Sidney Fine, *Sit Down: The General Motors Strike of 1936–37* (Ann Arbor: University of Michigan Press, 1969).

32. Quoted in a pamphlet by A. M. Stirton, "Getting Recognition: What It Means to a Union," 1912, Reel 19, IWW Film. On the syndicalist tinge to the CIO, see the dissenting views of David Brody, "Radical Labor History and Rank-and-File Militancy," *Labor History* 16, no. 1 (Winter 1975): 124; and Milton, *The Politics of U.S. Labor,* 107.

33. Membership figures for the CIO are from confidential reports by Philip Murray to the CIO executive board regarding per capita tax payments from its affiliated unions. AFL figures, also based on per capita dues, are from reports filed by each of the affiliated unions. The AFL membership figures for 1936 are based on subtracting some 800,000 members who were then enrolled in what would shortly become CIO unions. See Walter Galenson, *The CIO Challenge to the AFL: A History of the American Labor Movement, 1935–1941* (Cambridge, Mass.: Harvard University Press, 1960), 585–87. James Green places the CIO's membership at 4 million sometime after the 1937 sit-down strike wave. There is no source cited for this much higher figure. See James Green, *World of the Worker: Labor in Twentieth-*

Century America (New York: Hill and Wang, 1980), 158. Similarly, Art Preis reports, also without citation, that the CIO added 400,000 to the 3.7 million members it claimed during its first two years of existence. See Art Preis, *Labor's Giant Step: Twenty Years of the CIO* (New York: Pathfinder Press, 1964), 72. Altogether different membership totals are cited by Tomlins, whose figures, drawn from earlier research by Leo Troy and Leo Wolman, show both the AFL and the CIO growing by just under one million members from 1936 to 1940. Tomlins also challenges the view of the AFL as a stodgy defender of craft unionism, arguing instead that many AFL affiliates were open to industrial structures and that they played a vital and independent role in rebuilding American labor during the 1930s. See Tomlins, "AFL Unions in the 1930s."

34. Galenson, *The CIO Challenge*, 604.

35. This is not to minimize the significance of the more favorable political climate created by Roosevelt's election in 1932. Organized labor, particularly the newly formed industrial organizing committee of the AFL, took full advantage of such key legislative weapons as the Wagner Act of 1935. But it was the escalating struggle inside the workplace that consumed the attention of union leaders and liberal policy advisers alike. See Michael Goldfield, "Worker Insurgency, Radical Organization, and New Deal Labor Legislation," *American Political Science Review* 83, no. 4 (December 1989): 1257–82. Also see Preis, *Labor's Giant Step*.

36. For CIO leaders, the importance of political engagement grew in proportion to the growing backlash against labor. Thus the CIO did not form its Political Action Committee until July 1943, in direct response to the antiunion Smith-Connally Act, which was passed by Congress only a few weeks before. With the election of a Republican Congress in 1946, followed by passage of the "slave labor" Taft-Hartley Act a year later, the CIO, and even the AFL, attached a higher priority to politics, if for no other reason than self-defense. Still the electoral arena remained secondary to the point of production as the preferred site of struggle for both CIO and AFL leaders. See Robert H. Zieger, *The CIO, 1935–1955* (Chapel Hill: University of North Carolina Press, 1995), 180–88, 241–52. On the role of the CIO in politics, see James Caldwell Foster, *The Union Politic: The CIO Political Action Committee* (Columbia: University of Missouri Press, 1975); and David Plotke, *Building a Democratic Political Order: Reshaping American Liberalism in the 1930s and 1940s* (Cambridge: Cambridge University Press, 1996). The CIO's organizational and political efforts are also covered in David Brody, *Workers in Industrial America: Essays on the Twentieth-Century Struggle* (New York: Oxford University Press, 1980); Rhonda F. Levine, *Class Struggle and the New Deal: Industrial Labor, Industrial Capital, and the State* (Lawrence: University of Kansas Press, 1988); and Lizabeth Cohen, *Making a New Deal: Industrial Workers in Chicago, 1919–1939* (New York: Cambridge University Press, 1990).

37. Kim Moody, *An Injury to All: The Decline of American Unionism* (London: Verso, 1988); George Rawick, "Working Class Self-Activity," *Radical America* 3, no. 2 (March-April 1969): 23–31.

38. The "logic" of contract unionism is argued by Aronowitz, *False Promises,* chap. 4. For a compelling critique, see Herb Mills and David Wellman, "Contractually Sanctioned Job Action and Workers' Control: The Case of San Francisco Longshoremen," *Labor History* 28 (Spring 1987): 167–95.

39. On wildcat strikes, see the classic study by Alvin Gouldner, *Wildcat Strike* (Yellow Springs, Ohio: Antioch Press, 1954). Also see the more recent ethnographic studies of emergent strike activity by Fantasia, *Cultures of Solidarity.*

40. Wellman, *The Union Makes Us Strong.* It is not just unionized workers who routinely challenge industrial authority at work. Unorganized workers have devised some especially creative ways to resist, like the iron workers who, when told to perform a dangerous task on a high-rise building, downed their tools, held hands, and, citing their First Amendment rights, prayed for their safety. Such forms of resistance have been a recurring feature of American industrial relations. For other examples, see Stanley Bernard Mathewson, *Restriction of Output Among Unorganized Workers* (New York: Viking Press, 1931); and Harry Braverman, *Labor and Monopoly Capitalism* (New York: Monthly Review Press, 1974).

41. Ralf Dahrendorf, *Class and Class Conflict in Industrial Society* (Stanford: Stanford University Press, 1955); Clark Kerr, John T. Dunlop, Frederick H. Harbison, and Charles A. Myers, *Industrialism and Industrial Man: The Problems of Labor and Management in Economic Growth* (Cambridge, Mass.: Harvard University Press, 1960).

42. Stanley Weir, "U.S.A.: The Labor Revolt," in Zeitlin, *American Society, Inc.,* 487–524; Aronowitz, *False Promises,* chaps. 1, 7.

43. Figures on work stoppages in 1970 are from David M. Gordon, "Capital vs. Labor," in Zeitlin, *American Society, Inc.,* 532. The government task force is quoted in *Work in America,* Report of a Special Task Force to the Secretary of Health, Education, and Welfare (Cambridge, Mass.: MIT Press, 1973), xvi, 11.

44. See Jeremy Brecher and Tim Costello, eds., *Building Bridges: The Emerging Grassroots Coalition of Labor and Community* (New York: Monthly Review Press, 1990); Paul Johnston, *Success While Others Fail: Social Movement Unionism and the Public Workplace* (Ithaca: ILR Press, 1994); Sam Gindin, "Notes on Labor at the End of the Century: Starting Over?" *Monthly Review* 49, no. 3 (July-August 1997): 140–57; and Kim Moody, *Labor in a Lean World* (London: Verso, 1997).

45. On the changing composition of organized labor, both at the top and at the bottom, see Peter Meiksins, "Same as It Ever Was: The Structure of the Working Class," *Monthly Review* 49, no. 3 (July-August 1997): 31–45; Michael Goldfield, "Race and Labor in the United States," *Monthly Review*

49, no. 3 (July-August 1997): 80–97; and Robin D. G. Kelley, "The New Urban Working Class and Organized Labor," *New Labor Forum* 1 (Fall 1997): 6–18.

46. With the election in 1995 of new leadership at the top of the AFL-CIO and renewed organizing activity at the bottom, much has changed since 1991 when labor could be dismissed, in the words of a longtime supporter, as "too old, too arthritic, to be a cause." This supporter continued, "I try to think of the AFL-CIO in the year 2001. But I cannot do it. The whole idea is too perverse." See Thomas Geoghegan, *Which Side Are You On: Trying to Be for Labor When It's Flat on Its Back* (New York: Penguin Books, 1991). The two observers are Steven Fraser and Joshua B. Freeman, "Introduction," in Fraser and Freeman, eds., *Audacious Democracy: Labor, Intellectuals, and the Social Reconstruction of America* (Boston: Houghton Mifflin, 1997), 1. For contrasting perspectives on American labor's future, see Seymour Martin Lipset, "American Union Density in Comparative Perspective," *Contemporary Sociology* 27, no. 2 (March 1998): 123–25; and Ruth Milkman, "The New Labor Movement: Possibilities and Limits," *Contemporary Sociology* 27, no. 2 (March 1998): 125–29.

47. For an understanding of labor as a "mighty force" capable of disrupting the national economy, see the empirical analysis of union density by Howard Kimeldorf and Maurice Zeitlin, "How Mighty a Force? The Internal Differentiation and Relative Organization of the American Working Class," in Maurice Zeitlin, ed., *How Mighty a Force? Studies of Workers' Consciousness and Organization in the United States* (Los Angeles: Institute of Industrial Relations, University of California, 1983), 1–64.

48. Arthur B. Shostak, *Robust Unionism: Innovations in the Labor Movement* (Ithaca: Cornell University Press, 1991); Brecher and Costello, *Building Bridges.*

49. John J. Sweeney, "America Needs a Raise," in Fraser and Freeman, *Audacious Democracy,* 18–19.

50. Barry Bluestone and Bennet Harrison, *The Deindustrialization of America: Plant Closings, Community Abandonment, and the Dismantling of Basic Industry* (New York: Basic Books, 1982); James P. Womack, Daniel T. Jones, and Daniel Roos, *The Machine that Changed the World: The Story of Lean Production. How Japan's Secret Weapon in the Global Auto Wars Will Revolutionize Western Industry* (New York: HarperPerennial, 1991). Militant strikers in Flint, Michigan, forced GM to agree to return metal stamping dies that had been removed from the plant only a few days earlier. See *NYT,* June 12, 1998, 1, C2.

51. On the regional shift in unionization, see Goldfield, *Decline of Organized Labor,* 17–19, 139–44. The quotes on Las Vegas are from a story in *NYT,* April 27, 1998, 10.

52. *NYT,* April 27, 1998, 10.

Bibliography

Archives and Institutes

Abelson, Paul. Papers. Kheel Center for Labor-Management Documentation and Archives, M. P. Catherwood Library, Cornell University, Ithaca, New York.

American Federation of Labor Records: The Samuel Gompers Era. Papers. Microfilm. Sanford, N.C.: Microfilming Corporation of America, 1979.

Bell, Daniel. Papers. Tamiment Institute, New York University, New York, New York.

Federal Bureau of Investigation. Papers. Record Group 65, National Archives, Washington, D.C.

Federal Bureau of Investigation. Report of unidentified agent, dated April 15, 1922, received through a Freedom of Information Act request dated June 30, 1994, by Howard Kimeldorf.

Federal Mediation and Conciliation Service. Papers. Record Group 280, Washington National Records Center, Suitland, Maryland.

Harris, Abram. Papers. Abram Harris Collection, Moorland-Spingarn Research Center, Howard University, Washington, D.C.

Hotel and Restaurant Employees' International Union. Records. Hotel and Restaurant Employees' International Union International Headquarters, Washington, D.C.

Industrial Workers of the World. Papers. Walter P. Reuther Library, Archives of Labor and Urban Affairs, Wayne State University, Detroit, Michigan.

Industrial Workers of the World. Records. Kheel Center for Labor-Management Documentation and Archives, M. P. Catherwood Library, Cornell University, Ithaca, New York.

Inglis, Agnes. Papers. Labadie Collection, Special Collections Library, University of Michigan, Ann Arbor, Michigan.

International Longshore and Warehouse Union. Papers. International Longshore and Warehouse Union Research Library, San Francisco, California.

National Women's Trade Union League of America. Papers. Kheel Center
    for Labor-Management Documentation and Archives, M. P. Catherwood
    Library, Cornell University, Ithaca, New York. Microfilm.
New York. Lusk Committee Hearings, New York State Archives, Albany,
    New York.
Saposs, D. J. Papers. Archives Division, State Historical Society of Wiscon-
    sin, Madison.
Stokes, Rose Pastor. Papers. Tamiment Institute, New York University, New
    York, New York.
Taylor, Fred Walter. Papers. The Historical Society of Pennsylvania, Phila-
    delphia.
Thompson, Fred. Papers. Walter P. Reuther Library, Archives of Labor
    History and Urban Affairs, Wayne State University, Detroit, Michigan.
Urban Archives. Newspaper clipping file. Temple University, Philadelphia,
    Pennsylvania.
U.S. Department of Justice. Papers. Record Group 60, National Archives,
    Washington, D.C.
U.S. Shipping Board. Papers. Record Group 32, National Archives, Wash-
    ington, D.C.
U.S. War Department. Papers. General Staff, Military Intelligence Division,
    Record Group 165, National Archives, Washington, D.C.

Oral Histories

Alvarez, Manuel. Tape-recorded interview with Howard Kimeldorf. May 11,
    1989, New York, New York.
Benjamin, Herbert. Transcript of interview. 1976. Oral History Collection,
    Columbia University, New York, New York.
Biginski, Joe. Tape-recorded interview with Howard Kimeldorf. May 3,
    1989, Philadelphia, Pennsylvania.
Kane, Joe. Tape-recorded interview with Howard Kimeldorf. May 2, 1989,
    Philadelphia, Pennsylvania.
Kelly, Edward. Telephone interview with Howard Kimeldorf. March 10,
    1990, Ann Arbor, Michigan.
Lever, Jack. Transcript of interview with Herbert Hill. May 29, 1968,
    Solebury, Pennsylvania. Blacks in the Labor Movement Oral History Pro-
    ject, Walter P. Reuther Library, Archives of Labor and Urban Affairs,
    Wayne State University, Detroit, Michigan.
Margolin, Julius. Tape-recorded interview with Jon Bloom. December 30,
    1983. Oral History of the American Left Collection, Tamiment Institute,
    New York University, New York, New York.
Moocke, James. Tape-recorded interview. N.d. "Delaware River Oral His-
    tory Project," Independence Seaport Museum, Philadelphia, Pennsylva-
    nia.

Moses, Abraham. Tape-recorded interview with Greg Williams and Ed Kirlin. May 12, 1980. "Delaware River Oral History Project," Independence Seaport Museum, Philadelphia, Pennsylvania.

Nicas, Demosthenes. Tape-recorded interview with Howard Kimeldorf. May 6, 1989, Bronx, New York.

Rubin, Jay. Tape-recorded interview with Howard Kimeldorf. May 7, 1989, Newton, Connecticut.

Wagner, Otto. Transcript of interview by D. J. Saposs. June 5, 1919, New York, New York.

Periodicals

Daily Worker
Fellow Worker
Food Worker
Free Voice
Hotel Worker
Industrial Pioneer
Industrial Worker
International Hotel Work
International Socialist Review
Labor Action
Labor Unity
Marine Worker
Messenger
Mixer and Server
Monthly Labor Review
Negro World
New York Call
New York Herald
New York Sun
New York Telegram
New York Times
New York Tribune
New York World
One Big Union Monthly
Philadelphia Evening Bulletin
Philadelphia Inquirer
Philadelphia Public Ledger
Philadelphia Tribune
Rebel Worker
Shape-Up
Solidarity

Survey
Voice of the People (New Orleans)

Books, Articles, and Dissertations

Abbott, Andrew. "From Causes to Events: Notes on Narrative Positivism."
   Sociological Research and Methods 20, no. 4 (May 1992): 428–55.
Abercrombie, Nicholas, Stephen Hill, and Bryan S. Turner. The Dominant
   Ideology Thesis. London: Allen & Unwin, 1980.
Althusser, Louis. Essays in Self-Criticism. London: New Left Books, 1976.
American Federation of Labor. American Federation of Labor Records: The
   Samuel Gompers Era. Microfilm. Sanford, N.C.: Microfilming Corpora-
   tion of America, 1979.
Aminzade, Ronald. "Historical Sociology and Time." Sociological Methods
   and Research 20, no. 4 (May 1992): 456–80.
Annunziato, Frank. "Commodity Unionism." Rethinking Marxism 3, no. 2
   (Summer 1990): 8–33.
Arneson, Eric. "Biracial Waterfront Unionism in the Age of Segregation."
   In Waterfront Workers: New Perspectives on Race and Class, ed. Calvin
   Winslow, 19–61. Urbana: University of Illinois Press, 1998.
———. "Crusaders Against Critics: A View from the United States on the
   'Rank and File' Critique and Other Catalogues of Labour History's Al-
   leged Ills." International Review of Social History 35, no. 1 (1990): 106–
   27.
———. "It Ain't Like They Do in New Orleans: Race Relations, Labor
   Markets, and Waterfront Labor Movements in the American South." In
   Racism and the Labour Market: Historical Studies, ed. Marcel van der
   Linden and Jan Lucassen, 57–100. New York: Peter Lang, 1995.
———. Waterfront Workers of New Orleans: Race, Class, and Politics,
   1863–1923. New York: Oxford University Press, 1991.
Aronowitz, Stanley. False Promises: The Shaping of American Working Class
   Consciousness. New York: McGraw-Hill, 1973.
Ash, Roberta. Social Movements in America. Chicago: Markham, 1972.
Asteroff, Janet. "The Intrusion of Ideology: Wobbly Marine Workers of Phil-
   adelphia, 1913–1926." Unpublished seminar paper (1975). Fred Thomp-
   son Papers, Walter P. Reuther Library, Archives of Labor History and
   Urban Affairs, Wayne State University, Detroit, Michigan.
Barnes, Charles B. The Longshoremen. New York: Russell Sage Foundation,
   1915.
Baron, Ava, ed. Work Engendered: Toward a New History of American La-
   bor. Ithaca: Cornell University Press, 1991.
Baxandal, Rosalyn Fraad. Words of Fire: The Life and Writing of Elizabeth
   Gurley Flynn. New Brunswick: Rutgers University Press, 1987.

Bell, Daniel. *The End of Ideology: On the Exhaustion of Political Ideas in the Fifties.* Glencoe: Free Press, 1960.

Bernstein, Irving. *Turbulent Years: A History of American Workers, 1933–1941.* Boston: Houghton Mifflin, 1970.

Bettleheim, Charles. *Class Struggles in the U.S.S.R. First Period: 1919–1923.* New York: Monthly Review Press, 1976.

Bird, Stewart, Dan Georgakas, and Deborah Shaffer, eds. *Solidarity Forever: An Oral History of the IWW.* Chicago: Lake View Press, 1985.

Bluestone, Barry, and Bennet Harrison. *The Deindustrialization of America: Plant Closings, Community Abandonment, and the Dismantling of Basic Industry.* New York: Basic Books, 1982.

Bodnar, John. "Immigration, Kinship, and the Rise of Working-Class Realism in Industrial America." *Journal of Social History* 14, no. 1 (Fall 1980): 45–65.

Bohn, Frank. "The Strike of the New York Hotel and Restaurant Workers." *International Socialist Review* 13 (February 1913): 620–21.

Bonacich, Edna. "A Theory of Ethnic Antagonism: The Split Labor Market." *American Sociological Review* 37, no. 5 (October 1972): 547–59.

Braverman, Harry. *Labor and Monopoly Capitalism.* New York: Monthly Review Press, 1974.

Brecher, Jeremy. *Strike!* Greenwich, Conn.: Fawcett, 1972.

Brecher, Jeremy, and Tim Costello, eds. *Building Bridges: The Emerging Grassroots Coalition of Labor and Community.* New York: Monthly Review Press, 1990.

Bridges, Amy. "Becoming American: The Working Classes in the United States before the Civil War." In *Working-Class Formation: Nineteenth-Century Patterns in Western Europe and the United States,* ed. Ira Katznelson and Aristide Zolberg, 157–96. Princeton: Princeton University Press, 1986.

Brier, Stephen, supervising ed. *Who Built America? Working People and the Nation's Economy, Politics, Culture, and Society.* Vol. 2: *From the Gilded Age to the Present.* New York: Pantheon, 1992.

Brissenden, Paul. "The I.W.W.: A Study of American Syndicalism." Ph.D. dissertation, Columbia University, 1919.

Brody, David. "Labor History in the 1970s: Toward a History of the American Worker." In *The Past Before Us: Contemporary Historical Writing in the United States,* ed. Michael Kammen, 252–69. Ithaca: Cornell University Press, 1980.

———. "Radical Labor History and Rank-and-File Militancy." *Labor History* 16, no. 1 (Winter 1975): 117–26.

———. "Reconciling the Old Labor History and the New." *Pacific Historical Review* 62, no. 1 (February 1993): 1–18.

———. *Workers in Industrial America: Essays on the Twentieth-Century Struggle.* New York: Oxford University Press, 1980.

Brooks, John Graham. *American Syndicalism: The I.W.W.* New York: Macmillan, 1913.

Brown, Myland Rudoph. "The I.W.W. and the Negro Worker." Ed.D. dissertation, Ball State University, 1968.

Burawoy, Michael. *Manufacturing Consent: Changes in the Labor Process under Monopoly Capitalism.* Chicago: University of Chicago Press, 1979.

———. *The Politics of Production: Factory Regimes under Capitalism and Socialism.* London: Verso, 1985.

Carlson, Peter. *Roughneck: The Life and Times of Big Bill Haywood.* New York: W. W. Norton, 1983.

Clawson, Daniel. *Bureaucracy and the Labor Process: The Transformation of U.S. Industry, 1860–1920.* New York: Monthly Review Press, 1980.

Clements, Laurie. "Reference Groups and Trade Union Consciousness." In *Trade Unions under Capitalism,* ed. Laurie Clements and Tom Clarke, 309–32. Atlantic Highlands, N.J.: Humanities Press, 1978.

Cobble, Dorothy Sue. *Dishing It Out: Waitresses and Their Unions in the Twentieth Century.* Urbana: University of Illinois Press, 1991.

———. " 'Drawing the Line': The Construction of a Gendered Work Force in the Food Service Industry." In *Work Engendered: Toward a New History of American Labor,* ed. Ava Baron, 216–42. Ithaca: Cornell University Press, 1991.

———. "Sisters in the Craft: Waitresses and Their Unions in the Twentieth Century." Ph.D. dissertation, Stanford University, 1986.

Cobble, Dorothy Sue, and Alice Kessler-Harris. "The New Labor History in American History Textbooks." *Journal of American History* 79, no. 4 (March 1993): 1534–45.

Cohen, Lizabeth. *Making a New Deal: Industrial Workers in Chicago, 1919–1939.* New York: Cambridge University Press, 1990.

Cole, Peter. "Shaping Up and Shipping Out: The Philadelphia Waterfront During and After the IWW Years, 1913–1940." Ph.D. dissertation, Georgetown University, 1997.

Commons, John R. "Types of American Labor Unions: The 'Longshoremen of the Great Lakes." *Quarterly Journal of Economics* 20 (November 1905): 59–85.

Conlin, Joseph R. *Big Bill Haywood and the Radical Union Movement.* Syracuse: Syracuse University Press, 1969.

———. *Bread and Roses Too: Studies of the Wobblies.* Westport, Conn.: Greenwood Press, 1969.

Connel, Carol, and Kim Voss. "Formal Organization and the Fate of Social Movements: Craft Association and Class Alliance in the Knights of Labor." *American Sociological Review* 55 (April 1990): 255–69.

Consumers' League. *The Work of the Consumers' League of the City of New York, 1915.* New York: n.p., 1916.

Cornfield, Daniel B. "Union Decline and the Political Demands of Organized Labor." *Work and Occupations* 16, no. 3 (August 1989): 292–322.

Countryman, Edward. "American Liberalism and the Problem of American Socialism." In *Why Is There No Socialism in the United States?* ed. Jean Heffer and Jeanine Rovet, 87–100. Paris: Ecole des Hautes Etudes en Sciences Sociales, 1988.

Cronin, James E., and Carmen Sirianni, eds. *Work, Community, and Power: The Experience of Labor in Europe and America, 1900–1925.* Philadelphia: Temple University Press, 1983.

Dahrendorf, Ralf. *Class and Class Conflict in Industrial Society.* Stanford: Stanford University Press, 1955.

Davis, Mike. *Prisoners of the American Dream: Politics and Economy in the History of the U.S. Working Class.* London: Verso, 1986.

———. "The Stop Watch and the Wooden Shoe: Scientific Management and the Industrial Workers of the World." In *Workers' Struggles, Past and Present: A "Radical America" Reader,* ed. James Green, 83–100. Philadelphia: Temple University Press, 1983.

Dawson, Andrew. "History and Ideology: Fifty Years of 'Job Consciousness.'" *Literature and History* 8 (Autumn 1978): 223–42.

———. "The Parameters of Craft Consciousness: The Social Outlook of the Skilled Worker, 1890–1920." In *American Labor and Immigrant History, 1877–1920s: Recent European Research,* ed. Dirk Hoerder, 135–55. Urbana: University of Illinois Press, 1983.

DeCaux, Les. *The Living Spirit of the Wobblies.* New York: International Publishers, 1978.

Dick, William. *Labor and Socialism in America: The Gompers Era.* Port Washington, N.Y.: Kennikat Press, 1972.

Diggins, John Patrick. *The Rise and Fall of the American Left.* New York: W. W. Norton, 1992.

DiMaggio, Paul J., and Walter Powell. "The Iron Cage Revisited: Institutional Isomorphism and Collective Rationality in Organizational Fields." *American Sociological Review* 48, no. 2 (April 1983): 147–60.

Dolgoff, Sam. *Fragments: A Memoir.* Cambridge: Refract Publications, 1986.

Dubofsky, Melvyn. *Industrialism and the American Worker, 1865–1920.* Arlington Heights, Ill.: AHM Publishing, 1975.

———. "The Origins of Western Working-Class Radicalism, 1890–1905." *Labor History* 7, no. 2 (Spring 1966): 131–54.

———. "The Rise and Fall of Revolutionary Syndicalism in the United States." In *Revolutionary Syndicalism: An International Perspective,* ed. Marcel van der Linden and Wayne Thorpe, 203–20. Aldershot, U.K.: Scolar Press, 1990.

————. *We Shall Be All: A History of the Industrial Workers of the World,* 2d ed. Urbana: University of Illinois Press, 1988.

————. *When Workers Organize: New York City in the Progressive Era.* Amherst: University of Massachusetts Press, 1968.

Edwards, P. K. *Strikes in the United States 1881–1974.* Oxford: Basil Blackwell, 1981.

Eley, Geoff, and Keith Nield. "Why Does Social History Ignore Politics?" *Social History* 5, no. 2 (May 1980): 249–71.

Ernst, Daniel R. *Lawyers Against Labor: From Individual Rights to Corporate Liberalism.* Urbana: University of Illinois Press, 1995.

Estey, James A. *Revolutionary Syndicalism: An Exposition and a Criticism.* London: P. S. King and Son, 1913.

Fantasia, Rick. "Class Consciousness in Culture, Action, and Social Organization." *Annual Review of Sociology* 21 (1995): 269–87.

————. *Cultures of Solidarity: Consciousness, Action, and Contemporary American Workers.* Berkeley and Los Angeles: University of California Press, 1988.

Filippelli, Ronald, ed. *Labor Conflict in the United States: An Encyclopedia.* New York: Garland, 1990.

Fine, Sidney. *Sit Down: The General Motors Strike of 1936–37.* Ann Arbor: University of Michigan Press, 1969.

Fink, Leon. *Workingmen's Democracy: The Knights of Labor and American Politics.* Urbana: University of Illinois Press, 1983.

Flynn, Elizabeth Gurley. *I Speak My Own Piece: Autobiography of "The Rebel Girl."* New York: Masses & Mainstream, 1955.

————. *The Rebel Girl: An Autobiography. My First Life (1906–1926).* New York: International Publishers, 1973.

Foner, Eric. "Why Is There No Socialism in the United States?" *History Workshop* 17 (Spring 1984): 57–80.

Foner, Philip S. *History of the Labor Movement in the United States.* Vol. 4: *The Industrial Workers of the World, 1905–1917.* New York: International Publishers, 1965.

————. "The IWW and the Black Worker." *Journal of Negro History* 55, no. 1 (January 1970): 45–64.

————. *Organized Labor and the Black Worker, 1619–1973.* New York: Praeger, 1974.

Forbath, William H. *Law and the Shaping of the American Labor Movement.* Cambridge, Mass.: Harvard University Press, 1991.

Ford, Earl C., and William Z. Foster. *Syndicalism.* Chicago: Charles H. Kerr, 1990. Originally published as a pamphlet in 1912.

Form, William H. "Job Unionism versus Political Unionism in Four Countries." In *American Working Class: Prospects for the 1980s,* ed. Irving Louis Horowitz, John C. Leggett, and Martin Oppenheimer, 214–30. New Brunswick: Transition Books, 1979.

———. *Segmented Labor, Fractured Politics: Labor Politics in American Life.* New York: Plenum Press, 1995.

Foster, James Caldwell. *The Union Politic: The CIO Political Action Committee.* Columbia: University of Missouri Press, 1975.

Foster, William Z. *From Bryan to Stalin.* London: Lawrence & Wishart, 1937.

Fraser, Steve. "The 'New Unionism' and the 'New Economic Policy.'" In *Work, Community, and Power: The Experience of Labor in Europe and America, 1900–1925,* ed. James E. Cronin and Carmen Sirianni, 173–96. Philadelphia: Temple University Press, 1983.

Fraser, Steven, and Joshua B. Freeman. Introduction. In *Audacious Democracy: Labor, Intellectuals, and the Social Reconstruction of America,* ed. Steven Fraser and Joshua B. Freeman, 1–12. Boston: Houghton Mifflin, 1997.

Freeman, Harold. *Toward Socialism in America.* Cambridge, Mass.: Schenkman Publishing, 1980.

Friedman, Gerald. "The State and the Making of the Working Class." *Theory and Society* 17, no. 3 (May 1988): 403–30.

Fusfeld, Daniel R. *The Rise and Repression of Radical Labor in the United States, 1877–1918.* Chicago: Charles H. Kerr, 1980.

Galenson, Walter. *The CIO Challenge to the AFL: A History of the American Labor Movement 1935–1941.* Cambridge, Mass.: Harvard University Press, 1960.

Gambs, John S. *The Decline of the I.W.W.* New York: Columbia University Press, 1966.

Garlock, Jonathan. *Guide to the Local Assemblies of the Knights of Labor.* Westport, Conn.: Greenwood Press, 1982.

Geary, Dick. "Identifying Militancy: The Assessment of Working-Class Attitudes Towards State and Society." In *The German Working Class 1888–1933: The Politics of Everyday Life,* ed. Richard J. Evans, 220–46. London: Croom Helm, 1982.

Geoghegan, Thomas. *Which Side Are You On: Trying to Be for Labor When It's Flat on Its Back.* New York: Penguin Books, 1991.

Georgakas, Dan. "The Greeks in America." *Journal of the Hellenic Diaspora* 14, nos. 1–2 (Spring-Summer 1987): 5–53.

Giddens, Anthony. *The Class Structure of the Advanced Societies.* New York: Harper & Row, 1973.

Gindin, Sam. "Notes on Labor at the End of the Century: Starting Over?" *Monthly Review* 49, no. 3 (July-August 1997): 140–57.

Gitelman, H. M. "Perspectives on American Industrial Violence." *Business History Review* 47, no. 1 (Spring 1973): 1–23.

Goldfield, Michael. *The Decline of Organized Labor in the United States.* Chicago: University of Chicago Press, 1987.

———. "The Failure of Operation Dixie: A Critical Turning Point in

American Political Development?" In *Race, Class, and Community in Southern Labor History*, ed. Gary M. Fink and Merl E. Reed, 167–89. Tuscaloosa: University of Alabama Press, 1994.

———. "Race and Labor in the United States." *Monthly Review* 49, no. 3 (July-August 1997): 80–97.

———. "Worker Insurgency, Radical Organization, and New Deal Labor Legislation." *American Political Science Review* 83, no. 4 (December 1989): 1257–82.

Goldthorpe, John H. "The Uses of History in Sociology: Reflections on Some Recent Tendencies." *British Journal of Sociology* 42, no. 2 (June 1991): 211–30.

Gompers, Samuel. *Labor and the Employers*. New York: E. P. Dutton, 1920.

———. *Seventy Years of Life and Labor: An Autobiography*, ed. and introd. Nick Salvatore. Ithaca: Cornell University Press, 1984. Originally published 1924.

Gordon, David M. "Capital vs. Labor." In *American Society*, ed. Maurice Zeitlin, 525–38. Chicago: Markham, 1971.

Gould, Roger V. *Insurgent Identities: Class, Community, and Protest in Paris from 1848 to the Commune*. Chicago: University of Chicago Press, 1995.

Gouldner, Alvin. *Wildcat Strike*. Yellow Springs, Ohio: Antioch Press, 1954.

Gramsci, Antonio. "Americanism and Fordism." In Antonio Gramsci, *Selections from the Prison Notebooks*, ed. and trans. Quintin Hoare and Geoffrey Nowell Smith, 277–318. New York: International Publishers, 1971.

Green, James R. "The Brotherhood of Timber Workers, 1910–1913: A Radical Response to Industrial Capitalism in the Southern U.S.A." *Past and Present* 60 (August 1973): 161–200.

———. "Comments on the Montgomery Paper." *Journal of Social History* 7, no. 4 (Summer 1974): 530–35.

———. *World of the Worker: Labor in Twentieth-Century America*. New York: Hill and Wang, 1980.

Greene, Julia. " 'The Strike at the Ballot Box': The American Federation of Labor's Entrance into Election Politics, 1906–1909." *Labor History* 32, no. 2 (Spring 1991): 165–92.

Greenstone, David J. *Labor in American Politics*. Chicago: University of Chicago Press, 1969.

Griffin, Larry. "Narrative, Event-Structure Analysis, and Causal Interpretation in Historical Sociology." *American Journal of Sociology* 98, no. 5 (March 1993): 1094–1133.

Griffin, Larry, Michael Wallace, and Beth Rubin. "Capitalist Resistance to the Organization of Labor Before the New Deal: Why? How? Success?" *American Sociological Review* 51, no. 2 (April 1986): 147–67.

Grob, Gerald N. *Workers and Utopia: A Study of Ideological Conflict in the American Labor Movement 1865–1900*. Chicago: Quadrangle Books, 1969.

Grossman, James R., ed. *Black Workers in the Era of the Great Migration, 1916–1929.* Microfilm. Frederick, Md.: University Publications of America, 1985.

Gulick, Charles A., and Melvin K. Bers. "Insight and Illusion in Perlman's *Theory of the Labor Movement.*" *Industrial and Labor Relations Review* 6, no. 4 (July 1953): 510–31.

Halliburton, R., Jr. *The Tulsa Race War of 1921.* San Francisco: R and E Research Associates, 1975.

Hamilton, W. I. *Promoting New Hotels: When Does It Pay?* New York: Harper & Brothers, 1930.

Hammond, Thomas Taylor. *Lenin on Trade Unions and Revolution, 1893–1917.* New York: Columbia University Press, 1957.

Harrington, Michael. *Socialism.* New York: Bantam, 1972.

Hartz, Louis. *The Liberal Tradition in America: An Interpretation of American Political Thought Since the Revolution.* San Diego: Harcourt Brace Jovanovich, 1955.

Hattam, Victoria Charlotte. *Labor Visions and State Power: The Origins of Business Unionism in the United States.* Princeton: Princeton University Press, 1993.

Haydu, Jeffrey. *Between Craft and Class: Skilled Workers and Factory Politics in the United States and Britain, 1890–1922.* Berkeley and Los Angeles: University of California Press, 1988.

———. "Employers, Unions, and American Exceptionalism: A Comparative View." *International Review of Social History* 33, no. 1 (1988): 25–41.

———. *Making American Industry Safe for Democracy: Comparative Perspectives on the State and Employee Representation in the Era of World War I.* Urbana: University of Illinois Press, 1997.

Haywood, Big Bill. *The Autobiography of William D. Haywood.* New York: International Publishers, 1929.

Hershberg, Will. "American Marxist Political Theory." In *Socialism and American Life,* vol. 1, ed. Donald Drew Egbert and Stow Persons, 487–522. Princeton: Princeton University Press, 1952.

Hinton, James. *The First Shop Stewards' Movement.* London: Allen & Unwin, 1973.

Hirsch, Eric L. *Urban Revolt: Ethnic Politics in the Nineteenth-Century Chicago Labor Movement.* Berkeley and Los Angeles: University of California Press, 1990.

Holton, Bob. *British Syndicalism, 1900–1914: Myths and Realities.* London: Pluto Press, 1976.

Horowitz, Morris A. *The New York Hotel Industry: A Labor Relations Study.* Cambridge, Mass.: Harvard University Press, 1960.

Horowitz, Ruth L. *Political Ideologies of Organized Labor.* New Brunswick: Transaction Books, 1978.

Hotel and Restaurant Employees' International Alliance and Bartenders

International League of America. *Proceedings of the General Convention,* various years, 1913–41.

Hoxie, Robert. *Trade Unionism in the United States.* New York: D. Appleton, 1920.

Hughes, Lois Peirce. "Opportunities for Women in the Modern Hotel." *Journal of Home Economics* 13 (April 1921): 151–56.

Hyman, Richard. "Workers' Control and Revolutionary Theory." In *The Socialist Register,* ed. Ralph Miliband and John Saville, 241–78. London: Merlin Press, 1974.

International Longshoremen's and Warehousemen's Union. *Proceedings of the Second Annual Convention of the International Longshoremen's and Warehousemen's Union,* April 3–14, 1939.

International Longshoremen's Association. *Proceedings of the Convention,* various years, 1914–27.

Isserman, Maurice. " 'God Bless Our American Institutions': The Labor History of John R. Commons." *Labor History* 17, no. 3 (Summer 1976): 309–28.

Jacoby, Russell. "Political Economy and Class Unconsciousness." *Theory and Society* 5, no. 1 (January 1978): 11–18.

Jacoby, Sanford M. "American Exceptionalism Revisited: The Importance of Management." In *Masters to Managers: Historical and Comparative Perspectives on American Employers,* ed. Sanford Jacoby, 173–200. New York: Columbia University Press, 1991.

Jensen, Vernon H. *Hiring of Dock Workers and Employment Practices in the Ports of New York, Liverpool, London, Rotterdam, and Marseilles.* Cambridge, Mass.: Harvard University Press, 1969.

Johnston, Paul. *Success While Others Fail: Social Movement Unionism and the Public Workplace.* Ithaca: ILR Press, 1994.

Joseph, Antoine. "The Solidarity of Skilled Workers: Creating a Logic of Particularism." *Journal of Historical Sociology* 6, no. 3 (September 1993): 288–310.

Josephson, Mathew. *Union House Union Bar: The History of the Hotel and Restaurant Employees and Bartenders International Union AFL-CIO.* New York: Random House, 1956.

Katznelson, Ira. "The 'Bourgeois' Dimension: A Provocation about Institutions, Politics, and the Future of Labor History." *International Labor and Working-Class History* 46 (Fall 1994): 7–32.

———. *City Trenches: Urban Politics and the Patterning of Class in the United States.* New York: Pantheon, 1981.

———. "Working-Class Formation: Constructing Cases and Comparisons." In *Working-Class Formation: Nineteenth-Century Patterns in Western Europe and the United States,* ed. Ira Katznelson and Aristide Zolberg, 3–41. Princeton: Princeton University Press, 1986.

Kaufman, Stuart Bruce. *Samuel Gompers and the Origins of the American*

Federation of Labor, 1848–1896. Westport, Conn.: Greenwood Press, 1978.

Kazin, Michael. *Barons of Labor: The San Francisco Building Trades and Union Power in the Progressive Era*. Urbana: University of Illinois Press, 1987.

———. "A People Not a Class: Rethinking the Political Language of the Modern U.S. Labor Movement." In *Reshaping the U.S. Left: Popular Struggles in the 1980s*, ed. Mike Davis and Michael Sprinker, 257–86. London: Verso, 1988.

———. *The Populist Persuasion: An American History*. New York: Basic Books, 1995.

———. "Struggling with the Class Struggle: Marxism and the Search for a Synthesis of U.S. Labor History." *Labor History* 28, no. 4 (Fall 1987): 497–514.

Kelley, Robin D. G. "The New Urban Working Class and Organized Labor." *New Labor Forum* 1 (Fall 1997): 6–18.

———. *Race Rebels: Culture, Politics, and the Black Working Class*. New York: Free Press, 1994.

Kelly, John. *Trade Unions and Socialist Politics*. London: Verso, 1988.

Kerr, Clark, John T. Dunlop, Frederick H. Harbison, and Charles A Myers. *Industrialism and Industrial Man: The Problems of Labor and Management in Economic Growth*. Cambridge, Mass.: Harvard University Press, 1960.

Kimeldorf, Howard. "Ben Fletcher." In *American National Biography*. Forthcoming.

———. "Bringing Unions Back In (Or Why We Need a New Old Labor History)." *Labor History* 32, no. 1 (Winter 1991): 91–103.

———. *Reds or Rackets? The Making of Radical and Conservative Unions on the Waterfront*. Berkeley and Los Angeles: University of California, 1988.

Kimeldorf, Howard, and Maurice Zeitlin. "How Mighty a Force? The Internal Differentiation and Relative Organization of the American Working Class." In *How Mighty a Force? Studies of Workers' Consciousness and Organization in the United States*, ed. Maurice Zeitlin, 1–64. Los Angeles: Institute of Industrial Relations, University of California, 1983.

Kolko, Gabriel. "The Decline of American Radicalism in the Twentieth Century." *Studies on the Left* 6, no. 5 (September-October 1966): 9–26.

Larrowe, Charles P. *Shape-Up and Hiring Hall: A Comparison of Hiring Methods and Labor Relations on the New York and Seattle Waterfronts*. Berkeley and Los Angeles: University of California Press, 1955.

Lash, Scott. *The Militant Worker: Class and Radicalism in France and America*. Rutherford, N.J.: Fairleigh Dickinson University Press, 1984.

Laslett, John H. M. "The American Tradition of Labor Theory and Its Relevance to the Contemporary Working Class." In *The American Working*

Class: Prospects for the 1980s, ed. Irving Louis Horowitz, John C. Leggett, and Martin Oppenheimer, 3–30. New Brunswick: Transaction Books, 1979.

Laurie, Bruce. *Artisans into Workers: Labor in Nineteenth-Century America.* New York: Hill and Wang, 1989.

Lembcke, Jerry. *Capitalist Development and Class Capacities: Marxist Theory and Union Organization.* New York: Greenwood Press, 1988.

———. "Labor History's 'Synthesis Debate': Sociological Interventions." *Science and Society* 59, no. 2 (Summer 1995): 137–73.

Lenin, V. I. "What Is to Be Done?" In *Essential Works of Lenin,* ed. Henry M. Christman, 53–175. New York: Bantam Books, 1966.

Levine, Louis. "The Development of Syndicalism in America." *Political Science Quarterly* 28, no. 3 (September 1913): 451–79.

Levine, Rhonda F. *Class Struggle and the New Deal: Industrial Labor, Industrial Capital, and the State.* Lawrence: University of Kansas Press, 1988.

Lipset, Seymour Martin. *American Exceptionalism: A Double-Edged Sword.* New York: W. W. Norton, 1996.

———. "American Union Density in Comparative Perspective." *Contemporary Sociology* 27, no. 2 (March 1998): 123–25.

———. *The First New Nation: The United States in Historical and Comparative Perspective.* Garden City, N.Y.: Anchor Books, 1967.

———. "Radicalism or Reformism: The Sources of Working-Class Politics." *American Political Science Review* 77, no. 1 (March 1983): 1–19.

Lipset, Seymour Martin, and Reinhard Bendix. *Social Mobility in Industrial Society.* Berkeley and Los Angeles: University of California Press, 1959.

Livesay, Harold C. *Samuel Gompers and Organized Labor in America.* Boston: Little, Brown, 1978.

Lowi, Theodore. "Why Is There No Socialism in the United States? A Federal Analysis." *International Political Science Review* 5, no. 4 (1984): 369–80.

Lynd, Staughton. *Living Inside Our Hope: A Steadfast Radical's Thoughts on Rebuilding the Movement.* Ithaca: Cornell University Press, 1997.

McAdam, Doug, John D. McCarthy, and Mayer N. Zald, eds. *Comparative Perspectives on Social Movements: Political Opportunities, Mobilizing Structures, and Cultural Framings.* New York: Cambridge University Press, 1996.

McCammon, Holly J. " 'Government by Injunction': The U.S. Judiciary and Strike Action in the Late 19th and Early 20th Centuries." *Work and Occupations* 20, no. 2 (May 1993): 174–204.

McCarthy, John D., and Mayer N. Zald. *The Trend of Social Movements in America: Professionalization and Resource Mobilization.* Morristown, N.J.: General Learning Press, 1973.

McConagha, William A. *Development of the Labor Movement in Great Britain, France, and Germany.* Chapel Hill: University of North Carolina Press, 1942.

McDonnell, Lawrence T. " 'You Are Too Sentimental': Problems and Suggestions for a New Labor History." *Journal of Social History* 17 (Summer 1984): 629–54.

McGirr, Lisa. "Black and White Longshoremen in the IWW: A History of the Philadelphia Marine Transport Workers Industrial Union Local 8." *Labor History* 37, no. 3 (Spring 1995): 377–402.

Mandel, Bernard. *Samuel Gompers: A Biography.* Yellow Springs, Ohio: Antioch Press, 1963.

Mann, Michael. *Consciousness and Action Among the Western Working Class.* London: Macmillan, 1973.

Marcus, Irwin. "Benjamin Fletcher: Black Labor Leader." *Negro History Bulletin,* 35 (October 1972): 138–40.

Marks, Gary. *Unions in Politics: Britain, Germany, and the United States in the Nineteenth and Early Twentieth Centuries.* Princeton: Princeton University Press, 1989.

Marshall, Gordon. "Some Remarks on the Study of Working-Class Consciousness." *Politics and Society* 12, no. 3 (1983): 263–301.

Mathewson, Stanley Bernard. *Restriction of Output Among Unorganized Workers.* New York: Viking Press, 1931.

Matles, James. *Them and Us: Struggles of a Rank and File Union.* Boston: Beacon Press, 1974.

Matza, David, and David Wellman. "The Ordeal of Consciousness." *Theory and Society* 9, no. 1 (January 1980): 1–27.

Meiksins, Peter. "Same as It Ever Was: The Structure of the Working Class." *Monthly Review* 49, no. 3 (July-August 1997): 31–45.

Merrill, Michael. "The Other Great Evasion: Samuel Gompers, the AFL, and Workers Power in the United States." Paper presented at the annual meeting of the Social Science History Association, 1993.

Milkman, Ruth. "The New Labor Movement: Possibilities and Limits." *Contemporary Sociology* 27, no. 2 (March 1998): 125–29.

———. "Organizing the Sexual Division of Labor: Historical Perspectives on 'Women's Work' and the American Labor Movement." *Socialist Review* 10, no. 1 (January-February 1980): 95–150.

Milkman, Ruth, ed. *Women, Work and Protest: A Century of U.S. Women's Labor History.* Boston: Routledge and Kegan Paul, 1985.

Mills, Herb, and David Wellman. "Contractually Sanctioned Job Action and Workers' Control: The Case of San Francisco Longshoremen." *Labor History* 28 (Spring 1987): 167–95.

Milton, David. *The Politics of U.S. Labor: From the Great Depression to the New Deal.* New York: Monthly Review Press, 1982.

232 Bibliography

Mink, Gwendolyn. *Old Labor and New Immigrants in American Political Development: Union, Party, and State, 1875–1920.* Ithaca: Cornell University Press, 1986.

Monds, Jean. "Workers' Control and the Historians: A New Economism." *New Left Review* 97 (May-June 1976): 81–104.

Montgomery, David. "The 'New Unionism' and the Transformation of Workers' Consciousness in America, 1909–1922." *Journal of Social History* 7, no. 4 (Summer 1974): 509–29.

———. "The Past and Future of Workers' Control." In *Workers' Struggles, Past and Present: A "Radical America" Reader,* ed. James Green, 389–405. Philadelphia: Temple University Press, 1983.

———. "Thinking about American Workers in the 1920s." *International Labor and Working Class History* 32 (Fall 1987): 4–24.

———. "To Study the People: The American Working Class." *Labor History* 21, no. 4 (Fall 1980): 485–512.

Moody, J. Carroll, and Alice Kessler-Harris, eds. *Perspectives on American Labor History: The Problems of Synthesis.* Dekalb: Northern Illinois University Press, 1989.

Moody, Kim. *An Injury to All: The Decline of American Unionism.* London: Verso, 1988.

———. *Labor in a Lean World.* London: Verso, 1997.

National Adjustment Commission. "In the Matter of the Demands of the Longshoremen of the North Atlantic Coast Ports as to Wages, etc.," September 30—October 3, 1918, New York City. Typewritten copy, Houghton Library, Harvard University.

Nelson, Bruce. "The 'Lords of the Docks' Reconsidered: Race Relations among West Coast Longshoremen, 1933–61." In *Waterfront Workers: New Perspectives on Race and Class,* ed. Calvin Winslow, 155–92. Urbana: University of Illinois Press, 1998.

———. *Workers on the Waterfront: Seamen, Longshoremen, and Unionism in the 1930s.* Urbana: University of Illinois Press, 1988.

New York Senate. *Part 1: Revolutionary and Subversive Movements Abroad and at Home, Volume I.* Joint Legislative Committee Investigating Seditious Activities, New York Legislative Documents, 144th sess., 1921, vol. 17, no. 50. Albany: J. B. Lyon, 1921.

Northrup, Herbert. *Organized Labor and the Negro.* New York: Harper and Brothers, 1944.

Oestreicher, Richard J. "Urban Working-Class Political Behavior and Theories of American Electoral Politics, 1870–1940." *Journal of American History* 74, no. 4 (March 1988): 1257–86.

Ollman, Bertell. "Toward Class Consciousness Next Time: Marx and the Working Class." *Politics and Society* 3, no. 1 (Fall 1972): 1–24.

Orren, Karen. *Belated Feudalism: Labor, the Law, and Liberal Development in the United States.* Cambridge: Cambridge University Press, 1991.

Parkin, Frank. *Marxism and Class Theory: A Bourgeois Critique.* New York: Columbia University Press, 1979.

Pelling, Henry. *American Labor.* Chicago: University of Chicago Press, 1960.

Perlman, Selig. *A Theory of the Labor Movement.* New York: Macmillan, 1928.

Perrone, Luca. "Positional Power, Strikes and Wages." *American Sociological Review* 49, no. 3 (June 1984): 412–26.

Peterson, Larry. "The One Big Union in International Perspective: Revolutionary Industrial Unionism, 1900–1925." In *Work, Community, and Power: The Experience of Labor in Europe and America, 1900–1925,* ed. James F. Cronin and Carmen Sirianni, 49–87. Philadelphia: Temple University Press, 1983.

Plotke, David. *Building a Democratic Political Order: Reshaping American Liberalism in the 1930s and 1940s.* New York: Cambridge University Press, 1996.

Preis, Art. *Labor's Giant Step: Twenty Years of the CIO.* New York: Pathfinder Press, 1964.

Preston, William, Jr. *Aliens and Dissenters: Federal Suppression of Radicals, 1903–1933.* Cambridge, Mass.: Harvard University Press, 1963.

———. "Shall This Be All? U.S. Historians versus William D. Haywood et al." *Labor History* 12, no. 3 (Summer 1971): 435–53.

Przeworksi, Adam. "Proletariat into a Class: The Process of Class Formation from Karl Kautsky's *The Class Struggle* to Recent Controversies." *Politics and Society* 7, no. 4 (1977): 343–401.

Rawick, George. "Working Class Self-Activity." *Radical America* 3, no. 2 (March-April 1969): 23–31.

Reis, Elizabeth. "The AFL, the IWW, and Bay Area Italian Cannery Workers." *California History* 64, no. 3 (Summer 1985): 175–91.

Roberts, James S. "The New Labor History in America: Problems and Prospects." *Archiv für Sozial Geschichte* 23 (1983): 523–39.

Rock, Paul. "Some Problems of Interpretative Historiography." *British Journal of Sociology* 27, no. 3 (September 1976): 353–69.

Roediger, David R. *The Wages of Whiteness: Race and the Making of the American Working Class.* London: Verso, 1991.

Rogin, Michael. "Voluntarism: The Political Functions of an Anti-political Doctrine." *Industrial and Labor Relations Review* 15, no. 4 (July 1962): 521–35.

Rosenberg, Daniel. *New Orleans Dockworkers: Race, Labor, and Unionism, 1892–1923.* Albany: State University of New York Press, 1988.

Rubin, Beth. "Class Struggle American Style: Unions, Strikes, and Wages." *American Sociological Review* 51, no. 5 (October 1986): 618–33.

Rubin, Jay, and M. J. Obermeirer. *Growth of a Union: The Life and Times of Edward Flore.* New York: Comet Press, 1943.

Rubin, Lester. *The Negro in the Longshore Industry.* Report No. 29, The

Racial Policies of American Industry. Philadelphia: Industrial Research Unit, Wharton School, University of Pennsylvania Press, 1974.

Rudwick, Elliott, ed. *The East St. Louis Race Riot of 1921.* Microfilm. Frederick, Md.: University Publications of America, 1985.

Russell, Maud. *Men Along the Shore.* New York: Brussel & Brussel, 1966.

Salerno, Salvatore. *Red November, Black November: Culture and Community in the Industrial Workers of the World.* Albany: State University of New York Press, 1989.

Sampson, Leon. *Towards a United Front.* New York: Farrar and Rinehart, 1933.

Saposs, David. *Left-Wing Unionism: A Study of Radical Policies and Tactics.* New York: International Publishers, 1926.

Savage, Marion Dutton. *Industrial Unionism in America.* New York: Ronald Press, 1922.

Sayers, George, and Robert Price. *Profiles of Union Growth.* Oxford: Basil Blackwell, 1980.

Schneider, Linda. "The Citizen Striker: Workers' Ideology in the Homestead Strike of 1892." *Labor History* 23, no. 1 (Winter 1982): 47–66.

Scott, James. *Weapons of the Weak: Everyday Forms of Peasant Resistance.* New Haven: Yale University Press, 1985.

Scranton, Philip. "The Workplace, Technology, and Theory in American Labor History." *International Labor and Working-Class History* 35 (Spring 1989): 3–22.

Seidman, Harold. *Labor Czars: A History of Labor Racketeering.* New York: Liveright, 1938.

Selzick, Philip. *The Organizational Weapon.* New York: McGraw-Hill, 1952.

Seraile, William. "Ben Fletcher, I.W.W. Organizer." *Pennsylvania History* 46, no. 3 (July 1979): 213–32.

Sewell, William H., Jr. "Classes and Their Historical Formation: Critical Reflections on E. P. Thompson's Theory of Working-Class Formation." In *E. P. Thompson: Critical Perspectives,* ed. Harvey J. Kaye and Keith McClelland, 50–77. Cambridge: Polity, 1990.

———. "Three Temporalities: Toward an Eventful Sociology." In *The Historic Turn in the Social Sciences,* ed. Terrence J. McDonald, 245–80. Ann Arbor: University of Michigan Press, 1997.

Sexton, Patricia Cayo. *The War on Labor and the Left: Understanding America's Unique Conservatism.* Boulder: Westview Press, 1991.

Shefter, Martin. "Trade Unions and Political Machines: The Organization and Disorganization of the American Working Class in the Late Nineteenth Century." In *Working-Class Formation: Nineteenth-Century Patterns in Western Europe and the United States,* ed. Ira Katznelson and Aristide Zolberg, 197–276. Princeton: Princeton University Press, 1986.

Shostak, Arthur B. *Robust Unionism: Innovations in the Labor Movement.* Ithaca: Cornell University Press, 1991.

Sider, Gerald M. "Cleansing History: Lawrence, Massachusetts, the Strike for Four Loaves of Bread and No Roses, and the Anthropology of Working-Class Consciousness." *Radical History Review* 65 (Spring 1996): 48–83.

Skocpol, Theda, and Margaret Somers. "The Uses of Comparative History in Macrosocial Inquiry." *Comparative Studies in Society and History* 22, no. 2 (April 1980): 174–97.

Soffer, Benson. "A Theory of Trade Union Development: The Role of the 'Autonomous' Workman." *Labor History* 1, no. 2 (Spring 1960): 141–63.

Solow, Herbert. "The New York Hotel Strike." *Nation*, February 28, 1934, 239–41.

Sombart, Werner. *Why Is There No Socialism in the United States?* Ed. C. T. Husbands, trans. Patricia M. Hocking and C. T. Husbands. White Plains, N.Y.: International Arts and Sciences Press, 1976. Originally published 1906.

Somers, Margaret R. "We're No Angels: Realism, Rational Choice, and Relationality in Social Science." *American Journal of Sociology* 104, no. 3 (November 1998): 722–84.

Spargo, John. *Syndicalism, Industrial Unionism and Socialism.* New York: B. W. Huebsch, 1913.

Sperro, Sterling D., and Abram L. Harris. *The Black Worker: The Negro and the Labor Movement.* New York: Atheneum, 1974. Originally published 1931.

Sproule, George F., comp. and arr. *The Port of Philadelphia: Its Facilities and Advantages.* Harrisburg, Penn.: Board of Commissioners of Navigation for the River Delaware and Its Navigable Tributaries, 1914.

Stein, Jeff. "Ben Fletcher: Portrait of a Black Syndicalist." *Libertarian Labor Review* 3 (1987): 30–33.

Stein, Judith. *The World of Marcus Garvey: Race and Class in Modern Society.* Baton Rouge: Louisiana State University Press, 1986.

Stepan-Norris, Judith. "The Integration of Workplace and Community Relations at the Ford Rouge Plant, 1930s–1940s." *Political Power and Social Theory* 11 (1997): 3–44.

Stepan-Norris, Judith, and Maurice Zeitlin. " 'Red' Unions and 'Bourgeois' Contracts?" *American Journal of Sociology* 96 (March 1991): 1151–1200.

———. " 'Who Gets the Bird?' or, How the Communists Won Power and Trust in America's Unions." *American Sociological Review* 54 (1989): 503–23.

Sturmthal, Adolf. "Comments on Selig Perlman's *A Theory of the Labor Movement.*" *Industrial and Labor Relations Review* 4, no. 4 (July 1951): 483–96.

———. *Tragedy of European Labor, 1918–1939.* New York: Columbia University Press, 1943.

Sweeney, John J. "America Needs a Raise." In *Audacious Democracy:*

Labor, Intellectuals, and the Social Reconstruction of America, ed. Steven Fraser and Joshua B. Freeman, 13–21. Boston: Houghton Mifflin, 1997.

Taft, Philip. "On the Origins of Business Unionism." *Industrial and Labor Relations Review* 17, no. 1 (October 1963): 2–39.

Taft, Philip, and Philip Ross. "American Labor Violence: Its Causes, Character and Comparative Perspectives." In *Violence in America: Historical and Comparative Perspectives,* ed. Hugh Davis Graham and Ted Robert Gurr, 1:221–301. New York: Bantam, 1969.

Tanner, Amy E. "Glimpses at the Mind of a Waitress." *American Journal of Sociology* 13, no. 1 (July 1907): 48–55.

Therborn, Goran. "Why Some Classes Are More Successful than Others." *New Left Review* 138 (March-April 1983): 37–55.

Thernstrom, Stephen. "Socialism and Social Mobility." In *Failure of a Dream? Essays in the History of American Socialism,* ed. John H. M. Laslett and Seymour Martin Lipset, 408–26. Rev. ed. Berkeley and Los Angeles: University of California Press, 1984.

Thompson, E. P. "The Moral Economy of the English Crowd in the Eighteenth Century." *Past and Present* 50 (February 1971): 76–136.

Thorpe, Wayne. *"The Workers Themselves": Revolutionary Syndicalism and International Labour, 1913–1923.* Dordrecht: Kluwer, 1989.

Tilly, Charles. *From Mobilization to Revolution.* New York: Random House, 1978.

Tomlins, Christopher L. "AFL Unions in the 1930s: Their Performance in Historical Perspective." *Journal of American History* 65, no. 4 (March 1979): 1021–42.

———. "How Who Rides Whom: Recent 'New' Histories of American Labour Law and What They May Signify." *Social History* 21, no. 1 (January 1995): 1–21.

———. *The State and the Unions: Labor Relations, Law, and the Organized Labor Movement in America, 1880–1960.* Cambridge: Cambridge University Press, 1985.

Tridon, Andre. *The New Unionism.* New York: B. W. Huebsch, 1913.

Tuttle, William M. *Race Riot, Chicago in the Red Summer of 1919.* New York: Atheneum, 1970.

U.S. Bureau of the Census. *Thirteenth Census of the United States Taken in the Year 1910.* Vol. 4: *Population, Occupational Statistics.* Washington, D.C.: GPO, 1914.

———. *Fourteenth Census of the United States Taken in the Year 1920.* Vol. 4: *Population 1920, Occupations.* Washington, D.C.: GPO, 1923.

U.S. Department of Health, Education, and Welfare. *Work in America: Report of a Special Task Force to the Secretary of Health, Education, and Welfare.* Cambridge, Mass.: MIT Press, 1973.

U.S. Department of Justice. *Department of Justice Investigative Case Files.* Microfilm. Bethesda, Md.: University Publications of America, 1989.

U.S. Department of Labor, Division of Negro Economics. *Negro Migration in 1916–17.* Washington, D.C.: GPO, 1919; reprint, New York: Negro Universities Press, 1969.

U.S. Maritime Commission. *Report on Volume of Water-borne Foreign Commerce of the United States by Ports of Origin and Destination.* Washington, D.C.: GPO, 1923, 1926.

U.S. Senate. *Reports of the United States Immigration Commission, 1907–1910, Immigrants in Industries, part 16: Sugar Refining, vol. 15.* 61st Cong., 2d sess. Washington, D.C.: GPO, 1911.

———. *Testimony Submitted by the Commission on Industrial Relations.* 64th Cong., 1st sess. Washington, D.C.: GPO, 1916.

U.S. Shipping Board, Marine and Dock Industrial Relations Division. *Marine and Dock Labor: Work, Wages, and Industrial Relations During the Period of the War.* Washington, D.C.: GPO, 1919.

U.S. War Department, Military Intelligence Division. "Investigation of the Marine Transport Workers and the Alleged Threatened Combination Between Them and the Bolsheviki and Sinn Feiners." In *U. S. Military Intelligence Reports: Surveillance of Radicals in the United States, 1917–1941.* Microfilm. Frederick, Md.: University Publications of America, 1984.

U.S. Women's Bureau, U.S. Department of Labor. *The Effects of Labor Legislation on the Employment Opportunities of Women.* Bulletin of the Women's Bureau, No. 65. Washington, D.C.: GPO, 1928.

van der Linden, Marcel, and Wayne Thorpe, eds. *Revolutionary Syndicalism: an International Perspective.* Aldershot, U.K.: Scolar Press, 1990.

Vanneman, Reeve, and Lynn Weber Cannon. *The American Perception of Class.* Philadelphia: Temple University Press, 1987.

Voss, Kim. *The Making of American Exceptionalism: The Knights of Labor and Class Formation in the Nineteenth Century.* Ithaca: Cornell University Press, 1993.

Wallace, Michael. "Aggressive Economism, Defensive Control: Contours of American Labour Militancy." *Economic and Industrial Democracy* 10, no. 1 (February 1989): 7–34.

Wallace, Michael, Beth A. Rubin, and Brian T. Smith. "American Labor Law: Its Impact on Working-Class Militancy, 1901–1980." *Social Science History* 12, no. 1 (Spring 1988): 1–29.

Weir, Stanley. "U.S.A.: The Labor Revolt." In *American Society, Inc.: Studies of the Social Structure and Political Economy of the United States,* ed. Maurice Zeitlin, 487–524. Chicago: Rand McNally College Publishing, 1977.

Wellman, David. *The Union Makes Us Strong: Radical Unionism on the San Francisco Waterfront.* Cambridge: Cambridge University Press, 1995.

Wilensky, Harold L. "Class, Class Consciousness, and American Workers." In *American Society, Inc.: Studies of the Social Structure and Political*

Economy of the United States, ed. Maurice Zeitlin, 450–62. Chicago: Rand McNally College Publishing, 1977.

Wilentz, Sean. "Against Exceptionalism: Class Consciousness and the American Labor Movement, 1790–1920." *International Labor and Working-Class History* 26 (Fall 1984): 1–24.

Wolman, Leo. *The Growth of American Trade Unions 1880–1923.* New York: National Bureau of Economic Research, 1924.

Womack, James P., Daniel T. Jones, and Daniel Roos. *The Machine that Changed the World: The Story of Lean Production. How Japan's Secret Weapon in the Global Auto Wars Will Revolutionize Western Industry.* New York: HarperPerennial, 1991.

Wood, Ellen Meiksins. "The Politics of Theory and the Concept of Class: E. P. Thompson and His Critics." *Studies in Political Economy* 9 (Fall 1982): 45–75.

Wortman, Roy T. *From Syndicalism to Trade Unions: The I.W.W. in Ohio, 1905–1950.* New York: Garland, 1985.

Wright, Richard R., Jr. "The Negro in Pennsylvania: A Study in Economic History." Ph.D. dissertation, University of Pennsylvania, 1912.

Zeitlin, Jonathan. "From Labour History to the History of Industrial Relations." *Economic History Review* 40, no. 2 (1987): 159–84.

Zeitlin, Maurice, and Howard Kimeldorf. "Editors' Introduction." *Political Power and Social Theory* 4 (1984): xi–xiii.

Zieger, Robert. *The CIO, 1935–1955.* Chapel Hill: University of North Carolina Press, 1995.

Index

employers to cause tension, 30, 184n11. *See also* labor force composition; race relations; racism

Ettor, Joseph, 35, 107–9, 112

European labor: contrast with U.S. labor, 4, 10, 158, 160, 174n25, 210n12; movements in, 12, 90, 172n17

exclusionary membership practices, 25, 56, 111, 132; AFL use of, 87–88, 130, 162; AFL vs. IWW's use of, 2, 15–17, 38; IWW avoidance of, 21, 47. *See also* inclusiveness

Fair, James, 31, 40, 53, 72

Federation of Hotel Guilds, 144

Fellow Worker, 62

Fields, B. J., 145

Fletcher, Benjamin, 39, 40, 49–53, 61–63, 78, 79, 83, 193n81

Flore, Edward, 143, 147

Flynn, Elizabeth Gurley, 39, 107–10, 117

Food Worker, 143, 148

Food Workers Industrial Union (FWIU), 6, 114, 141–44, 146, 147, 150; Local 110, 147; Local 119, 143, 144, 147, 148

Foster, William F., 179n42

Fournigault, Andre, 144

Free Voice, 133–35, 142, 144

garment district, 138–40

Garriga, Miguel, 146

Garvey, Marcus, 70–71, 85

gender: division of labor by, 127, 136; ideology, 91, 104, 116, 121, 135; and unionization, 2, 6, 115, 121, 135, 139, 149

German Waiters Union, 93

Giovannitti, Arturo, 107–8

Gitlow, Benjamin, 145

Gompers, Samuel, 2, 4, 13, 109, 160; antilabor activities of, 124–25; relationship of to Marxism, 170n8

government, U.S.: Employment Service, 120, 121; imprisonment of IWW leaders, 49, 52, 112; investigations of subversive activities by, 5, 51, 120–21, 124; Justice Department, 52–55, 154; labor legislation, 54, 161, 164, 213n35; lack of impartiality with unions and employers, 25, 49, 51, 57, 60, 75, 83, 84, 134, 159; lack of repression by in New York, 112; National Adjustment Commission, 55, 58; repression by, 10, 49, 53, 70, 84, 85, 120, 159, 172n15; Shipping Board, 54–60, 75, 80–84; surveillance by FBI, 52, 53, 58, 68, 69, 84; surveillance by Office of Naval Intelligence, 51, 55; surveillance by Shipping Board, 60, 74, 77; surveillance by

War Department, 53, 124; task force on labor (1973), 165; Treasury Department, 64. *See also* industrial relations; legal system; police

Gramsci, Antonio, 16, 155, 208n8

Great Depression, 115, 140, 142, 150

Green, Joseph, 53

Harrington, Michael, 8

Harris, Abram, 22

Hartz, Louis, 9

Haywood, "Big Bill," 3, 102, 103, 160

Hegarty, Michael, 127

Hembosy, William, 36

Hill, Joe, 187n59

Hinz, Frank, 110–12

Hotel and Restaurant and Cafeteria Workers, 137; membership figures of, 137; strike by, 138–39

Hotel and Restaurant Employees National Alliance (HRE), 94–97, 102, 105, 106, 109, 111, 114–51, 154, 155, 157; convention of, 94, 136, 140, 148, 204n50; leadership in, 97, 147; Local 1, 94–96, 105, 117–19, 124, 127–29, 131–36, 140, 149, 154; Local 1 membership, 95, 129, 131; Local 3, 95; Local 5, 96, 97; Local 5 membership, 97, 131; Local 16, 134, 142–44, 147–48; Local 719, 128, 140; Local 719 membership, 131; and separate local for waitresses, 136

Hotel and Restaurant Workers Industrial Union, 117

hotel industry, 87–89, 114–51, 154; employers in, 107–8, 120; Hotel Men's Association, 101, 102, 123, 124; unionism in, 6, 7, 95, 167; workers in, 87–90, 96, 103, 109, 119, 120. *See also* culinary industry

Hotel Worker, 119, 120, 126, 130

immigrants. *See* ethnicity

inclusiveness, 21, 106, 134, 155, 156; of the IWW, 21, 31. *See also* exclusionary membership practices

industrial relations: federal regulation, 51–52, 143, 164; mediation, 136, 145; unions' cooperation with employers, 28, 139, 142, 144, 162

Industrial Solidarity, 43

Industrial Worker, 79

Industrial Workers of the World (IWW), 1–20, 154–58, 162–63; constitution of, 31, 63–65, 67–68, 73; convention of, 37, 68, 85; dissention within, 35, 55–68; General Executive Board (GEB), 55, 61–63, 65, 68, 97; lack of race-consciousness in, 31, 50, 71–72, 82, 85, 193n81; leaders, 28,

Text: Caledonia
Display: Caledonia
Composition: Binghamton Valley Composition
Printing and binding: Maple-Vail

DATE DUE

NOV 1 2 2007					